GALANTIÈRE

For Emma,

Mark Lewis

Overlook Press LLC
West Palm Beach, Florida

ISBNs:
978-0-9991002-0-2 (Paperback)
978-0-9991002-2-6 (Hardcover)
978-0-9991002-9-5 (E-book)

GALANTIÈRE

The Lost Generation's Forgotten Man

Mark I Lurie

Contents

Preface

Eda Galantière was my father's first cousin—my first cousin once removed. She was pleasant, petite, quiet, reticent. I have vague recollections of her. I didn't know she had a brother; no one in the family spoke of him and, to my knowledge, no one, except Eda, ever saw him. So when Eda died in 1982, that might have ended the subject. But, about a decade ago, my sister, Patti Sowalsky, told me that, apparently, Eda's brother, Lewis Galantière, had been a figure in twentieth-century American literature. Patti asked me to see what I could discover. Five years passed before I got around to it. An internet search revealed that Lewis's papers were stored at Columbia University's Butler Rare Books and Manuscripts Library and, with a call to the manuscript librarian, Tara C. Craig, I found them waiting for me when I arrived in the summer of 2012. There were thousands of pages of correspondence, photographs, and government documents; enough to lure me into a four-year investigation of Lewis's life. Few people who knew Lewis were still living, but the twentieth-century custom of personal letter writing, in addition to Lewis's work product, official documents, and newspaper articles, revealed a great deal. And from those things, I stitched together this book, in which I have tried to reconstruct the self-fabricated man that Lewis became.

Lewis was born in 1895, into an era in which new technologies were being introduced—electricity, the telephone, movies, automobiles, machine guns, and, soon, airplanes—technologies that would forever change the way people lived, worked, and killed each other. It was a time when, in America, anything seemed possible, especially to a bright boy who, having been told by the Chicago settlement house movement that he could become anyone he wanted to be, made his choices early on and then tenaciously pursued them.

During the first six decades of the twentieth century, Lewis seemed to be magically present and a consequential participant at crucial moments in history. He guided Hemingway through his first years in Paris, when the author was unknown and desperate for recognition; helped James Joyce and Sylvia Beach launch *Ulysses;* started John Houseman in his theatrical career; saw Antoine de Saint-Exupéry through his wartime exile in America, as his friend and as his collaborator and translator in life and in print. He was a playwright, a literary and cultural critic, author, Federal Reserve Bank economist, director of the French Branch of the Office of War Information, ACLU Director, Counselor to Radio Free Europe and, at a crucial time in its history, president of PEN America, the writers advocacy organization.

Today, to the few who know his name, he is a cipher. To the fewer still who think they know him, he is not what they think.

This biography captures, through previously unpublished love letters to Lewis from Iris Barry (the first director of MOMA's Film Library), the cultural volatility and bigotry of the 1920s avant-garde. It unveils, through Lewis's aides-mémoire and the files of the Hoover Institute, how he was prevented from reforming Radio Free Europe's Hungarian desk, with the calamitous result that, days later, that desk's broadcasters urged the Hungarian people to take up arms in bloody and futile resistance against the Soviets. And it contains a newly discovered letter from Hadley Hemingway to Lewis revealing her impressions of *A Moveable Feast* and of Ernest. But more, *Galantière* chronicles the first half of the twentieth century through the experiences of one whose senses were fully awake to its unfolding history and who played a part in the shaping of that history.

CHAPTER 1

LEWIS AND ERNEST AND HADLEY

LEWIS SCOOPED A HANDFUL OF mail from the pile on his desk and riffled through it, his eyes scanning the senders' names on the envelopes. He recognized some as American bankers, undoubtedly asking him to impress on the French that their war loans must be repaid. And some as French officials, reminding him that the loans *had* been repaid with the blood of their country's youth along the Somme and the Marne and the Meuse. And, of course, there were the inquiries from all quarters about whether the reparations scheme, agreed to in the Treaty of Versailles and not yet three years old, was being circumvented, by whom, and in what ways. Then the address on one envelope caught his eye and quickened his pulse. It was a letter from the novelist Sherwood Anderson, whom Lewis had gotten to know while working as a book salesman in Chicago. Sherwood and his wife had visited Lewis in Paris the previous summer. Lewis eagerly sliced open the envelope:

November 28, 1921

My dear Lewis: A friend of mine and a very delightful man, Ernest Hemingway, and his wife are leaving for Paris.[1] They will sail December 8th and go to Hotel Jacob, at least temporarily. Hemingway is a young fellow of extraordinary talent and, I believe, will get somewhere. He has been a quite wonderful

> newspaper man, but has practically given up newspaper work for
> the last year. Recently he got an assignment to do European
> letters for some Toronto newspaper for whom he formerly worked,
> and this is giving him the opportunity he has wanted, to live
> in Europe for a time. I have talked to him a great deal about
> you and have given him your address. I trust you will be on the
> lookout for him at the Hotel Jacob along about the 20th or 21st
> of December.
>
> [Ernest's] wife [Hadley] is charming. They will settle down to
> live in Paris, and [I] am sure you will find them great playmates.
> As I understand it, they will not have much money, so that they
> will probably want to live over in the Latin Quarter. However,
> Hemingway can himself find quarters after he gets there, and the
> Hotel Jacob will do temporarily.[2]

What Sherwood's letter left unsaid was that Hemingway was coming to Paris in the desperate hope that there, at last, he would find a literary voice. The stories he had written—mostly about his exploits as a military ambulance driver melded with the war stories of others—had, so far, been rejected. The *Saturday Evening Post* had refused them all. And his income, aside from what Hadley's trust fund brought in, was the small stipend of a features writer for the *Toronto Star* newspaper.

Three weeks later, Lewis detoured from his usual route to the International Chamber of Commerce, where he held the post of secretary to the U.S. commissioner. Crossing over to the Left Bank of the Seine, he stopped in at the Hotel Jacob, saw that the Hemingways had registered, and left them an invitation to come to his apartment at 24 Quai de Béthune the next day. Ernest wrote to Sherwood Anderson:

> Well here we are. And we sit outside the Dome Cafe, opposite
> the Rotunde that's being redecorated, warmed up against one of
> those charcoal braziers and it's so damned cold outside and the
> brazier makes it so warm and we drink rum punch, hot, and the
> rhum enters into us like the Holy Spirit ...
>
> We had a note from Louis Galantière this morning and will call
> on him tomorrow.[3]

On that next evening, Ernest and Hadley set out for the broad promenade that frames the Seine's southern embankment and whose name changes with each passing bridge: the Quai Saint Michel...the Quai de Montebello...the Quai de la Tournelle...their hedgerow of green canvas and wood stalls filled with paintings, stamps, and rare books: things that the devastation of the Great War had made plentiful and that the vendors, weary after their day in the cold, were eager and reluctant to sell. Ernest and Hadley walked across the Pont de la Tournelle to the Île Saint Louis, turned right, counted down the address numbers of the seventeenth-century five-story stone residences, entered number 24 and knocked. As the door opened, Ernest reached into his pocket to retrieve a letter of introduction—one of several such letters that Sherwood had addressed to Lewis and to Gertrude Stein, Ezra Pound, Sylvia Beach, and others.

The person who opened the door surprised Ernest. He had the appearance of a midlevel bookkeeper: thin, about five foot five and 130 pounds, black hair combed smooth, a carefully trimmed square moustache and rimless glasses. Ernest pushed the note back into his pocket, unconvinced that this little fellow was the person of consequence that Sherwood had described. Lewis, observing Hemingway's indecision, deduced what was going on. He would bide his time.

That Friday evening's plan was to reconnoiter the Left Bank for a suitable apartment. The trio walked through the fifth and sixth arrondissements of Paris, referred to as the Latin Quarter, but nothing Hemingway saw satisfied his wants and self-imposed budget.[4] They ended up at the Café Michaud, then an epicurean restaurant, where Lewis bought the newlyweds dinner and entertained them with his repertoire of cultural insights. The conversation eventually got around to Ernest's passion—boxing—and his description of how, on the voyage over, he had fought and beaten another American in a three-round exhibition match.[5] Lewis's experience with the sport had been a few lessons at a California Army camp, Camp Kearny, two years earlier. His instructor, George Blake, a former professional boxer and now a popular referee, was a man whose self-effacing nature and homespun way of speaking had made a firm impression upon Lewis, one that he enjoyed imitating:

> "Well, Lewis" he says, "let's go put on the feed bag."... "Can he hit? Why he couldn't hit water if he fell out of the boat." In telling a smutty story: "so then he went upstairs to take a ride in the midnight handicap..." [6]

Hadley listened avidly but, over the course of the evening, Ernest grew resentful of this little man who was so damned charming. He told Lewis that he had two pairs of regulation boxing gloves in his hotel room and that the two of them should do some friendly sparring after dinner. Lewis, although probably alarmed by the invitation, played the good sport, or maybe felt obliged not to appear a coward. The Hotel Jacob was just a few doors down from the restaurant and it was Friday night. No ready excuse was at hand.

The three went to the Hemingways' room, Ernest and Lewis laced-up, and Hadley, serving as ringmaster, called out the bell for the first round. The two men stepped forward. At six feet tall, Ernest loomed over Lewis. The men circled, tapping gloves here and there, tentatively parrying, weaving, skipping, and dodging, in a display of form over substance until Hadley called the end of the round. Lewis retired to his corner, unlaced one glove, and put on his glasses, unaware that Ernest was approaching. As Lewis turned, he offered a clear target for Ernest's sucker punch that caught him squarely on the face, breaking his glasses.

With that, the incipient friendship might have ended. That it did not was attributable, on Lewis's part, to his neither wanting to disappoint his friend Sherwood Anderson nor to have people think that he was the sort who couldn't "take it." Or perhaps he thought he had it coming. On Ernest's part, he could not afford to burn a bridge before he had crossed it. Despite that rocky start, over the coming five years, Lewis and Ernest formed a friendship that was sometimes enjoyable, always intense, and often turbulent for reasons that had nothing to do with the mutual respect and affection they came to share.

During the last week of December, Lewis, Ernest, and Hadley scouted the cold rainy streets of the Latin Quarter for an apartment and Ernest finally settled on a fourth-floor two-room apartment with a tiny kitchen, a coal-burning fireplace, and a makeshift toilet wedged in a bend of the staircase. The address was 74 Rue du Cardinal Lemoine and the rent was about $20 a month—the equivalent of $280 in 2017.

As Sherwood Anderson suggested, Ernest introduced himself to Gertrude Stein, Sylvia Beach, and Ezra Pound, giving to each Sherwood's letter of introduction. Ezra Pound was a poet-author-publisher and self-styled musician, whom Ernest initially assessed to be a pompous and affected (in a too literary way) pretender. He ridiculed Pound in an article he intended to send to the *Little Review*, a leading literary digest of the day, and handed the piece to Lewis for his critique. At the time, in addition to his work as secretary to the International Chamber of Commerce (ICC) commissioner, Lewis wrote a weekly column—the "Paris News Letter"—that appeared in the *New York Tribune*, as well as pieces for other literary journals. Ernest was hoping that Lewis would praise the deftness with which he skewered Pound the poseur but, instead, Lewis asked whether Ernest knew that Pound had been serving, without pay, as foreign editor to the *Little Review*. The magazine would never print the piece and, if it ever saw the light of day, Pound would be infuriated, his many friends would be offended, and Hemingway would become a pariah. As Ernest later explained,

> I almost ended it with Ezra before the friendship really
> began. He was an affected sort and when I first got to Paris I
> caricatured him for "The Little Review." If Lewis Galantière
> hadn't talked me out of publishing that parody, Ez's ire
> would've had his Van Dyke spontaneously combusting and he

> *wouldn't have published my first little book,* Three Stories and
> Ten Poems*...*[7]

Ernest tore up the satire and, moreover, came to adopt Pound's theory about writing:

> *Use no superfluous words, no adjective which does not reveal
> something ...*[8]

"He's teaching me to write and I'm teaching him to box," Ernest wrote to Lewis.[9] It was Pound who persuaded Hemingway of the importance of spare, deliberate prose. Lewis's writing differed from Pound's and Hemingway's. It was not prolix, but did not leave anything unsaid that might result in imprecision. By early 1923, Lewis acknowledged that Ezra Pound had taken over Ernest's mentorship:

> *Ernest Hemingway, who was sent to me a year ago by Sherwood
> Anderson...escaped from me and is now being hatched by Mother
> Pound.*[10]

On November 5, 1922, Lewis mentioned Hemingway in his "Paris News Letter" column. He was the first credentialed literary critic to write about Hemingway's potential:

> *Under the editorial direction of Mr. Ezra Pound, a new venture,
> the Three Mountains Press, 19 Rue d'Antin, is about to publish
> the following books: "Indiscretions," by Pound;..."The Great
> American Novel," by Carlos Williams;...and "Blank," by Ernest
> M. Hemingway. There are three Englishmen and three Americans
> (if Pound is to be reckoned with the latter. It is not certain
> that this would please him). Hemingway is a protégé of Sherwood
> Anderson, whose work I greatly admire and in whose continued
> development I have much faith.*[11]

Lewis sent Burton Rascoe, the *New York Tribune*'s literary editor, a copy of Ernest's *Three Stories and Ten Poems*, undoubtedly telling Ernest that Burton was the guy who could get it published. But when the book sat unread on Burton's desk,[12] Ernest, impatient with the glacial progress of his career, groused in a letter to Edmund Wilson, literary editor at the *Toronto Sun*:

To EDMUND WILSON, Toronto, 11 November 1923

Dear Mr. Wilson:

... I am sending you Three Stories and Ten Poems.

... Being an unknown name and the books unimposing, they would probably be received as by Mr. Rascoe who has not yet had time, after three months, to read the copy Galantière sent him. (He could read it all in an hour and a half.) ...

If you are interested could you send me the names of four or five people to send it to to get it reviewed? It would be terribly good of you...

Thanking you very much whether you have the time to do it or not.

Yours sincerely,

Ernest Hemingway[13]

Ernest redirected his resentment of Burton Rascoe's indifference onto Lewis and that resentment helped kindle his outrage when a Christmas 1923 *New York Times Book Review* article appeared titled "Paris, the Literary Capital of the United States." The article hailed Lewis as the most "well thought of" among the American authors in Paris, and it made no mention of Hemingway:

Customs inspectors at the Gare Saint Lazare have been puzzled by the troop of little black boxes that seem to arrive with every boatload of Americans...[T]he little black cases are portable typewriters, brought to Paris by the literary insurgents of America. Each one represents, potentially, the Great American novel. Chicago must surrender its leadership as the literary capital of America to Paris ...

Louis Galantière, Paris literary correspondent of The New York Tribune who, when not in the throes of translating Jean Cocteau's Le Grand Ecart for an American publisher, is deciding which of the two titles shall grace the cover of his first novel soon to be finished. Galantière's work is so well thought of here that those in the know will not be surprised if he is awarded the prize, last year given to Raymond Radiguet for Le

Diable Au Corps... Galantière is an American citizen of French extraction.[14]

The article went on to mention Sinclair Lewis, Willa Cather, Gilbert Seldes, Gertrude Stein, Ezra Pound, Carl Van Vechten, Frederick O'Brien, Robert Service, Edith Warton, Edna St. Vincent Millay, Harold Stearns, John Willard, Janet Flanner, and many others, but there was not one word about Hemingway. That is, except for a demeaning allusion that Hemingway probably inferred was being directed at him. Like many other American writers, Hemingway spent his days at the Café du Dome, a favorite hangout for American expats, where he shared ideas with other authors and did much of his writing. He would have had good reason to believe that this acerbic observation in the *Times Book Review* article was directed precisely at him:

> In addition to all these writers who come to do serious work in Paris and who really spend at least six hours a day (every day) at their work there is always to be found day or night a group of "young ineffectuals" at the well-known Café du Dome. These are the literateurs who spend their time worrying about when they will start their books. While they worry, of course, the saucers under their liqueurs pile up with amazing speed and the hours flit by on wings.

In the weeks that followed, sparks of resentment made it clear to Lewis that Ernest felt that he had been betrayed. To set things right, Lewis wrote a twenty-two-hundred-word essay lauding Hemingway's newly published book of short stories, *In Our Time*. The European edition of the *Chicago Tribune*[15] carried it on April 27, 1924:

> He came to me more than two years ago with a letter from Sherwood Anderson which he put back into his pocket immediately after showing it to me, so that I never properly knew what it said...
>
> The maturity of Hemingway's work consists in the suppression of the instinct to revolt, in the possession of a sense of

proportion which leads to a careful, frequently a poetic,
constatation without commentary ...

For my part, I counsel you to buy the book [In Our Time]. There
isn't much in it, but what you will find is superbly done.
Hemingway is finding himself. He knew how to write from the
beginning, and he is learning now what he wants to say. With
a bit of patience, with less regard for immediate publication
and more attention to the organization of his thoughts and his
emotions on a scale greater than any he has thus far employed,
Hemingway has every chance to jump at a bound into the front
line of American writers.

The piece was published under Lewis's Paris nom de plume, "Lewis Gay."[16] (Lewis's use of a pen name may have been to separate his literary opinions from his work at the International Chamber of Commerce.) That same weekend, a second article by Lewis, "American Books in France," appeared in the literary journal *The American Mercury*. In it, he placed Hemingway in the same echelon as Joyce, Pound, and Williams:[17]

The European edition of the Chicago Tribune includes a weekly
magazine section on Sundays in which American literature is
discussed and reviewed...In addition, Shakespeare & Co., the
Three Mountains Press, and the Contact Publishing Company are
active publishers of the writings of James Joyce, Ford, Pound,
William Carlos Williams, Mina Loy, Robert McAlmon, Ernest
Hemingway, and others.

Lewis took Ernest aside and showed him the *Chicago Tribune* and *American Mercury* articles before they went to press, confident that Ernest would be pleased to know Lewis was in his corner. What Lewis did not know was that Ernest, having reached the end of his rope, had just sent off for publication a venomous screed attacking literary critics in general and Lewis in particular:

An American citizen, not yet thirty five years old, of French-
German-Jewish parentage, writing in the Paris Sunday Literary
Supplement of the World's Greatest Newspaper under the name of
Louis Gay says:

> *"Remember that less than twenty years ago the reading matter*
> *to be found in the home of the average American of means—the*
> *American who sent his boys to college—was composed almost*
> *entirely of the New England Poets, the Christian Register*
> *and the Youth's Companion."*

As Mr. Gay is frequently denunciatory, rarely unpersonal, and
always insistent on the lack of a cultural background of almost
everyone of whom he writes, the above selection from his article
will have a certain biographical significance in the critical
study of American Criticism which should be written to carry to
its end the present phenomenon on American letters.[18]

Ford Madox Ford published Ernest's diatribe in the May 1924 edition of
The Transatlantic Review.[19]

At this point, it may have come to Ernest's mind that an apology was in
order but, given his machismo instincts, that would be a last resort. Instead,
Ernest was inclined to either laugh off his mischief, as would a schoolyard
bully, or to set things right by somehow, in some way, coming to Lewis's aid.
Ernest did both; the first in a note to Ezra Pound:

May 2, 1924

Dear Ezrah:

... Galantière has a big Yahticle in The American Mercury...

Galantière in the Chi Tribune Sunday mag. sets out to prove
that the mantle of Abe Lincoln, Wm. Dean Howells, Hamlin
Garland, Sherwood Anderson and yourself is descending upon me.
The article takes up some space. In the same week, unknowing
he was preparing this blurb, I prove in a squib for Ford that
Galantière is a little Jewish boy and a fool.[20]

Ernest's chance to come to Lewis's defense came two weeks later and involved Lewis's girlfriend, Dorothy Butler.

Dorothy was a lithe, attractive girl who had grown up in Chicago and,
in her early teens, had trained with Andreas Pavley and Serge Oukrainsky,
who were then notable dance instructors.[21] Dorothy's professional career

had been in the chorus of the Manhattan Opera Theater's productions of "The Wanderer" and "Chu Chin Chow" in 1916 and 1917, respectively.[22]

Ernest and Hadley had gotten to know Dorothy during the summer of 1922, when she and Lewis joined Ernest and Hadley and Bill Bird and his wife, Sally, for a hike through Germany's Black Forest.[23] (Bill Bird headed the Consolidated Press Association's local operations.) Starting out in Strasbourg on August 3, the six had gone to Triberg to fish, stayed overnight at the Gasthaus Roessle, and then spent ten days hiking through the forests. Ernest later described the outing in three stories for *The Toronto Daily Star*: "German Inn-Keepers," "A Paris-To-Strasbourg Flight," and "German Inflation."

Left: Lewis and Dorothy; right: Ernest and Hadley.

The expedition was the first time that the Hemingways spent more than a casual moment with Dorothy Butler, and the experience confirmed their first impression that she seemed always to be casting herself as the lead in a play in which others had supporting roles.[24] This was an annoying narcissism to which Ernest was especially attuned in others but seemed not to recognize in himself. When it later appeared that Lewis had ended the affair, Ernest was delighted and shared the news with Harriet Monroe, editor of *Poetry* magazine:

November 16, 1922

I don't know whether you ever knew Lewis Galantière when he lived in Chicago. He has just undergone a very trying love affair with a girl from Illinois who is over here getting cultured. She's just left town and we have all cheered up.

But Dorothy returned, and during the ensuing year, Ernest and Hadley's dislike of her intruded upon their friendship with Lewis. When Lewis confided that he was going to propose to Dorothy, Hadley told him that she thought Dorothy was selfish and would not likely marry him. Things came to a head on May 23, 1924, the month before Lewis and Dorothy's wedding, when Dorothy wrote to Hadley to say that the discord between the two couples had not been her (Dorothy's) doing because, unlike Lewis, *she* had been "perfectly square and open and above board."

Dear Hadley,

I am about to explode in righteous indignation.—The worm has turned—Lewis has put me in the position of the boobish kid who stays to face the music while the rest run away. Once too often—I think he needs a lesson in having the courage to stick to his convictions, or else to give them up openly,—change his mind, and take a different tack.

You and Ernest have said so many times,...that Lewis was "so different" since he has been in love with me,—the inference being that I was the cause of the break in the friendship— ...it seems to me I've been the only person who's been perfectly square and open and above board...

... Lewis told me last winter..."Hadley...said you were selfish ..." Naturally that made me furious—I wanted to have things out with you and not keep on piling up resentment, but Lewis persuaded me not to, and that perhaps it wouldn't work—

... Lewis has been cowardly...about saying one thing behind your back, and acting another...I just wanted to tell you that I have been consistent, and that, in spite of appearances, I have nothing to do with snatching Lewis's friendship away from you.[25]

As Hadley was about to reply, Ernest took the pen from her hand and wrote,

Dear Dorothy—

You are certainly consistent.

Your letter in which you accuse Lewis, whom you are going to marry, of cowardice and double dealing...is entirely consistent.

As you grow older, for no matter what age we are we do grow older, you will be more and more disgusted at the lack of this sincerity in others. But on the other hand you cannot expect me when disgusted by you or your behavior to order you out of the house, even for the sake of sincerity. Such intensity of living makes life so difficult. Even though I kissed you, Dorothy, Even while I kissed you, I never liked you but was willing to make the effort to like you for the sake of seeing Lewis occasionally. I made this effort successfully numberless times. Finally it could no longer be made. That was quite a relief. Still I wanted to keep up appearances to hold together the difficult social fabric.

As for Hadley's telling Lewis you were selfish I am sure she was quite sincere. I believe my own language on that occasion was that you were a selfish bitch and that he would be a good deal better off in the hands of Dr. Fernandez[26] than married to you. This view I still hold in general although the language is no doubt immoderate.

Now that you have completely busted the social fabric, which you will appreciate as you grow older, and Dorothy you will grow older, as a necessity for making human intercourse bearable, by your letter you will no doubt in the interest of frankness and consistency be very glad to know what I really think of you.

Dorothy, I will never tell you. As a matter of fact I don't know what I think of you. I haven't thought about the subject for some time.

Lewis came over to see some of my stuff because I put him in the embarrassing position of asking him to come and paying for his drink as he sat defenseless in front of the Café du Dome. Lewis is both gentle and nice and fonder than I am of being found dead beside his guns in some bitter fought social field. Also, as you chivalrously put it, he was interested to see what I was writing.

Do not get Ritzy Dorothy about my answering your letter to
Hadley. I know it was not addressed to me. I answer it because
I am amused by writing a funny letter. It is funny is it not?
Perhaps you do not think so. Nevertheless each time I read it
over I get a good laugh. In fact I am loath to send it. But I
will keep a copy. You may have the original.

To make the manuscript more valuable I will sign it,

Affectionately yours,

Ernest Hemingway. [27]

If Lewis learned of these letters, he was not deterred. He married Dorothy the following month at the Hotel Ritz in Paris. Dorothy's mother, Alice Carter Butler, attended, as did Dorothy's two brothers who survived the Great War (a third had been killed). No one from Lewis's family came, and there is no evidence that anyone from his family was invited. Or informed. On the French marriage certificate, Dorothy identified her parents as Hubert Wilson and Alice Carter Butler, and Lewis identified his as Joseph Galantière and Cécile Lurie.[28] The *Chicago Tribune European Edition* reported the nuptials and identified the guests; the Hemingways were not among them. They either had not attended or the newspaper had thought them not worth mentioning.[29]

A BRIDE IN PARIS

Mrs. Lewis Galantiere of Paris, formerly Miss Dorothy Butler of Glencoe, Ill. Her marriage took place at the Hotel Ritz, Paris, recently.

If Ernest was not invited, it would have been especially hard on him because, as much as he detested Dorothy, he admired her mother. Everyone did. Alice was an unaffected, warm and intelligent woman, who was said to have possessed "a soul that refused to compromise with ugliness, tawdriness, base thoughts or emotions."[30] Hemingway saw in Alice the female embodiment of the protagonists he would later write about: a woman who embraced life and persevered, while tuberculosis remorselessly set about killing her. One example of Alice's fortitude: when Benito Mussolini became Italy's prime minister in October 1922, she traveled to Italy to interview him. He kept her waiting for days and, although ill, she did not relent. The interview was published in the *Chicago Tribune, Paris Edition*.

As Alice saw death was approaching, she returned home to Chicago and, from there, wrote to Dorothy on September 19, 1924:

> I am better every day, but pleurisy takes a long time. Now, dearest, good night. Hold Lewis' head against you the way I used to, and tell him I love him much for him and, oh, so infinitely more because you and he love each other. Take care of him as he does of you. I want to see a deeper light in the blue and the brown eyes. I want to feel that you are both closer to me because you are closer to each other. I dare not think how I miss you. Untellable love. Mama.[31]

Hemingway's fondness for Alice moved him in November 1924 to write an empathetic note to Dorothy when she embarked from Paris to be with her mother at the end. Dorothy and Lewis misconstrued Ernest's note as a softening of his opinion of Dorothy, and responded in kind:

> November 28, 1924 [from Dorothy]
>
> Dear Ernest,
>
> I was very touched with your sweetness and sympathy—you know I appreciated from the bottom of my heart. And the books are going to help me through the trip—
>
> You and Hadley, I feel sure, are sad about my darling mother—I can't believe it—

We'll come to see you if we may, when I get back.

Dorothy[32]

November 30, 1924 [from Lewis]

Dear Ernest:

Here is a note Dorothy scribbled for you Friday evening.

I got her off on the Mauretania, on Saturday. This morning I have a wire saying that Mrs. Butler died Sunday.

I'd like to see Hadley & you one of these days when I get straightened out. Just now I feel all messed up inside. We are living, by the way, at 42 rue Jouffroy, which is in the Plaine-Monceau, near the Bd. Malesherbes.

I hope Hadley is getting better and that you & the heir [Hemingway's infant son, Bumby] are well.

Yours ever, Lewis.

But Ernest's contempt for Dorothy hadn't waned. On December 6, 1924, he wrote to William "Bill" Smith, his closest friend and the best man at his wedding to Hadley:

Dear Boid

... It's so god damn swell to know that we will have some of the old genuwind together again. Because Boid the number of genuwind all Caucasian white guys in the world is limited. I should say that maybe there were 5 or 6 at the most. That may be an exaggerated figure. There'd probably be a number more if they didnt marry foecal matter in various forms. There's a guy named Lewis Galantière over here was a priceless guy and he has been hooked and married by the most absolute copper plated bitch in the world and he aint a good guy any more. And with casualties like that in the thin red line of white guys we have to keep the ranks close together. There is an awful one is damned near married to Dos Passos. He's a guy you'd like.[33]

In 1925, Sylvia Beach hosted a Thanksgiving dinner. The Galantières were there, as were the James Joyces, the Hemingways, and other notables including the estimable Paul Robeson. A few days later, Ernest relocated his family to Schruns, Austria, for the winter, where they were joined by Hadley's friend Pauline Pfeiffer. At Schruns, Ernest completed *The Sun Also Rises* and Pauline and F. Scott Fitzgerald persuaded him to bring the book to Scribners. Ernest sailed to New York, signed a contract with the firm, and returned through Paris, where Pauline met and seduced him.

Lewis and Dorothy and Ernest and Hadley met again at Sylvia Beach's the following spring for a Walt Whitman exhibit.[34] Hadley suspected that Ernest and Pauline were lovers and, a month later, Ernest confirmed it, unleashing a season of anguish and tears for both of them. Hadley moved, with their son, to an apartment of her own and handed Ernest an ultimatum, in writing:

> If Pauline Pfeiffer and Ernest Hemingway do not see each other for 100 days, and if at the end of that time Ernest Hemingway tells me that he still loves Pauline Pfeiffer, I will, without further complication, divorce Ernest Hemingway.[35]

Pauline accepted the challenge and returned to the United States to serve her hundred-day banishment of not "seeing" Ernest. She wrote to him daily, and also wrote to Hadley, in an unrealistic attempt to keep her friendship. Ernest spent the ensuing weeks alone, tormented by the need to choose but sometimes fantasizing that the two women might be persuaded to share. Scott Fitzgerald warned him about choosing Pauline over Hadley:

> You need the shining qualities of Hadley. Her buoyancy. Neither Pauline nor her money can provide that ...[36]

> [Pauline] would probably bring you some positive things, but she would also bring you remorse. Don't try living with remorse—remorse will break your goddamn heart.[37]

After seventy-five days, Hadley ended Ernest's suffering and told him in a letter that she wanted a divorce. Ernest wrote back that Hadley was the best, the loveliest person he had ever known, but he did not ask her to take him back.[38] In the same letter, he promised Hadley the royalties from *The Sun Also Rises*.

For Ernest, the day he yielded to Pauline marked the end of the time when his life still seemed ordered, loving, and benign. His last work, *A Moveable Feast*, was an homage to those early, intense Paris years, and an airing of the sour unrelenting guilt with which he had lived since his betrayal of Hadley:

> to really love two women at the same time, truly love them, is the most destructive and terrible thing that can happen to a man when the unmarried one decides to marry. The wife does not know about it and trusts the husband. They have been through really difficult times and share those times and have loved each other and she finally trusts the husband truly and completely. The new one says you cannot really love her if you love your wife too. She does not say that at the start. That comes later when the murder's done...You break all promises and you do everything you knew that you could never do nor would want to do...
>
> ... You love both and you lie and hate it and it destroys you and every day is more dangerous...but you live day to day as in a war. Everyone is still happy except you when you wake in the middle of the night. You love them both now and you are gone. Everything is split inside of you and you love two people now instead of one.
>
> ... When I saw my wife again standing by the tracks as the train came in by the piled logs at the station, I wished I had died before I ever loved anyone but her. She was smiling, the sun on her lovely face tanned by the snow and sun, beautifully built, her hair red gold in the sun, grown out all winter awkwardly and beautifully..."Oh Tatie" she said, when I was holding her in my arms, "you're back and you made such a wonderful successful trip. I love you and we've missed you so."[39]

A Moveable Feast was published posthumously. Three decades and as many wives after Hadley, on a Sunday morning in July, Ernest had placed the ends of a double-barrel shotgun to his forehead and pushed the trigger. When *A Moveable Feast* was published, the *New York Times* asked Lewis to review the book. Lewis titled the piece "There is Never Any End to Paris":

*Love of his young wife shines softly in his revelation of an
adoring, undemanding nature, achieved through the extraordinary
felicity and tenderness of the dialogue he lends Hadley—a true
triumph of Hemingway's art...*

*...in the final section, bearing the lyrical title, "There is
Never Any End to Paris,"...this masterly artist...plead[s] his
case with the wife he left 30-odd years before...*

*Par délicatesse, j'ai perdu ma vie,[40] this, though in a raging
tone, is Hemingway's last cry. Pathetic defense on the part of
a man who sought to show—and, by an art in which credibility
triumphs over verisimilitude, long persuaded us—that fortitude
is the highest virtue, and that the savage is noble, is laconic,
severe, animated by a sense of honor. And yet, in this baffling
character there is something that goes deeper than pathos.*

*More than anything else, the book is a chant of love addressed
to his first wife. He knew that in the invincible armor of her
candor she possessed a strength greater than his own and forever
denied him. Two natures struggled in the breast of this Faust—
and they died in each other's grasp, so to say, the lower nature
resisting with its last breath. Because there was this struggle,
we must speak of tragedy, not of pathos.[41]*

"There is Never Any End to Paris" drew letters from appreciative readers but, most significantly, one from Hadley, which has lain undiscovered because it was written under her new married name, Mrs. Paul Scott Mowrer. Following her divorce, Hadley had gotten on with her life so that, by the time of Ernest's death, the immediacy of the innumerable moments together had merged into a larger perspective, from which she both admired and pitied the man she had once known:

May 28, 1964

Dear Lewis:—

*I cannot let your review of EMH's "Movable Feast" pass
unremarked and unappreciated by me. For all this is about the
good place I seem always to have held in his esteem. I do thank
you—and in spite of the fact that it is unnervingly joy bringing.*

For this I am, by Ernest and the book & by you in your review, overestimated.

Even more satisfactory and potent is your saying—on account of his desperate struggle with his own lower nature—one must feel that his life was tragic rather than full of pathos—and that the writing is far from being casual—calculated to the nth degree—superb writing, closely thought to mean various things to the few people pointed at—

Thanks, Louis—and what a wonderful writer you are—

Affectionately, Hadley[42]

· CHAPTER 2 ·

FROM THE CHICAGO GHETTO TO THE CHICAGO RENAISSANCE

THE EVENTS THAT HAD PLACED Lewis in Paris in January 1920 had their start in 1888, when his father, Joseph, and Joseph's two brothers immigrated to Chicago from Riga, Latvia. They were three Jewish men among the hundreds of thousands who bid good riddance to the Tsar's May Laws, pogroms, and military conscription. Chicago was then a city on the threshold of modernity. Starting out as the waterway that connected the Atlantic Ocean and New York's Erie Canal to the Mississippi River and states to the west, by the 1880s Chicago had grown into the country's central rail hub for the transporting of meat, grain, and manufactured goods. Telephone service had been around for a decade and electrical service was introduced the year that the Galantières arrived.

Joseph and his wife, Cecilia, took a room in one of the tenements in Chicago's Jewish section, south of downtown. There they earned a subsistence living making cigars and cigarettes in that room, by hand.[43] Tobacco products were an entry level business for immigrants and the second leading such occupation after dry goods.

Lewis was Joseph and Cecilia's first child. Born on October 10, 1895, he exhibited a remarkable intelligence from an early age. Fortunately, this was the era of the Chicago settlement house movement, when primary school teaching and curricula were excellent and free. Lewis was allowed to take courses that matched his abilities and, by the time he was a teenager, he had learned French and had studied and could competently discuss the works of eighteenth- and nineteenth-century English, French, and German authors, philosophers, and poets. His teachers predicted that he would attend a university and then go on to obtain a doctorate. They told him that a man with determination, a sense of purpose, and intelligence could accomplish anything. A popular image of the day was the photograph of President "Teddy" Roosevelt, clothed in a white suit, sitting at the controls of a steam shovel in an excavation cut of the Panama Canal. This was the twentieth century; anything was possible.

And yet, at each day's end, Lewis returned from school to the tenement apartment that was all that his father's income could afford. In the heat of summer, the air in the single room was thick with the smell of fermenting leaf and the outgassing of garbage and manure from the simmering streets. The stench clung to his clothing and hair. In the winter, the acrid fumes of indoor coal stoves and the aroma of roasting onions had the same effect. It angered Lewis that he had to live in those conditions when others at the school had long since escaped them. But what angered him more was the disappointing man who was his father: this uneducated, perpetually unsuccessful man who dressed in old-world garb, spoke with a thick Yiddish accent, and whose uninformed, incoherent opinions Lewis had to listen to, let alone respond to. For Joseph's part, the infant he had adored had grown into the youth who now intimidated him and whose undisguised resentment wounded him. Joseph knew he was not and would never be the father that Lewis wanted him to be. Eventually, a silent truce descended between them.

Market Street in the Chicago ghetto, circa 1905.

A typical Chicago tenement interior.

Unlike Lewis's father, his uncles Charles and Jacob Galantière had done well in Chicago. They opened a book bindery—the family's trade in Latvia—and it had thrived, buoyed by the 1893 World's Fair. A fourth brother, David, emigrated from Riga and joined the business. The bindery earned enough for the three brothers to purchase homes in the suburbs, where Joseph, Cecilia, and their children (who now included a daughter, Eda, and another son, Jacob) sometimes visited for holiday dinners, knowing they could not reciprocate.[44] But even the bindery could not withstand the 1908 run on bank deposits that followed the Knickerbocker Bank crisis. The bindery's list of clientele contracted to the point where the business could support only one of the three brothers. David, the youngest, bought out the other two.

Jacob, Charles, and Joseph moved their households to Los Angeles to make a fresh start and in the hope that, as the city's advertisements were then promising, the Pacific air would cure the tuberculosis that Joseph had contracted in the tenements. Jacob and Charles used their bindery money to start up a retail tobacco store. They put Joseph on the payroll, telling him he should work only to the extent that he was able. But Joseph's paycheck was not enough to support Cecilia and the children, and Jacob and Charles made it clear to Lewis that he would have to contribute to the family's support. Lewis, at the age of thirteen, went to work, forfeiting further grade school education.

Lewis's first job in Los Angeles was as a clerk for the Santa Fe Railroad, a position that allowed him the time to continue his reading of French, English, and German literature. He kept a journal of written passages he found interesting or useful, and practiced interjecting them into his conversations and correspondence. He also spent time at the local "talking machine" store, listening to symphonic recordings and learning about the composers' lives and music. In the early twentieth century, 78 rpm disks were displacing larger, more fragile, and more expensive cylinders, but customers still purchased their records from the store that sold the players, and they expected that the store's salesman would be conversant with the orchestral and operatic works available. In 1910, Irvine Andrews, owner of the Andrews Talking Machine Company, hired Lewis to be his salesman. The store's clientele, which included that city's financially well-to-do, were bemused when the fifteen-year-old lad spoke to them with practiced erudition. Customers came to know him by name, and some invited him to join the Los Angeles Union League Club. Lewis accepted their invitation.

The Union League had been formed during the American Civil War to support the Union and the Republican Party. By the turn of the century, the political purposes of the league had waned but its social and public service purposes remained. The Los Angeles club membership boasted that its members comprised the thousand most successful men in the city. They were lawyers, judges, oil men, politicians, architects, doctors, building contractors, civil engineers, railroad executives, and manufacturers. As one article indicated, they were the men who had "made good" in Los Angeles. Most had attended college. In 1911, the club moved into a new home, a nine-story building in downtown Los Angeles. It had a large private dining room with a full-time staff of cooks, kitchen support, and white-gloved waiters; a library; a billiard room; a card room; a bar room; and fifty-eight private sleeping rooms with steam heat and hot and cold running water.[45] As a club resident, Lewis, now sixteen, used the opportunity to observe how successful men behaved: their words, silences, pauses, and intonations; what they would talk about and what they would not; how they dressed, ordered food, tasted wine, and treated staff; which bread plate and water glass setting was whose; the purpose of each dining utensil. The Union League Club became Lewis's laboratory for practicing decorum, nuance, and manners but, especially, for sculpting his public persona. He had a keen ear for speech patterns, cadences, and pronunciation, and his impressions of fellow club members were delightfully entertaining. Always deferential and interesting, the members came to appreciate the young man with an encyclopedic recall of literature, music, and art. At the Union League Club, Lewis rehearsed playing (and sometimes overplaying) the cultured one.

L. H. GALANTIERE

UNION LEAGUE BUILDING

Some attorney members of the club urged Lewis to consider a career in the law and furnished him with certificates of good moral character that were a University of Southern California Law School requirement. Lewis was admitted for the summer 1911 session, notwithstanding that the minimum admission age was eighteen. Other school prerequisites were either a diploma from a four-year high school or (more relevant to Lewis) passing examinations in English, a foreign language, science, algebra and plane geometry, and U.S. history and civics.[46] Lewis must have passed those tests because he was admitted. But the summer's law school experience revealed to him that he would be happier doing something in the uncrowded and arcane field of literature than he would as another lawyer in a field crowded with ambitious young men.

Lewis continued in his efforts at self-education and in 1914 wrote his first published article. It was titled "Machine-Made Musical Appreciation" and appeared in the February 1916 issue of *The Music Student* magazine. Lewis drew from what he had learned at the Andrews Talking Machine Company and, in the piece, invited readers to share in the conceit that they—like he—were more cultured than "the man in the street":

One of the greatest factors in the education of the public toward appreciation of music has been that modern "Apollo," the "talking machine," to use its popular name. By the public I mean the man in the street; the man for whom music affords the only view of the finer side of life,—this man and his family.

He knows Shaw through the newspapers, Galsworthy not at all, and would never have known Maeterlinck if the Belgian mystic had not written "The Blue Bird." Speak to him of Monet or Renoir, and he is blank. Abbey, Blashfield, Borglum, Davies, Homer, St. Gaudens, or others among leaders in American painting and sculpture probably are strange to him.

But talk of music and you find him voluble..."Records" and record makers he knows. His appreciation of music has grown with the distribution of the talking machine.[47]

In the spring of 1914, the Los Angeles Public Library system offered, for the first time, a librarian training program. Admission entailed an examination that assessed applicants' knowledge of Western culture. Here are sample questions:[48]

Make an outline of English literature from the time of Chaucer, giving the periods with approximate dates, and the principal writers in each.

Who painted the following:

The Last Judgment

The Golden Staircase

Sistine Madonna

Frescoes portraying the legends of the Holy Grail

The Last Supper

Madonna of the Chair

The Horse Fair

Name

Two living violinists

Four living composers of opera and the name of an opera by each

One director of an orchestra

Two symphonies with their composers

Two oratorios with their composers

Fourteen students passed the exam and were admitted. The school's "Circular of Information" described their backgrounds and attributed to Lewis (the only boy in the class) "one year University of Chicago." The university has no record of Lewis's having attended.[49] Lewis's year at the Los Angeles Library School was the entirety of his college-level education in comparative literature and literary criticism. One of his instructors, Helen E. Haines, who was forty-two when she and Lewis met, would remain his closest confidante until her passing almost half a century later.[50]

With his library school degree in hand, Lewis returned to Chicago and a position as a salesman at Kroch's bookstore. At the turn of the century, bookstores in New York City, Philadelphia, Chicago, Paris, and London were meeting places for aspiring authors and literary critics and, in Chicago, Kroch's was that place. Its success was attributed to "Papa" Adolph Kroch's knowledge and taste in literature, especially about books in foreign languages. Literary critics, authors, and poets gravitated to him.[51] There were the poets Carl Sandburg, Edgar Lee Masters, and Harriet Monroe; reporters Ben Hecht and Ring Lardner; novelist Theodore Dreiser; and the literary critics Margaret Anderson, editor of *The Little Review*; Martyn Johnson, editor of *The Dial*; Floyd Dell of the *Friday Literary Review*, and, importantly, Burton Rascoe, then the literary editor of the *Chicago Tribune*.

Kroch's bookstore was the epicenter of what came to be known as the Chicago Renaissance: the realistic writing style that depicted the twentieth century's materialism through characters drawn unromantically, sparely, and precisely.

Within this throng, Burton Rascoe and Lewis found each other. Sharing a love of books, they often lunched together, revealing their literary discoveries[52] and sparring over their critiques of authors.[53] The two were sometimes joined by Sherwood Anderson, another of Kroch's customers. The forty-year-old Anderson was completing a short-story collection he intended to title *Winesburg, Ohio*, about the psychology of midwestern small-town folks, written in a "realistic" literary voice. In three years, the book would bring Anderson national critical acclaim and, for the first time in his life, substantial royalties, but, in his memoirs, it was not that breakthrough that he most cherished but, instead, the summer of 1916:

> It was during that summer that I met Carl Sandburg. I was introduced to him by Ben Hecht and we went for a long afternoon's walk through the factory district on Chicago's West Side...

> Through Ben Hecht I also met Henry Justin Smith of the News, Burton Rascoe, then doing books for the Tribune, and Lewis Galantière, who was to become a lifelong friend. We were all from the Middle West. We were all full of hope.[54]

In those days, the influential literary journal was neither *Kirkus Reviews* nor the *Saturday Review of Literature* (neither of which then existed) nor the *New York Times Book Review* nor *Publishers Weekly*. It was *The Dial*. For an author or critic to be published in its pages was a mark of legitimacy. *The Dial*'s October 1917 edition carried Lewis's review of *Some Modern Belgian Writers*. He was twenty-two years old. That same year, Guy Holt introduced Lewis to the novels of James Branch Cabell. Lewis thought them superb and sent Cabell a self-described "shamefully effusive" letter, prompting Cabell to write to Holt:

> *Who, to begin with, is Galantière? He writes a charming letter,
> exactly the sort one hungers to receive, but, in view of his
> unusual literary discernment, I cannot but suspect his sanity.*[55]

Lewis and Cabell began a correspondence that continued into the early 1920s. It was marked by Lewis's fulsome praise except in one instance, in April 1919, when he faulted Cabell for the sexual references in *Beyond Life*, saying that they were an "unnecessary disfigurement of the beauty" of the book. (In fact, Cabell had been inspired by his uncle's pornography collection.) In one letter, Lewis suggested that Cabell write a book about the interrelationships between the fictional characters in Lichfield, the home of Cabell's stories. Cabell did, and in 1921 dedicated his book *The Lineage of Lichfield* to Lewis.[56]

A second Chicago newspaper, the *Chicago Examiner*, competed with Burton Rascoe's *Chicago Tribune*. In its December 15, 1917, review of the best books of the year, the *Examiner* turned to the twenty-two-year-old Lewis (who was now adding an accent mark to his last name). The paper printed Lewis's year-end review under the banner headline "H'M!—LET'S SEE!—SAYS LEWIS GALANTIÈRE." In the *Examiner* piece, Lewis melded lengthy self-deprecation and certitude, first describing his reluctance to offer opinions and then delivering them with gusto.[57] One could sense in his writing that a door had been opened. He reveled in his new role as a literary authority.

And then it ended. Suddenly. In early 1918, without explanation, Lewis left the Kroch's Bookstore and Chicago. The March 2, 1918, *Publishers Weekly* printed a terse announcement, written by Kroch, under the caption PERSONAL NOTES:

> *L. H. Galantière is no longer connected with A. Kroch & Co.,
> Chicago.*[58]

Lewis's friends were perplexed as to the cause for his departure. Lewis hesitated, but then gave his explanation to a few—those who he thought would probably find out anyway: Kroch had announced to his employees that he was going to conduct a store inventory that Lewis knew would reveal that many of the store's books were in his apartment. Kroch saw the appropriations as theft and fired Lewis on the spot.[59] Lewis insisted that Kroch had misconstrued his motives; that he had only borrowed the books in order to read them. That was what Lewis told Burton Rascoe in a March 9 letter in which he also gratuitously speculated that Kroch was Jewish:

> Kroch, by the way is not Viennese. He is from Luxembourg, in Galicia, and since he is not a Pole, and there are no Germans there, and he speaks German with a Polish accent, he must be a Jew. He's pretty foxy, the old boy, but people have been so decent to me that every time he speaks of me to any of his customers he is using a little more rope with which to hang himself.[60]

This was the age of eugenics—the pseudoscience of individual and racial genetic superiority[61]—under which the U.S. Supreme Court would soon declare constitutional the forced sterilization of people (mostly women and disproportionately black and native American) deemed unworthy of procreation. Nazi Germany would later invoke eugenics to justify killing persons and races it thought genetically inferior: those lives the state considered not worth living. Slurring Jews was de rigueur among intellectuals and, for Lewis, who concealed his own Jewish origins from Burton, disparaging Jews was both a form of misdirection and an allusion to their mutual superiority.[62]

After the Kroch incident, Lewis returned to Los Angeles and lived with his parents and sister in a two-story duplex on Kensington Road. During the two years of his absence, his father's tuberculosis had worsened[63] and he died ten months later, at the age of fifty-one.[64] With his passing, Joseph Galantière metamorphosed, under the ministrations of his son's pen, from an unschooled, shtetl-grown, Yiddish-speaking failed cigar maker into a collegial mentor, a man expert in the classics:

January 9, 1919

Dear Burton:

... Burton, old top, I lost my father last week. He died because he had no lungs left in his body. He was a beautiful spirit, a fine gentleman, and a wonderful pal. I am sorry you couldn't have known him; everyone who came into contact with him gained something in tenderness and wisdom. I have gone on with my work regularly enough, but I am really so distracted in mind, so dazed, that I marvel at the way I finish each day's work.

I will tell you what I am reading: (and have read)—Homer, both epics: Sophocles in Greek and English with my father's notes...

... I read a great deal, as you may suspect, with my father, and almost for the first time in my intellectual life I felt this summer in acute personal sensation, a moving appreciation of the sublime and letters. And I am afraid that in this hurdy-gurdy life of ours no one will arise to achieve it...it will take hours for me to tell you what influence the concentrated reading of the Greeks in my father's company has done to my mind...

Now that father is dead a great many things have changed for me. For one thing, he left nothing; the family lived on an annuity that expired, unfortunately, with him, and it is up to me to take care of my mother and sister. My brother, I imagine, will be able to help very little.[65]

Lewis's subsequent letters would embellish upon the posthumous fiction of his father's erudition.[66]

CHAPTER 3

ON TO PARIS

THE UNITED STATES HAD BEEN in the war for a year when Lewis returned to Los Angeles. The army had rejected him as being too short, too light, and his vision too poor for combat and, according to a letter Lewis sent Burton Rascoe, the Canadian Army had rendered the same verdict. He took a job with the San Diego Library, which loaned him out to the army library at Camp Kearny (now the Marine Corps Air Station Miramar, located about six miles north of downtown San Diego). From there, Lewis drove a Ford-truck lending library between the Southern California military camps. The work was pleasant and undemanding and allowed him the time to read and review books. From 1917 through 1919, his reviews were published in the *Los Angeles Times*, the *Chicago Tribune*, the *New Republic,* and the *Little Review.*

Lewis on the steps of the Camp Kearny library, June 23, 1919. Image courtesy of Burton Rascoe Papers, Kislak Center for Special Collections, Rare Books and Manuscripts, University of Pennsylvania.

During the war, the American Library Association's "War Service" managed a program under which public civilian libraries funded and operated thirty-two military training camp libraries. In the summer of 1918, the head of the ALA War Service, Herbert Putnam, recruited Lewis to manage those camp library activities. Lewis agreed, telling Burton Rascoe, "I can't slack, of course."[67]

But by November, the war was over and Lewis was told to stop what he was doing and await further orders. The operational doldrums left Lewis with time to brood about his future and about how, at twenty-two, his life still seemed directionless. His insecurities surfaced in words of boastful self-deprecation he wrote to Burton Rascoe:[68]

> I know a sufficient smattering to make me "remarkable" (as
> it goes among these ignorant Californians) in conversation.
> Conversation! There you are: some one should hire me, like a
> parrot, to speak. My memory is stored with a thousand allusions,
> grave and humorous, applicable to any subject, droll and dry to
> hear, from smut to sublimity, from the origin of 'baiser mon cul'
> [kiss my ass] to 'the multitudinous laughter of the sea'. Pah![69]

The demobilization orders that finally came informed Lewis that he had been chosen to close down camp libraries throughout the country. He started in California and moved on to camps in Kansas, Texas, Georgia, and Kentucky. At each installation, he inventoried their books, furniture, and office supplies and arranged for their disposition. It was a routine exercise until San Antonio, when an excruciating toothache intervened:

> To Sherwood Anderson
>
> November 6, 1919
>
> Dear Sherwood,
>
> ... God punished me. When I rode into camp Funston, Kansas (a
> hell of a place!) he sent the dull ache and to my right jaw. My
> first night was spent awake and in misery, and for 72 hours I
> suffered the tortures of the most successfully damned until I
> got to San Antonio one midnight and got emergency treatment (a

*lancing of the gum). The next morning, my abscessed tooth with
all appurtenances thereunto belonging, including all rights,
tenements and hereditaments, were forcibly ejected from the
premises of my right jaw forever and ever, Amen. Jesus Christ!
What a siege. It cost me five pounds of goodly flesh and a heap
o' blood and for five days I couldn't chew even bread. Now I'm
in a happier frame of mind—the DTs had disappeared; my vision is
normal...*

Ever yours, Lewis[70]

Lewis went to New York City to recover and, while there, cast about for a job for the day when his war service would end. Sherwood Anderson's *Winesburg, Ohio* had been released in June to national acclaim[71] and seeing the author's name in every newspaper and magazine admonished Lewis that he was still a prodigy without a profession.

Lewis stayed at the Brevoort Hotel (since demolished), one block north of Washington Square, from which he wrote to Burton Rascoe that he had decided he wanted to become a literary columnist specializing in translations, something "meaty." He did not want a "Paris Letter" because *that* was too superficial, desultory, and thin[72] (the irony being that, within a few years, that very thing—a "Paris News Letter"—would be his destiny).

He visited with Harold Stearns, H. L. Mencken and Waldo Frank, all of whom judged that he knew too little American history. They handed him some books to read, one of which, Frank's own *Our America*, stung Lewis with observations that may have been too insightful for comfort:

*The psychological history of the Jew in the United States is
the process of his rather frenzied conformation to the land of
his new opportunity: the sharpening of his means to power, the
perfecting of his taste for comfort, the suppression of the
mystical in his heart...*

*... [The Jew] knew that the best defense from the subtle
promptings of his race lay in the passionate devotion to
rational pursuits...And everything he did, he did a little more
intensely, a little more like the fanatic, than his brothers...*

Jews of this sort have played a great part in the recent
intellectual life of the United States. They are bitter, ironic,
passionately logical. And the camps of the Enemy fascinate them
so, they cannot keep away. They become critics of the arts. They
consort with artists [and] *study the anatomy of aesthetics.*[73]

Lewis next saw Stearns four months later, after the man had lost everything important to him: his wife (in childbirth), all his money, and custody of his son, who was sent to live with his mother-in-law in California. In Paris, Lewis would take pity on Stearns and give him lodging and money.

In the summer of 1920, Lewis held the title of "Assistant Director of Army Libraries." He had been placed in charge of a training school at Camp Grant, Illinois, about eighty miles west of Chicago, where soldiers could study to become librarians. The curriculum included five lectures given by Lewis supplemented by the lectures of invited speakers,[74] one of whom was Frederick Paul Keppel, the former dean of Columbia College and currently the third assistant secretary of war.

Dr. Keppel had just accepted the post of administrative commissioner of the U.S. legation to the ICC in Paris. The ICC commissions were being created to represent their countries' private business and financial institutions in matters of international debt repayments, trade, and participation in the reconstruction of Europe. Its members would include Belgium, Denmark, France, Great Britain, Italy, Luxemburg, Netherlands, Poland, Sweden, and the United States. Dr. Keppel's job would be to liaise between the ICC's Paris headquarters,[75] the U.S. Chamber of Commerce in Washington, and European bankers, politicians, and businessmen. His posting was to commence January 1, 1921, and he was looking for someone to serve as his assistant. The candidate had to be able to think and write coherently, have administrative abilities and be conversant in French. Dr. Keppel offered Lewis the position and Lewis accepted. His new title would be "Editorial Secretary for the American Commission of the ICC" and his address 33 Rue Jean Goujon, Paris. Lewis completed a passport application that described him as twenty-five years old, five feet five inches, with brown hair, Roman nose, round chin, oval face, fair complexion and "mustached." His mother, Cecilia, attested to his date and place of birth in an affidavit that she signed in Denver, Colorado, where, after Joseph's death, she had gone to live with her older brother, Henry Lorie.

When Lewis told his friends of his plans, Sherwood Anderson asked him to look for someone in Paris to translate *Winesburg, Ohio*, and Sinclair Lewis asked him to do the same for his satire of American life, *Main Street*, which was then on the threshold of success. Sinclair wrote to his friend and publisher, Alfred Harcourt:

> November 26, 1920
>
> Dear Alf:
>
> ... Lewis Galantière, an intelligent chap I know here in Washington, friend to Sherwood Anderson, Guy Holt, Burton Rascoe, et al., is going to France, to be stationed there on a business mission. He insists that Main Street must be translated into French. He seems to know something of French publishers and of the proper approach. He is a fine lad and I have given him a card to Spingarn so that he may talk over this with him.
>
> Corking, 17,000 already. We'll get that 100,000.
>
> Thaznuff
>
> sl[76]

Lewis resigned from the army on December 1, 1920 and, a week later, set sail for France on *La Lorraine*, a ship that had earned its place in history eight years earlier when her crew had transmitted wireless warnings of icebergs to the *Titanic*. Now *La Lorraine* was making scheduled runs between New York City and the port of Le Havre at the mouth of the Seine.

Lewis described the nine-day crossing as "unendurable," his nausea having welled and ebbed as the coal-fired ship plodded through the winter Atlantic.[77] In Paris, he settled into the apartment of a Chicago friend, Helene Edel,[78] in Auteuil, an hour's walk west of his office. Although the apartment was unattractive, its setting, Paris's sixteenth *arrondissement,* was and remains verdant and lovely. Lewis's job at the ICC was to help U.S. companies win contracts for the reconstruction of French roads, bridges, utilities, and industries[79] and to advocate on behalf of American banks for the repayment of their war loans. Lewis had neither experience nor expertise in these matters but found the job to be well suited to his abilities and learned quickly.[80]

At the ICC, Lewis's romantic imaginings of France—the impressions and hopes that he had been nurturing since his settlement house days—became real. The joie de vivre and the *dignité* of his ICC coworkers, especially those who had suffered cruel losses in the war, earned his respect:

> We had a luncheon mess, a popote, in the basement of the handsome town house of the Marquis de Villeroy in which we were lodged. The stenographers would take turns managing the mess, buying the food, and overseeing the cooking. There, around one large oilcloth-covered table, we lunched together—office boys, typists, clerks, and officials. As often as his engagements permitted, Mr. Keppel lunched with us, and I know that he never had as good a time when he lunched elsewhere. The war of 1914-18 was fresh in everyone's mind. All the men at the table had participated in it and told stories about it, from the brilliant Normalien[81] Captain René Arnaud, to the squat, sandy-haired office manager, Sergeant Sauvaget.
>
> I myself used to tell them Negro dialect stories in French (Lord knows where I got that grotesque notion), and I shall never forget Mr. Keppel's yelp of astonishment when one of the secretaries, Madeleine Charvagat, called to me from the other end of the table, "Oh, Monsieur Galantière, chantez-nous encore, 'Zese bones going to rise again.'" It appears that I sang "American folk songs" at that table.[82]

The "brilliant Normalien" of whom Lewis spoke was René Arnaud. René had fought in the goriest battles on the Somme. Called up in early September 1914, he had been promoted to 2nd lieutenant after three months in recognition of his abilities and because of the annihilation of the French officers who preceded him.

René Arnaud, 1919.

René was the embodiment of the soul of France: courageous, modest, incorruptible and fatalistic: the model Frenchman, made more endearing by his admiration of Lewis's knowledge of art, literature, and philosophy and his fluency in English, French, and German. Lewis flattered René by attributing to him a greater cultural knowledge than Lewis knew he possessed— saying "As you know, René" and "As you will recall" when referring to some arcane cultural allusion that René would not have known or recalled. It was a gentle vanity—manipulative but ingratiating.

For René, after the horrors of the trenches, life at America's ICC offices was a haven. He saw in Lewis, his boss, a man of letters, a man of conscience, a generous man who obviously loved and admired the French people in general and him in particular. In March 1932, René would name Lewis godfather to his second son, Michel Pascal *Lewis* Arnaud. During his lifetime, Lewis would meet the boy only once, in the early 1970s, when René and Michel sat at Lewis's table at the Century Association in New

York. There, the young man was impressed by the deference shown his elderly godfather by the association members who approached the table to pay Lewis their respects.[83]

Soon after he arrived in Paris, Lewis kept a promise he had made to Sherwood Anderson: he found someone to translate *Winesburg, Ohio*. His choice was Madame Marguerite Gay who, having read the novel while visiting the American Library in Paris, was keen to do the job.[84]

In May, Sherwood, his wife, Tennessee (or "T"), and the journalist Paul Rosenfeld came to Paris and stayed for the summer.[85] Lewis greeted them at the Gare St. Lazare and brought them to the Hôtel Jacob et d'Angleterre at 44 Rue Jacob, on the left bank, where they paid the equivalent of less than a dollar a night. (This was the same hotel where, a year later, Ernest and Hadley Hemingway first took a room.) Lewis introduced Sherwood to Sylvia Beach; to James Joyce (who was then working on his magnum opus, *Ulysses*); and to Ezra Pound (who was then nurturing the talents of Joyce, T. S. Eliot, Robert Frost, and Iris Barry).[86] Sylvia Beach and Lewis brought Sherwood to the studio of the American doyen Gertrude Stein for a visit; both later described their meeting as memorable.[87]

Sylvia Beach was raising money to support James Joyce and his family while he was completing *Ulysses*. From what Lewis had seen of Joyce's work-in-progress, he was not impressed. Here, his May 17, 1921 letter to Burton Rascoe:

> By the way, a little American bookseller here [Sylvia Beach] is bringing out Joyce's _Ulysses_ complete at 150, 250 and 350 francs in respective editions, to run to 1000 copies. Joyce himself is a sad-faced, half blind Irishman with a burr, who is always sighing and drinking with Valéry Larbaud. He is not at all the rebel in life that he is on paper and I suspect him to be one of the few men of our day completely detached from schools of politics, schools of writing, schools of thought, and every damn thing else.[88]

I am anxious to see Ulysses (which will be ready in October),
though I must say that the two or three extracts from the Little
Review did not epate me.[89]

The prudishness that had prompted Lewis's criticism of Cabell six years earlier may have colored his first sampling of *Ulysses*, which explicitly depicted Joyce's youth in Ireland. But further reading of the book won him over so that, by the spring of 1921, he was both soliciting financial contributions to support Joyce (even though the author's perpetual impoverishment was largely his own doing) and inquiring stateside about possible publishers:

July 28, 1921

Dear Sylvia,

... Mencken is not encouraging about money for Joyce. He wrote
to Margaret Anderson [founder and editor of the literary
magazine the Little Review] and got the usual "watch this" reply.
[Quoting Mencken] Huebsch would be my one hope, if I were you...

Galantière[90]

Lewis asked Burton Rascoe to contribute:

October 20, 1921

Dear Burton,

... I want to write you about J. Joyce. He has been here some
time with the family—wife and two grown kids, and is financially
flat on his fanny. They live in one room, in the rue de
L'Université and haven't a sou. Literally, Joyce had two francs
when I saw him the other evening. I collected a few hundred for
him, and am looking for more. Do you know anyone in America who
would hold the hat for him (I have sent Mencken a line about
it). The money might be sent either to me or to Sylvia Beach,
Shakespeare & Co., 12 Rue de l'Odéon (Sylvia is publishing
his Ulysses). Maybe, too, you could spread the news of the
forthcoming book; it will be ready in November, run to 800 pages,
and will be handsomely presented in three editions (total 1000
copies): one ed. at 150 francs; a larger at 250 francs; a third
on Holland paper, signed by Joyce, at 350 francs. I expect to

> get a little money from Red [Sinclair] Lewis (who is at Pallanza,
> on Lake Maggiore)[91] and from Scofield Thayer who is in Vienna (I
> ran into him in Berlin last month). But I don't know to whom
> else to write.[92]

Ulysses was scheduled for publication on February 2, 1922, Joyce's forti-
eth birthday, but was delayed due to problems with the cover, so that only
two copies were released on that date. The following week, Joyce inscribed
number 282 to Lewis:

> To Lewis Galantière / James Joyce / Paris / 11 February 1922.[93]

When the book sold out through multiple printings, Lewis and James Joyce
spoke about collaborating on a lecture series about *Ulysses* for Lewis to
take on tour. And Sylvia Beach asked Lewis to write a guide about how to
read the work.[94] But Lewis declined to do either. He surmised that neither
would pay much and would intrude on his work at the ICC and occasional
writing jobs for the American market such as he here described in a letter
to Burton Rascoe:

> October 20, 1921
>
> Dear Burton:
>
> I did a job for Mencken the other day: wrote him an exhaustive
> treatise on Paris newspapers. He wanted it for the use of one
> Patterson, owner of the Baltimore Sun, and of Adams, its chief
> editor...I shall be able to get out of the distant & ugly Edel
> apartment in Auteuil on the 1st Nov. I have three rooms & a
> kitchen on the Quai de Béthune, in the Île Saint Louis, and am
> the envy of my friends. Come & stay with me, & eat with me at
> Mme Lecomte's good table.[95]

Madame Lecomte was proprietress of a restaurant—*Au Rendez-vous des
Mariniers*—at 33 Quai d'Anjou, on the north bank of the Île Saint Louis.
From 1904 to 1953 it was where the barge owners and washerwomen of
the district met for lunch. Lewis brought Ernest Hemingway to the place,
and it was there that Hemingway placed Jake Barnes and Bill Gorton in
The Sun Also Rises.[96]

Lewis complained to Burton about his "dog's life" existence, but it was a "dog's life" of a particularly Parisian variety:

> No books, no theater, a little music and, happily, some conversation at dinner in the wine shop by the river.[97]

Lewis's "three rooms & a kitchen on the Quai de Béthune" had its shortcomings but, as he told Sherwood in late November 1921, it also had its charms:

> I have moved into a small apartment on the Île Saint-Louis, on the other side of the island from the little "bistro" where we used to eat and, though I shall probably freeze there in the winter and have no bath-room nor any light except oil lamps and candles, I think I shall be happy there.[98]

The apartment became smaller when Lewis magnanimously let Harold Stearns move in while Stearns was writing *America and the Young Intellectual*, an examination of America's post–World War I generation. Stearns brought with him an unrelenting financial parasitism that eroded their friendship[99] and drained Lewis's wallet, already thinned by the nonpayment of a translation fee he had been counting on. Hoping to supplement his ICC wage, Lewis asked Burton Rascoe to consider publishing a regular newspaper column about the Paris literary scene:

> If I had a regular job of it; if someone gave me space monthly, say, and took my junk...Paris & its book world are immensely rich in material, and I make mental notes soon forgotten, of things worth space in America. I want to write about the frères Tharaud; about Pierre Mac Orlan; Giraudoux; Gourmont; new books; the Larbaud conference on Joyce; the Goncourt prize winner, Maran, a Nigger; and much else.[100]

Burton agreed to try a column or two in the *New York Tribune*'s weekly "Reviews of Books," and Lewis mailed the first piece on April 7, 1922. The *Tribune* carried it three weeks later under the banner "Paris News Letter."[101] Other "Paris News Letters" followed on May 2 and May 9, and Lewis waited for Burton's verdict, praying that he had not made a fool of himself. Word came in mid-May:

> Dear Lewis
>
> I have been so frightfully rushed on the new job that I have not had a chance to write to you. Your letters have been superb. Quite the best thing of the kind that has ever been published in English and that goes for the English literary magazines and supplements as well as for the American. I am extremely proud of you. My opinion of your Paris Letters is not only my own but it is quite generally shared and Ernest Boyd[102] asked me to tell you that he thought the same.
>
> Keep up the good work. My suggestion would be that you do it very much in the manner that you have been. Write anything that comes into your head and don't necessarily confine yourself to books. For instance, I enjoyed especially your paragraph about the Shoenberg Concert.[103]

Lewis replied:

> Dear Burton—
>
> Your letter of the 15th covers me with blushes, or should, if it weren't more extravagant than just. But I'm glad that you let me have something of a free hand.[104]

Emboldened, Lewis asked Burton to have the *Tribune* buy a French font, so that his American readers could "appreciate French notes that suggest France & French literature a little more intimately than the usual review." A week later, this came from Burton:

> I hope that by this time you have received my letter telling you that your pieces from Paris have been excellent. I don't very well see how it could be improved.[105]

And on June 12:

> You are making a great hit with your "Paris Letter." I hear comments from it on all sides.[106]

Over the next two years, Lewis wrote 140 weekly columns for the *New York Tribune* and 13 columns for the Paris edition of the *Chicago Tribune* under the pen name "Lewis Gay."[107] With the added income, he enjoyed a better existence than he had ever known. He was young, in Paris, in the thrall of life, and he had money.

In the early 1920s, Paris was home to the postwar avant-garde: men and women who intuitively understood that Europe's institutions and orthodoxies had been corrupt and decadent, and were ripe for replacement following the Continent's spasm of self-immolation. These artists, poets, composers, and authors did not know what new artistic esthetics would emerge from the ashes, but were confident that *they* would be their creators. Spontaneity, intuition, unadornment and unsentimental simplicity would be its hallmarks. For Americans observing this cultural revolution from the other side of the Atlantic, Lewis was their eyes and ears:

> PARIS (Special Correspondence),— The other night occurred the répetition générale of Rolf de Maré's Ballets Suédois...I saw Stanislavsky, Mme. Knipper-Tchekhova, Diaghileff, Strawinsky [sic], Merejkovsky, Bunin among the Russians; Satie, Roussel, Koechlin, five of "Les Six," the four protégés of Satie, who compose "'L'Ecole d'Arcueil," among the musicians; Picasso, Derain, Marie Laurencin, Fernand Léger, Gardner Hale, among the painters; Cocteau, Drieu la Rochelle, Clive Bell, John Peale Bishop, E.E. Cummings, Ezra Pound, James Joyce (and family), among the writers; Marcel L'Herbier, Jacque Catelain and Rodolfo Valentino, among the movie people; Lady Rothermere, Lady Colfax [her son Peter would become another of Lewis's friends] and a number of ambassadrices among the foreign swells.[108]

This was the fulfillment of the fantasy that Lewis had so long nurtured. Not yet thirty years old, he and his wife Dorothy were in their ascendancy.

Dorothy and Lewis.

· CHAPTER 4 ·

THE UNRAVELING

ON MARCH 17, 1924, THE *New York Tribune* bought the *New York Herald* and the merged papers became the *New York Herald Tribune*.[109] Soon thereafter, Burton Rascoe was fired from his job as the paper's literary editor and Lewis's "Paris News Letter" came to an end.[110] His last regular column appeared the month before he and Dorothy were married, and the income that had been supplementing his ICC salary suddenly stopped. Lewis made up some of the shortfall by completing his translation of Jean Cocteau's *The Grand Ecart* for G. P. Putnam's Sons and Cocteau's *Thomas the Imposter* for D. Appleton & Company. He wrote articles for H. L. Mencken's *Baltimore Sun*, including a March 1925 piece in which he assured American readers that France was not headed toward dictatorship, but the fees were too little to meet the expenses of his newly married state, and Lewis turned to Hemingway for help in finding a new post as book critic. Hemingway recommended him to Ernest Walsh, editor of the literary journal *This Quarter*:

> January 29, 1925
>
> ... Lewis Galantière...writes excellent criticism of French books and could do you very damned well as Paris correspondent. He also writes on American Literature. His stuff is published in the Dial, Am. Mercury, and he formerly did a Paris letter for the NY. Tribune. In English.

Write to him. I had a letter from him just yesterday, very blue because he wasn't writing anything.[111]

Ernest followed up with Walsh two months later:

March 28, 1925

... Think Galantière's stuff is first intelligent criticism of contemporary young Frenchman I've ever read.[112]

F. P. Keppell, the first commissioner of America's ICC legation, had left the post in July 1922 to become head of the Carnegie Foundation. In 1925 his successor, Basil Miles, was musing aloud about how useful it might be to have a trained economist on staff to take over for Lewis. Faced with the prospect that he might soon be unemployed, Lewis and Dorothy set out for New York on a one-week mission to find him a job. Old friends greeted him and Burton Rascoe hosted a welcome-home celebration. Lewis made the rounds of publishers, editors, and fellow critics who knew him or knew of him,[113] but no job offers materialized and he and Dorothy returned to Paris without prospects and with their bank account depleted. In October, Hemingway's first book, *In Our Time*, was published. Lewis declared it "magnificent"[114] and that same month asked Burton for a loan.[115]

On May 23, 1926, Lewis received a telegram—actually a "Marconi-Gram"—from ICC Commissioner Basil Miles, telling him that his days at the ICC were about to end:

Plan practically approved...Trained economist come Paris October first. Am in communication with Keppel regard your own future after that date in case you consider returning United States.[116]

Two days later, Commissioner Miles sent a letter that likely set Lewis's teeth on edge:

Mr. Burland [the ICC's new economist] shall be transferred...to Paris October 1st.

I talked to Dr. Keppel about you the other day and he and I agreed that it was probably better in the long run that you should anchor to something where your literary inclinations and

proved training would find a market. Dr. Keppel suggested that
you might be able to launch either in New York or Chicago—and
he said he had something fairly tangible for such a proposition
in St. Louis—a book shop which might specialize on modern
literature and particularly the foreign end of it. Perhaps some
kind of library work and research might be more palatable to
you, but the difficulty there seems to me to be the matter of
compensation...

With kind regards, Basil Miles[117]

Lewis was on borrowed time and in a sour mood:

May 25, 1926

Burton:

... I've been here six years, and I've decided that may be
what the trouble is. I should like to come home for good in,
say, October. Do you know if I could get a job in New York?
Unfortunately, I am one of these birds who can do 'anything.'
But you keep your eyes open, and meanwhile I'll snoop around by
mail.

... Last night we had Clive Bell and his ladyfriend to dinner.
Also Seldeses, Seward and [Dorothy] Parker, and the Bromfields
in the course of the evening. Dorothy and I adore Seward. Mrs.
Parker seems to me the most overrated person in the world as
dinnertable companion, wit, or whatever you like. She may have
a sterling character, and be an agreeable humorist, but her
fashion of cocking her head on one side and popping her eyes and
moaning something like "Ohhhhhh. May I reeeeally come again?
I do so love to come here." It's nauseating. And she has no
conversation whatever, but none.[118]

The Paris summer doldrums passed without any prospects of employment. Lewis wrote to Sherwood Anderson to say that he would be returning to the United States by the end of the year. He implied that it was a career choice:

I think I have had my fill of Europe, although living here is
surely more agreeable than at home. But I ought to get to work

seriously and the only jobs that would suit me as a permanent interest are to be found in New York.[119]

On August 29, 1926, the *New York Times* published a story about the effects of trade barriers on international commerce and monetary stability. The monograph was Lewis's last ICC project.[120] His former ICC boss, Frederick Keppel, arranged a job interview with Condé Nast, editor of *Vanity Fair* magazine.[121] Could Lewis be in New York City in a week? Lewis and his brother-in-law, George Butler, booked third-class accommodations aboard the *Caronia*. Lewis wrote to Burton, "I have no idea yet what I shall do if the Nast wire is a false alarm." It wasn't a false alarm, but Nast wasn't looking for another literary critic or journalist. Instead, he wanted Lewis to analyze his publishing business, including the magazine *Vanity Fair*, and recommend managerial improvements. With no other offers in hand, Lewis accepted.

Dorothy and Lewis hosted a farewell party at the apartment they had been occupying on Boulevard St. Michel. When an acquaintance, Carlos Drake, told Lewis he felt sorry for him having to leave Paris, Lewis enthused, "But I'm not sorry! I'm going home to conquer the big city!"[122] Before he left, Lewis promised Sylvia Beach that he would do what he could to stop the unauthorized publication of *Ulysses* in America. Joyce had been stripped of his intellectual property rights to *Ulysses* by a U.S. copyright code that withheld protection for books that had been banned for sexual explicitness. An American publisher, Samuel Roth, exploiting the vulnerability, had serialized *Ulysses*, sometimes with his own gratuitous edits, in a magazine he owned, *Two Worlds Monthly*.[123]

September 30, 1926 was Lewis's last day of work at the ICC. He pocketed his last paycheck and, with Dorothy, sailed from France at the end of October.[124] A New York hotel room was their residence for the first three months, and then an apartment on Waverly Place. Lewis wrote to Sylvia Beach with the news:

January 26, 1927

Dear Sylvia:

... We are in a state of terrible fatigue, Dorothy and I. Four days ago we finally moved from a hotel into the apartment we have taken on Waverly Place, and we have still books to shelve, curtains to put up, rugs to lay, and hundreds of little things to buy. What a country! Their labour-saving devices are a fraud, and their labourers are a menace to the peace of the middle-class citizenry. I am so sick of my folly in leaving Paris that I dare not think of it. (This between ourselves.)

... Dorothy has just called out that I am to give you her love (with which goes my own), and to say the candies were delicious,— which they were. Say also to Joyce that I have posted the copy of Ulysses to his cousin.

Affectionate greetings to Adrienne[125] (shakes 'and a zat!') And to the Antheils.

Dorothy joins me in sending love to you and Adrienne. Lewis[126]

His next letter was to his former Île Saint Louis neighbor, William "Bie" Bradley. Bie and his wife Jenny were literary agents who had often turned to Lewis for advice and help with translations. Lewis told them of his homesickness for Paris.

February 3, 1927

Dear Bie,

You are so right about Paris being the proper place for Dorothy and me. We have glided very smoothly into the social stream of New York, but the business of daily unholy living here is so difficult, so hectic, that I feel we shall never be entirely happy again until we are fixées in Paris once more. It is a pity— if I may be selfish about you—that you are not here this week, for, having now been installed in our apartment these ten days past, we should be ready to welcome you here in Waverly Place as you have so often welcomed us at Mario's et ailleurs.

[Condé] Nast has gone south for a few weeks, taking with him a 20,000-word survey of Vanity Fair which I completed in time for his departure. I do not know whether I should really pray

that it please him. If he likes it, I shall have a "career"
in his organization; if not, that may prove a way out of New
York in the direction of Paris. The survey is pretty severe as
regards the present management of the magazine, but I think it
entirely just. I think the old boy is openminded but it is very
difficult to estimate the openmindedness of any man about his own
creation,—or even about his own possessions, whether created by
him or not.

I have a little article by Ford on expatriates, with particular
attention to Hemingway, Pound, and Antheil. We shall use it in
our April issue, with a print of Hartmann's portrait...

I'll write you again, of course, when there is something to
write. For the moment, Dorothy and I are terribly fatigued,
after the trial of moving in and getting adjusted.[127]

Hemingway's *The Sun Also Rises* had been out for three months and had become a commercial success, its minimalist style, later described as the "Iceberg Theory," drawing a wide readership. There was a second printing in December, and more soon thereafter. As interest in the book grew, *Vanity Fair*'s editor, Frank Crowninshield, asked Lewis to persuade Ernest to write something for the magazine. Lewis's letter went out on January 6, 1927:

Dear Ernest,

I suppose that since [Heywood Campbell] Broun and the rest of
the great guys have told the World what the world could see
for itself if it would read—that The Sun Also Rises is a great
book,—everybody in America is asking you to write for the great
magazines of this country. I expect you to get so rich in a year
or two that you will begin to look like Henry Mencken, with a
fur coat and a long fat, black cigar in one corner of your face.

Frank Crowninshield would like to help you to this enviable
state. If you have two or three stories which are anywhere
from 1800 to 2500 words in length, which could be read by the
intelligent people who are reading The Sun Also Rises, will you
send them along to us. The stories need not be fiction, of course.
You can write about pretty nearly anything you please—except

abortion and allied subjects, maybe—We will dress you up in our
handsome 10 pt. Caslon.

Our friend, Mr. Anderson, told me I was wrong when I said you
were a great writer because, said he: "A man's gotta have
character to be a great writer and he hasn't got no character."
I agreed with him on both points but I nearly died laughing at
the notion that Sherwood might have thought that he was a great
writer precisely because he had character.

Write me a note one of these days, and give my love to one or
two people.

Yours, Galantière[128]

Lewis's allusion to Anderson concerned a recent rift between the two novelists. Hemingway's newfound success allowed him—or, maybe, compelled him—to ridicule some people who had helped him in his career. Donald Ogden Stewart (the model for Bill Gordon in *The Sun Also Rises*) put it this way: "The minute he began to have some sort of obligation to you… then is when he had to kill you."[129] In his early writing, Ernest had adopted Sherwood's naturalistic voice but, later, chafed at the thought that others would detect Anderson's influence. To dispel that notion, Ernest ridiculed Anderson in a 1925 satirical novella *Torrents of Spring*. Anderson thought the effort unworthy but never disparaged Hemingway's work or laid claim to credit for it.[130]

Ernest wrote back to Lewis to say he would entertain an offer from *Vanity Fair*, and Lewis replied:

March 7, 1927

Dear Ernest:

Letter received and contents noted, as I am learning to say.

Vanity Fair will pay you, upon acceptance of a MSS of 1000 to
2500 words, One Hundred Fifty Dollars. If your stuff takes with
the forward-looking readers of our most beautiful magazine, your
rate will go up with succeeding contributions.

*... When are you coming to New York? We have had a very gay
winter, despite the trouble and nerve-racking work of getting
ourselves installed. We found an apartment in December, moved
into it in January, and have to be out by April 1 because they
are going to tear the damned building down! More fun!*[131]

Dorothy and Lewis moved once again—the third time in four months—
to an apartment in a brownstone at 229 East Forty-Eighth Street.[132] That
was where they were living when Lewis completed the assignments Condé
Nast had given him and his work for the publisher ended. To earn a living,
Lewis returned to the reliable drudge work of translation. Considered a
nearly clerical vocation, translating paid little and Lewis had to do a lot of
them to earn a modest income. In the course of about a year, there were
five volumes from French to English and one from German into English:

Remy de Gourmont, *Dream of a Woman*, Liveright

Léon Daudet, *The Stupid XIXth Century*, Payson and Clark

Paul Morand, *Nothing but the Earth* R. M. McBride & Co.

Jeanne Maurice Pouquet, *The Last Salon*, Harcourt, Brace & Co.

Raymond Escholier, *Victor Hugo*, Payson and Clark

Jakob Wassermann, *Worlds' Ends*, Liveright

Lewis also worked on an original book-length satire about the gulf between
the French and American business ethos and social culture after the war.
France Is Full of Frenchmen was the closest Lewis would ever come to writing a novel for which he would not have a co-author. In a letter to Burton
Rascoe, he projected onto Burton *his own* inability to become invested in
writing fiction:

July 15, 1926

Burton:

*... You are, to my thinking, a man with a mercurial mind, an
inquisitive intelligence; you are a champion of ideas, not a*

creator of worlds or people. I haven't seen your novel, but
I'll bet that it is satirical and analytical; that you expose
and exploit foibles more than you create character or situation
even. Am I wrong? You may wish a million years to abandon your
interest in what the world is thinking and writing from month to
month, but you will never, never realize that wish.[133]

By the spring of 1927, it was clear to Lewis and to Dorothy that his career as a leading opinion-maker had run its course. They did not enjoy the deference in New York that they had been shown by the glitterati of Paris. While Hemingway's star had been ascending, Lewis, to whom she was anchored, had been reduced to a tradesman, doing translation work under contract. The Paris limelight that once illuminated the couple had sputtered out. So when Dorothy told Lewis that she was going to resume her career as a dancer in Paris, he didn't laugh or protest. He knew he had forfeited the right. And he knew that he wanted to be freed from the unrelenting job of reassuring Dorothy that he had a future; a matter about which he had his doubts. In July, Dorothy booked a passage on a steamship back to France.

Any respite that Lewis might have hoped for following Dorothy's departure did not occur, as abdominal pains and vomiting signaled acute appendicitis. An emergency appendectomy and then weeks of postoperative recuperation limited Lewis's work schedule and shrank his income. He wrote to Helen Haines, his former teacher at the Los Angeles Library School, and told her of his failed marriage, his money problems, and the detour that his career had taken. He asked whether she thought he should try writing for popular magazines. Helen commiserated, but told him that such magazine articles were unworthy of his talents. Helen spoke words of affirmation and encouragement the likes of which Lewis had not been hearing from Dorothy:

August 29, 1927

Dear Lewis:

No, I would not think you have a gift for popular magazine articles—your mind centers on philosophical or intellectual considerations...You are...indifferent to the obvious & the sentimental...You are always & essentially a "man of letters"; & somehow I am sure that as such you will find expression...

... I suppose, greater in New York than probably anywhere else... the actual physical difficulties of living...must make existence quite maddening. I am so sorry poor little Dorothy succumbed to it all—& it must have been much more dismal for you to go through operation & hospital sojourn without her. What troubles me most is the amount of intensive work you have loaded up on yourself—all these translations, within so short a time! I don't wonder you have the commissions, for you are a virtuoso in that field; but it seems a superhuman effort to carry out so much at once. [134]

Lewis recuperated from his appendectomy over the summer of 1927, alone, dejected, on a tight budget, and under the self-imposed pressure that comes from knowing that everything is at risk. Any hope for improving his reputation and his bank account now lay with *France Is Full of Frenchmen*. Royalties from that book, if any, would still be months off.

A reprieve from Lewis's loneliness came in September, during a visit to the offices of his publisher, Payson and Clark. There he ran into Iris Barry, an acquaintance from his Paris years, who was in the United States to get a first-hand look at the Hollywood film business for a London newspaper. Iris, like Hemingway, had been one of Ezra Pound's students and, like Lewis, she had helped Sylvia Beach with her distribution of *Ulysses*.[135] In 1927, Iris was married to the poet Alan Porter. And Lewis was still married to Dorothy.

Iris was a woman of passionate and yet strangely blindered emotions. She had had two children by the writer/painter Wyndham Lewis: a son, Robin, whom she had placed in the care of her mother, and a daughter,

Masie, born the following year and now in the home of a financially well-off childless couple, the Spencers. Lewis and Iris allowed themselves to fall in love, or at least to give in to an infatuation that was made more intense and poignant by the inevitability that, in November, Iris would return to England. Iris's letters are all that remain of that interlude; Lewis's to Iris were lost or destroyed. Lewis was thirty-two, Iris thirty-one. The first of Iris's letters that Lewis saved was dated Saturday, October 2, 1927.

> *Lewis, dearest Lewis,*
>
> *[I] lunched nicely and quietly with the Fairbankses* [Douglas Fairbanks and Mary Pickford] *who are human after all even if there is the prettiest air of White Lodge or Trianon about it—Fairbanks himself is a love, I think. She's a "remarkable woman" tout court, don't you think?...They quarreled sweetly about films and I flattered her, not him, which proved to be right.*
>
> *... Did I tell you, I apologize if I did, about little Jews I meet who tell me confidentially that the European directors are the most interesting, and add obsequiously that they, too, are Europeans. It is to laugh—or weep with shame.*
>
> *Alas, the box for room 134 was innocent of correspondence this evening. You will write soon: you needn't write at all: it is very delicious being torn by apprehension, shaken by longing, suffused with memories, filled with hopes of something so vague that it is hardly anything but just hope itself of seeing you again. Where? In a railway station, Jo's office, the Algonquin?*
>
> *... The film critic on the Daily Express not long ago coined (or did he steal) the word "californication." I don't see much trace of it still. They are as you indicated externally at any rate most horribly respectable.*
>
> *... I adore you enormously. Iris*[136]

Thursday, October 6

> *I terribly want you to finish the delicious, wise, tenderly wicked novel about the Americans [France Is Full of*

Frenchmen] partly because no one else is clever enough, or knows both sides of the medal enough, to do it, and more still because it will give me so much pleasure. [137]

Saturday evening, October 8

here are the sitting [pictures] for you. Can you imagine how I got my leg into just that position?

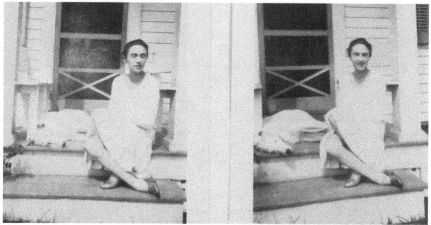

Iris Barry.

... Your letters are so good: they might not be, but they have your "disappearing" quality so nicely. Perhaps your reticences are one of the things that charmed me most: only people who talk as much as we do can avoid saying the things that are shocking. And how grateful one is for the not-said.

... You don't know how much I want to be with you: it's not your affair but my happiness...

I will be back in New York by the 25th or 26th and stay till Nov. 12th...naturally I won't hope to get more than small snatches of you, and shall only hope to get a big snatch during the weekend. That is if I am lucky. But it doesn't matter at all, really, so long as I just see you for one piece before I go. Gloomy words, before I go. Go I must. Hell.

And of course, as I said before, you wouldn't like me so well if I wasn't going, it would lose that exquisite transient, dream-like quality.

... You know I terribly need to be with you a little, only ever so little when you consider how long years are—you are so good to me, so lovely. I'm not a bit good to you, or don't feel I am, though you know I would be if you wanted it. I quite simply love you: just that.[138]

Wednesday, October 12

I just realized why writers like acrobats: it is the precision which enchants them...you must know how much I appreciate your particular dexterity, the human prestidigitation of behavior which is the loveliest thing of all the people that we like—the balancing trick of words, intonation, sous-entendus, when nothing enfin is said & everything communicated.

... Lewis, ...you know I am intoxicated with joy at knowing you. I shall wear the thought of you all through the London winter rain & fog & mud & sleet so like a red knitted muffler. I shall be so happy, sometimes so grief-stricken but that will be a pleasure too...

... Some things are awful to remember: not daring to ring up the day after we first met & feeling ill when I picked up the telephone—... oh, did you know how I was dying and how much I loved you? You did I think.[139]

Saturday, October 14

... After I go back to London I shall have to do without you: that seems as if it would be possible, but only because I am hoping to have some more of you when I return. From your letter it seems that I shall...

The way you end your letter, saying you are troubled by things that letters can't cure, may or may not have been responded to in this letter of mine. As you may well imagine, I have speculated not only on reading that, but all along... Darling Lewis...can you bear to be loved?[140]

When Iris returned to London that November, she reclaimed her daughter from the Spencers and brought her to London to live with her. The experiment failed in about a year. Iris place both of her children in a boarding school without revealing to either that they were sister and brother. In early 1930, she wrote to Lewis about these things.

March 10, 1930

> I expect I told you that I was summoned to fetch my daughter aged almost 8 away from her "home" because she was so naughty and went for her "parents" with a poker, etc., etc. She is now with the older cheeild [sic] but as they don't know and apparently no one else does that they are bro. and sis. They both have green eyes, the tender not the sea green type, but the boy's are apparently Chinese and go up which is quite horrible. I think not much of all this, it wasn't a successful effort. Both are really rather like Tallulah both to listen to and to see, though uglier. I like little blond cherubs not foreigners as these are—wops my god. Jesus. To think of it. I absolutely refuse to devote myself to them. Darling you will tear up this letter quite small or burn it won't you, because these things are not for public consumption.
>
> Iris[141]

Lewis wrote a review of Iris's novel *The Last Enemy* for the July 2, 1930, issue of the *New Republic*:

> Miss Barry has written a remarkable and very readable novel and has shown qualities of imagination, skill, assurance and compassion which make us look forward very eagerly to her future writing.[142]

Later that year, Iris and her husband, Alan Porter, moved to the United States, where Alan obtained a teaching position at Vassar. Iris and Lewis saw each other occasionally during that decade, sometimes in the company of their shared friends and acquaintances: Lincoln Kirstein, the architect Philip Johnson, composers Paul Bowles and Virgil Thomson, John Houseman, and Alfred Barr Jr., director of the new Museum of Modern

Art. They were also regulars at the Sunday salons in the homes of Kirk and Constance Askew.

Iris and Alan Porter remained married until 1934. Theirs was an odd arrangement. They had not spent their wedding night together and, during their marriage, Iris had taken other lovers, the occasional consequences of which she accepted:

> It was not difficult in London at that time to be aborted. One
> only needed money and the right address. I myself between 1925
> and 1928 arranged to have several abortions, including one which
> I shall never forget, as I came back to my flat the same evening
> to give a snack to the fellow (was he a journalist?, I can't
> remember) and so did though not feeling very good. Heaven help
> us, how content men are of themselves ('the lady is tired or not
> feeling so well')...at least that man never knew that I had been
> butchered that same day. How I really hate men.[143]

Alan and Iris divorced in 1934 and, that same year, she married a Wall Street financier Richard Abbot. In 1935, she created MoMA's film library and became its first curator and later its director.[144]

As Lewis was writing *France is Full of Frenchmen*, Dorothy, in Paris, was attempting to resume her career as a dancer. It had been more than a decade since she had been on the stage and she had not trained during her time with Lewis. Now, in her thirties, she was set to go for broke and return, not as a member of the chorus, but as the choreographer and sole performer in a recital at the Comédie de Champs Élysées, near the Pont de l'Alma. Her dance motif would be "modern," to the musical accompaniment of phonograph recordings of "Negro Spirituals and blues." Dorothy sent handbill announcements to the people Lewis and she had counted among their friends, including one to Gertrude Stein, whose copy appears below.

COMÉDIE DES CHAMPS-ELYSÉES 15 Avenue Montaigne — PARIS VIII
(Métro ALMA)

Vendredi 25 Novembre 1927 à 17 heures

MATINEE DE DANSES

donnée par

Dorothy **BUTLER**

(Mme GALANTIÈRE)

et consacrée exclusivement aux

NEGRO SPIRITUALS & BLUES

PHOTO SOBOL

PROGRAMME

I. SPIRITUALS

Swing low, Sweet Chariot
On my Journey
Bye and Bye
Hear de Lam's A'Cryin'
Rock Church Rock

II. SPIRITUALS

Steal Away
Ezekiel saw De Wheel
Water Boy
Goin' to tell God all my Troubles

III. BLUES

Shake That Thing
No Man's Mamma
How'm I doin' It
Whip it to a Jelly
Look were- the Sun done gone

IV. SPIRITUALS

Nobody Knows the Trouble I've seen
Sometimes I feel like a Motherless Child
Were You There.

Costumes exécutés par la Maison FERNANDE, 2, Rue Montaigne

PLACES de 8 à 40 frs. (droits compris) en location à partir du 18 Novembre

BILLETS au Théâtre des Champs-Elysées (Le Bureau de location est ouvert tous les jours de 11 heures à 19 heures sans interruption) et à l'American Express Co. 11, Rue Scribe.

Source: the Beinecke Rare Book and Manuscript Library, Yale University

Ford Madox Ford came, as did "Bie" and Jenny Bradley, the Galantières' neighbors when they lived on the Île Saint Louis.[145] Madox Ford's verdict of the performance was kind: "I've just been to Dorothy Galantière's dance matinee. It went off pretty well but she doesn't move about enough nor 'get across' altogether." The French critic Andre Levinson was less kind. He said that Dorothy had "sought in vain to relieve her entire lack of ability by a touch of suggestiveness" and advised that, in the future, she confine her performances to private salons.[146]

· CHAPTER 5 ·

1928-1934:
ENDINGS AND BEGINNINGS

LEWIS'S HOPE FOR SOLVENCY WAS tethered to the fate of *France Is Full of Frenchmen*. The book's plot was simple: the French wanted their war debts canceled and the Americans wanted them paid. The protagonists, members of the fictitious "American Foreign Affairs Committee," go to Paris representing U.S. banking and industrial interests and find that the Parisians' joie de vivre is seductive, but that their apparent lack of ambition is mystifying and their indifference to contractual promises is galling. For their part, the French envy the Americans' wealth but bridle at their obsession with efficiency, their self-subjugation to work, and their crassness. *France Is Full of Frenchmen* culminates with the American protagonist, Senator Wise, describing a banquet speech that he recently delivered to French businessmen and dignitaries, a speech he gave in French so that, he said, "there won't be any mistake about it":

> Madames et Monsoors. Je suis beaucoup interesser par les
> remarks de la dernier speaker le member de Cabinet de le French
> Government. Je no parler in le nom de my Government alors my
> remarks not official mais je will say a few words pour faire la
> situation clear. Dans le first place this speaker dire Amerique
> has no heroes except Lafayette, Rochambeau, etc. Je dire Oui
> Amerique has beaucoup better heroes includer Washington, Lincoln,

Franklin, Jefferson, Grant and a lot of others. Amerique jamais
need to importer son heroes de la France or de la Angleterre or
de la anywhere.

Dans le next place General Pershing said dans his Report
to Congress that when Americans arriver in 1917 les Allies
absolument on the run avec les Germans sinking tout le British
shipping et defeater les Allies armees all up and down la ligne.
Alors. Amerique sauver la democracy sauver les Allies sauver la
France et along comes ce Monsoor et has le nerve de dire that
we never won the war and how la France sauver nous where as a
matter de fact nous sauver them. Excepter pour Pershing tout les
Francais would be working for the Germans right this minute et
ca est le truth.

Dans le troisieme point is la question de la debts. All vous
people think les American streets paved avec gold and so on.
Absolument nonsense. Americans spend liberalment mais work tres
hard pour son argent. Et American Government very pauvre. Ce
Monsoor never heard of Coolidge je suppose et le policy de
economy nous pursuer pour 7 yrs. Si le French Government faire
le meme chose et decharger le armee et collecter la taxes et
make tout le mond cougher up they could payer la debt facilement.

Laisser moi tell you ce debt pas Government debt de tout.
American Government borrowed ce argent from American people
and forcer payer back. Le idea que le American people just put
son hand down dans son pocket et forker over le argent pour le
French loans est absolument ridicule. These pauvre Frenchmen
jamais heard about les 3 minute men je suppose. Comment nous
have trouble to collecter le argent avec speeches dans le movies
and le churches et le theaters. Dans all the factories sur pay
day nous make les ouvriers buy liberty bonds ou lose their jobs
ou knock them over the head or something. Amerique pas Shylock.
Pas sur votre life. Amerique damn good business man. American
Government signer sur le dotted ligne et keep son word. French
Government signer sur le dotted ligne et pas keep son word.
Voila le grand difference entre vous people and us people.

Dans le last place Je dire Amerique pas care for friends qui
no respecter their engagements. Nous respecter our engagements
et nous expecter everybody respecter his. Je dire la best thing
pour vous is to pay up and shut up. Alors Amerique make France

riche et prosperous et show France how to live dans la paix et
la efficiency. If France no payer up comme un gentleman without
squealing nobody knows what may happen especialment if vous
have un autre guerre avec somebody dans le future. Je parler ici
purement dans le interest de la France et je donner straight
stuff from the shoulder. I thank you.

When I got thru you could hear a pin drop in that place.

Lewis knew that *France Is Full of Frenchmen* was clever satire, but he also knew that it was not important literature. It did not speak of the human condition or embody immortal truths, and it was not poetic in form or imagery. It would be a book for the decade, but not one for the ages. Lewis dedicated *Frenchmen* to René Arnaud, his brother-in-spirit at the ICC, and handed it to Payson and Clark for publication. He had grown less sanguine about its success as his bank account balance had dwindled.

And then a call came from, of all places, the Federal Reserve Bank of New York (FRBNY). The bank needed someone experienced in dealing with Europe's bankers, economists, and politicians; someone fluent in French, German and English, who understood the social sensibilities of those societies; someone who could competently discuss the culture of those countries: their art, literature and music, as well as banking and economics. The job being offered was chief of the FRBNY's Foreign Research Division.[147] Its timing was exquisite. Lewis grasped the lifeline.[148]

At the time the bank called, in February 1928, the French economy was spiraling into hyperinflation. France had been printing money to pay for recurring national deficits on the assumption that, one day, German reparations would save their currency. In the meantime, the diminishing value of the franc impaired the country's capacity to repay its U.S. war loans or to purchase U.S. exports. Central bankers, led by the FRBNY, had to persuade an obstinate French government that substantial and immediate intervention was required.

Benjamin Strong, FRBNY's director, assigned Lewis to work with the Bank's second in command, Deputy Governor George L. Harrison. Their offices would be those of J. P. Morgan & Co., at 14 Place Vendôme in Paris. Lewis embarked for France that May. It was hard to believe, but he had been away for only fourteen months. It had seemed so much longer. Before embarking, he cabled Dorothy and asked her to meet him at the Gare Havre on the Rue Saint-Lazare on June 3. Dorothy wrote to Virgil Thomson to tell him of the news:

> Dear Virgil,
>
> ... I'm not advertising the fact that [Lewis] arrives Saturday
> because I'm afraid he's rushing right on—His cable tells me
> nothing but—meet me Havre-St. Lazare or will phone! He's been
> expecting to be sent over by the bank but not to Paris except
> en route. However you might cast your eye about the Deux Magots
> Sunday morning.
>
> Dorothy[149]

When Dorothy and Lewis met, he asked her for a divorce. Dorothy agreed, but her price was that he tell the Seine court that it was *she* who was divorcing *him* on grounds of desertion. Lewis agreed, even though everybody knew that Dorothy was then having an affair with the sculptor Roy van Aukon Sheldon.[150]

Throughout the month of June, Lewis and FRBNY Governors Strong and Harrison consulted with central bankers and advised French premier Poincaré as to how best to end the papering-over of France's deficits.[151] Their efforts culminated, on June 24, with the Chamber of Deputies and the Senate approving a three-part plan: the creation of a new standard franc (one fixed to the value of gold), new taxes, and a more balanced budget. Once implemented, the value of the franc immediately ceased its downward spiral and, over the coming months, vigorously gained in value. The *New York Times* congratulated the FRBNY for the "new community of thought" that had been integral to "the present happy moment in French finance."[152]

With that immediate task done, Lewis returned to New York, a rein-vigorated man. He had money to spend, renewed self-confidence, and was freed from his marriage to Dorothy, a fact heralded in the January 16, 1929, issue of the *Palm Beach Post*:

> Mrs. Dorothy Butler Galantière and Roy van Aukon Sheldon, fashionable society sculptor, are both bound for New York aboard the liner Cleveland. They will be married soon after their arrival in the United States, according to intimates here.
>
> Sheldon, who was well-known as a sculptor, is a widower. Mrs. Galantière is the daughter of the late Mrs. Alice Carter Butler, society and club woman of Evanston, Illinois, and has been on the stage. Coming to Paris, she met Galantière six years ago when he was at the height of his fame as a critic with extraordinary gifts.
>
> After their marriage, they entertained extensively, presenting to Parisians such literary and social figures as Lewis Bromfield, Clive Bell, Ford Madox Ford, Mr. and Mrs. F Scott Fitzgerald, Mr. and Mrs. Gilbert Seldes, and Sheldon himself.
>
> Soon after her return to New York [with Lewis in 1927], Mrs. Galantière came back to Paris where, with Sheldon's help, she appeared in a dance spectacle at the Champs Elysees Theater.
>
> Her dancing presentation of Negro "blues" aroused a sharp difference of opinion... Americans came to her aid, but she has not danced publicly since then.
>
> Her divorce from Galantière was on July 5, last. Since then, Sheldon has been most attentive to her.[153]

The Sheldon-Butler wedding drew a good turnout. The *New York Times* carried the story under the indelicate headline "Mrs. D. Galantière Weds." Ford Madox Ford was there, and remarked:

> The great feature of it was that Galantière was there, doing the honours. It was very impressive to hear him say to the bride: "I think I must be going now," and to hear her answer: "See you tomorrow!" It seemed rather cynical but who is one to judge.[154]

Dorothy would marry a third time but, by 1944, would again be single.[155]

In 1929, Scribners published Hemingway's second novel, *A Farewell to Arms*, and Lewis reviewed it for *Hound & Horn*, a new quarterly journal of the arts started by Lincoln Kirstein, still a Harvard undergraduate.[156] Why Lewis would have chosen this fledgling magazine for his review was linked to another of Lincoln Kirstein's interests: he was a cofounder of the *Harvard Society for Contemporary Art*,[157] which had just held a retrospective exhibition of the works of the painter Margarett Sargent McKean.[158] Margarett may have expressed her appreciation to Lincoln by securing Lewis's review for *Hound & Horn*.

Margarett was already an established artist. *Art News* had effused that she possessed an "amazing talent for leaving out of her delicate watercolors all that is not strictly essential," and Forbes Watson, a leading art critic of the day, rhapsodized that "Her subjects seem ready to step from their frames and become really alive."[159]

Margarett was tall, blue-eyed, dark-haired, slender, and elegant. She was smart, educated, driven, and competent. She was three years older and five inches taller than Lewis. And she was manic-depressive and an alcoholic. Lewis fell hopelessly in love with her. Their affair began in Margarett's summer home in Dorset, Vermont, and its trajectory is preserved in Lewis's many handwritten poems, letters, and musings.

Lewis was not Margarett's first extramarital affair. She had had sexual liaisons with men and women before Lewis, and would have them during and after him. Mrs. Henry Cabot (Emily) Lodge said of Margarett that "she took to affairs as easily as to brushing her teeth." Margarett's biography, written by her granddaughter, Honor Moore, captured her sexual voracity:

Attention still came to Margarett naturally, and to respond, she believed, transgressed nothing. She fixed you with her eyes, and if you looked back at her, the room disappeared. Then she began to talk, to smile at you, and you were riveted, fascinated, caught. She did not miss the erotic subtext to a smile or gesture.[160]

Ms. Moore allowed that it would be impossible to compile a complete list of the men and women Margarett had seduced. But, initially, Lewis was certain that he was *the one* for her, and that she was the one for him.

> a new passion, a new gentleness, a new sense of life and its
> possibilities and its meaning, a new vision of human happiness—
> all these things were born in me...

> ... When you said to me that you thought well of my mind,
> instantly it became one that might have been thought well of;
> when you told me I wrote poetically, my letters became those
> of a poet; when you saw distinction in me, it blossomed where
> before there had been none. I swear to you these things are true.
> I am not trying to denigrate what I was before: I know that even
> before I was a man of a certain culture, a certain gift for
> expression, a certain grace of manner, probably. But love does
> work "miracles"; your love made bloom.[161]

Lewis set out to win Margarett with expressions of fulsome and enduring love. He would, by increments, learn that these were the very kind of worshipful sentiments that Margarett found intolerable.

> I have a stubborn conviction that love should be simple, tender,
> and passionate...how can a person who truly loves, "lose"
> anything since it is after all the love we feel, rather than the
> love we receive, which is a great boon...That, I am beginning to
> discover, is what Goethe meant when (as I think I have quoted to
> you before), he wrote: "If I love you, what concern is that of
> yours?"[162]

> ... Love is a thing of pain for you isn't it? The burden of it
> is very great for you, when added to those you already carry...I
> remember vividly with what bitterness you said to me once, "I
> wish I had been able to love anybody two years"; and how sad I
> thought what you said.[163]

The more ardent Lewis became, the more Margarett was repelled. And the more she was repelled, the more obsessed and persistent Lewis became. When he had exhausted his variations on the themes of love, looking in vain for the key to her adoration, he tried to impress Margarett—or divert her—with the lore he had invented about his father:

> I remember you had spoken of dining or lunching with [a Mr.]...
> Motley...My father went to Göttingen University, which is in
> the old Kingdom of Hanover—(and I myself in school in Hanover).
> There is at Göttingen a tablet set up bearing the names of four
> Americans who were students there...My father and I were there
> one day when he came to fetch me home from Hanover to Paris. He
> showed me where he had lived as a student, where Bismarck lodged,
> the student club he had belonged to, and then ...he said with a
> smile, "and there is the reason why you were born in America."...
> The truth seemed to be that the tablet inspired father to hunt
> out the few Americans then at Göttingen, and become friends with
> them, and that one of them, a Chicagoan, became his very close
> friend and financed (or did something about financing) his oil
> expedition into Russia a half dozen years later.[164]

Lewis tried reasoning with Margarett, telling her that she did not need to yield to the misery that was her recurrent state of mind:

> The hardest thing for me to determine is whether or not you are
> really cruel. What I really seem to find in you is a strange
> amalgam of sadism—the love of inflicting pain—and masochism—the
> love of receiving it. There are some people whose desires are
> whipped to a climax only by the first; others only when they are
> being tortured. Occasionally there are people such as I imagine
> you to be who, when their desire to be whipped is not satisfied,
> turnaround in fury, seize the whip themselves, and gain their
> satisfaction and lashing the one by whom they would prefer to
> be hurt. (These terms are of course symbolic; I am accusing you
> "merely" of mental flagellation, not necessarily physical.)
>
> But your case—it is proper to speak of you as a "case" for you
> are a sick soul—and it is a little ironic that I used to speak
> of myself as physician to your soul—your case is infinitely
> more complex than this I have described. A minor complication
> seems to be your weak surrender to a constant state of pain
> and unhappiness. How you fell into the harmful habit I don't
> know, but you do not appear to be able to think of the world as

a normal place unless it appears to you dark, filled with pain, with frustration, with things gone wrong...

The truly saddest thing about you is your deep-seated belief in your incapacity for happiness—indeed for real accomplishment of any sort. As certain people grow dizzy and draw back from the edge of great heights, so you have bred in yourself a terror of happiness and accomplishment; a panic seizes you when you approach the frontier of either...

... You have put me into a state in which I must say to myself: has she softened now because her thirst for my heart's blood was quenched in our last rapture; has she licked her tiger-chops clean and come back to be stroked and to yawn and to play with me until a new thirst for my blood comes over, and again her swift-darting claw opens my breast?

... I know that it was for my sake I was told you did not love me. I know it was because you feared for me that you put the knife into my heart. I know that you sent me brutally away because you thought only thus would I be preserved from sharing your misery and becoming miserable too...

... I know that you have all the gifts of happiness. I know you have also those for misery, but I know, too, that these last can be obliterated before it is too late. You are sick, it is true; you are self-scorching; but at your core you are incorruptible.

Do as you like. I urge you not to surrender.[165]

But, by the end of July, Lewis knew he would never be more to Margarett than an expended indulgence, a tiresome emotional cinder circling the event horizon of her despair. He could not save her and, in his diary, he wrote that he would stop trying:

The end, truly the end! I am as dead to her as if I had never lived. This is the conclusion to which I am brought by an "objective" review of what happened...

... It is clear that she wished to be in subjection; that she sought in me—has sought in man all her life—someone who would at no instant let her see that his love was greater, and therefore more vulnerable, than hers. And having learned, slowly at first and then with speed of lightning, that I love her to the

point of adoration, not masterly (which was never in my mind, since I could not love anyone who would consent to be my slave, pick my things from the floor, and live in a kind of perpetual involuntary degradation), she became revolted by me.[166]

His last letter to Margarett was dated July 29, 1929:

My dear Margarett,

... Please send back all I have written you. I shall have to come for it if you don't, and that would be a most unpleasant business. But the letters are not yours; they were written to a phantom who, I thought, loved me and knew how to read them—not just how to read...

Lewis Galantière[167]

Lewis had hoped to transcend Margarett's despondency and her marriage to Shaw; to release her from both. But for Margarett, Lewis began as a diversion and ended as another of her burdens. The realization came late to Lewis:

I was kind, certainly; and she grew to hate, to loathe my kindness, because it made her feel culpable towards a man she was already through with. I taught her—she says—all she knows of sexual pleasure; but having experienced it, she doubtless wearied of it...

... I do not know what I did not give her, except the satisfaction of her desire for a master.[168]

Two months after the affair, Margaret sent Lewis a note. It was written on the letterhead of an East Gloucester art gallery but was sent in an envelope of the Massachusetts General Hospital in Boston, postmarked October 10, 1929:

It is all so terrible—

Lewis—can you release me from this—

The children are still untouched by it.

I am thankful for you.[169]

Shaw McKean divorced Margarett in 1947. Their son accompanied him to Reno for the decree. Margarett's drinking and depression worsened and she periodically underwent electroshock therapy. In 1949, she was legally committed to Baldpate Sanitarium and, when discharged later that year, resumed drinking. She was readmitted in 1955 and, in 1963, was admitted to Westwood Lodge, another sanitarium in the Boston area. A friend described Margarett's appearance at about that time:

> she had become monstrous fat, but she still had those marvelous eyes and the irresistible charm. Since then she has had numerous strokes, I believe, and I had no idea that she was still at all ambulatory.[170]

In 1966, at seventy-four, Margarett suffered a stroke that left her unable to draw or speak clearly. Her manic depression continued until the 1970s, when pharmacology helped. In the spring of 1973, she hosted a dinner party at her longtime family home—Prides—in Beverly, Massachusetts. Although wheelchair bound, Margarett was clear eyed, alert, and elegantly clothed and quaffed. Her nephew, the state's governor, attended. It was a glorious evening.

Lewis had done much of his letter writing and musing about Margarett[171] at the homes of Archibald MacLeish and Mina Kirstein, Lincoln's sister.[172] Mina lived in Ashfield, Massachusetts, about a two-hour drive south of Margarett's summer residence in Dorsett. Mina recalled those 1929 days in a letter she sent Lewis forty-three years later:

> those long ago days when you used to come to Ashfield and spend hours in the Blacksmith's Shop, first writing her letters and then exorcising your unhappiness by pages of writing in your diary. How very Proustian.[173]

Mina would not be the only person to compare Lewis to Proust.

Margarett Sargent's portrait of Lewis, 1929, courtesy of Honor Moore.

As for Lewis's review of *A Farewell to Arms*, when Hemingway read it, he thought it a betrayal:

June 30, 1930

To Archibald MacLeish

Dear Archie:

... Saw Galantière, author of "Brushwood Boy at the Front"—wanted him to check some French in a story I have in August Scribners. He did as much with aid of a dictionary. Maybe you'll like the story. He [Lewis] is a little fellow I trust as long as I'm in the room with him but while he has double-crossed me in mean and petty ways 3 times now I still like him—when I'm with him.

You Mac I feel the same way about when with and away from.[174]

The story in *Scribners Magazine* to which Hemingway alluded was "Wine of Wyoming." Ernest stopped in to see Lewis at the Algonquin Hotel—Lewis's home following his divorce from Dorothy—for help with his use of French idiom. Lewis did some editing and Ernest gave him his pocketknife in payment.

When describing *A Farewell to Arms*, Lewis had alluded to Kipling's "The Brushwood Boy," the story of an injured soldier and the woman in whose love he finds purpose. The comparison riled Hemingway, possibly because, in his mind, it equated *him* with a lesser character. While Lewis praised the book as Hemingway's best, his review was not uncritical:

In the descriptive passages, Hemingway shows for the first time that he can write by ear as well as by eye, so to say. Even the haphazard punctuation is not an obstacle to enjoyment of the fluidity and the rhythmical beauty of many of his periods. He has remembered, besides, all the lessons of his arduous, self-taught apprenticeship. Echoes are here of those steely paragraphs which comprised the first Paris publication of 'In Our Time,' and of much that he has learned since. Now and then there is a line of gibberish, of unfortunate Joyce or bad Stein; his eye for objects and excessive concern with detail lead him into dull cataloguing; his meticulousness about should and would (which does not prevent his using whom in the nominative) lures him into affectation; he sprays the words 'nice' and 'fine' and 'lovely' a bit too monotonously through his pages.

There are two Hemingways: the positive, creative talent
skillfully at work in a being who sees and understands the
anguish and bravery of men struggling with forces whose purpose
they cannot divine; and the negative, fearful writer with the
psychological impediments of a child afraid of the dark and
conjuring it away with a whistle as hopeless as it is off key.
From the first of these we may look for work of great merit.[175]

At the Federal Reserve Bank during that summer of 1929, Lewis monitored international currency and commodity trading patterns and gold movements by eliciting information from bankers and industrialists worldwide and reciprocating to the extent permitted by the bank: enough to keep the channels of communications open. One grain trader with whom Lewis frequently had lunch was John Houseman. (Four decades later, Houseman would win the Academy Award for Best Supporting Actor for his portrayal of the imperious Professor Charles W. Kingsfield in *The Paper Chase*, but in 1929 movies were not yet on his horizon.)

During their lunches, Houseman marveled to Lewis about his recent good fortune in the grain trading business and in love, his life having been directionless until a couple of years earlier, when he took a job with the Continental Grain Company in Saint Louis. Continental had furnished on-the-job training, and Houseman had met with such outlandish success that, when word got out, a private investor made him an extraordinary offer: to fund a new trading company, make John its president, and pay him an annual base salary of $275,000 (in 2017 dollars) plus 5 percent of the profits. John was twenty-six, and that sum was more money than he thought he would ever earn. He accepted the offer and formed the Oceanic Grain Corporation, based in New York.

At the time, John's stepbrother, Eric Siepmann, was working in Manhattan as an editorial writer for the *New York Post*. Eric was living with a stunning young painter named Magda Johann, whose sister was the actress Zita Johann. Eric, Magda and John went to the September 7th Broadway opening of *Machinal,* in which Zita was starring,[176] and John was besotted.

Within days, he and Zita became lovers and, that same month, were married. John signed a two-year lease on the penthouse apartment at 66 Fifth Avenue and had the place professionally decorated.

At the Oceanic Grain Corporation, John managed the business conservatively. He booked only fully protected grain transactions, locking in buyers and sellers for each trade and borrowing only what he needed to finance the intervals between the two. That first year, business was brisk and, by mid-August, Oceanic's loans had grown to thirty times the firm's declared capital. But every single loan was backed by one or more sales contracts.

On October 24, 1929, a date that came to be known as Black Thursday, John was on the floor of the Produce Exchange and observed when commodity prices started to fall. He was nervous but confident; his buyers were in place. And he remained confident until the first of his buyers delayed paying. The buyer explained that there was nothing he could do: *his* customers were walking away from their contracts. A second and a third buyer said the same thing, and then they all did. John tried to extend Oceanic's loans, but no financing could be had. Not at any price. John told his staff to defer creditors' payments for a week, then for two weeks. And then a month. He exhausted Oceanic's capital and then postdated the firm's checks. Finally, with no other options, he let the ringing phones go unanswered.

The end came in early 1930. Oceanic sold its few remaining assets and closed its doors, still owing $200,000, leaving John worse than penniless. His penthouse lease had sixteen months to run and he had borrowed $17,000 to invest in Oceanic, even though he hadn't been asked to do so. In a fortnight, he had ceased being (as he had once described himself) "the merchant prince." In 1930, he would earn $275.

John tried his hand at writing, something for which he had always presumed he had a talent. But six months passed without a useful word finding its way onto the page. At Zita's suggestion, the two collaborated on a play, a drama about unfulfilled love that they titled *The Lake*. The Berkshire Playhouse in Stockbridge, Massachusetts, agreed to produce it if Zita played the lead. She did, and the play ran for several performances. The *New York Times* attributed the authorship to John Houseman and "Joan Wolfe" (Zita's pseudonym).[177] At the close of summer, Zita joined the touring production of *Uncle Vanya*, leaving John behind in New York, and John called Lewis, looking for a collaborator to replace Zita. Lewis said he would help, to the extent that his work for the bank permitted. The result of their collaboration was a drawing room comedy—*Lovers, Happy Lovers*—based on Sacha Guitry's *L'Illusioniste*. According to John, Lewis was not happy with the genre but went along for the ride:

> Lewis protested periodically that such foolery was not for him, but he was having a good time; as a small fastidious man with thick glasses, he found vicarious satisfaction in the gambits of our philandering hero.[178]

In the end, John took credit for the play's structure and gave credit to Lewis for its dialogue. *Lovers, Happy Lovers* had an initial run in London, England that gave John cause for hope, as he described in his biography, *Unfinished Business*:

> "Lovers, Happy Lovers"... was touring the British provinces before coming into the West End of London. I rose before dawn after a sleepless night, went down with my coat over my pajamas to the newsstand on the corner, then burst triumphantly into the darkness of Galantière's room and read him the brief cabled report of our play's successful London opening. Lewis took the news more calmly than I did and was less disappointed when it closed after five weeks. In a note that accompanied their final statement, its managers assured us that they were in no way disheartened and intended to bring the play to New York soon after the turn of the year.

Next, a Broadway producer paid John and Lewis to adapt a French farce, *Trois et une* or *Three and One*. It opened in New York in mid-October 1933.

It had been a decade since the *New York Times* had declared that Lewis might be the most promising American writer in Paris. On December 3, 1933, the newspaper presented a piece about Lewis and John titled TWO WHO MADE "THREE AND ONE" that was an encore of journalistic fantasy:

> One is a banker and the other is a Parisian newspaperman. They met in 1928, quite by accident, over a second cup of coffee that lacked the warmth of the first and, in the argument that followed with the waiter, became acquainted. Two hours later they had rented room 603 at the Hotel Algonquin for the purpose of collaborating on a play. It turned out to be "Lovers, Happy Lovers."...The man, whose official address is the Federal Reserve Bank of New York, and the scribbler, who never had any address, have made their Broadway bow in the adaptation of "Three and One," from the French by Denys Amiel now on view at the Longacre Theatre.
>
> First, who is the big greenback man? He is Lewis Galantière and he was born forty years ago in Chicago during the World's Columbian Exposition. His father, a Frenchman with ideals and a comfortable income, had gone, according to his offspring, "in search of civilization." Why he picked out Chicago nobody has ever been able to answer.
>
> However, young Lewis was taken back to France, where he was educated. Later he was sent to schools in Germany and he wound up in the American Army during the war. He was the interpreter at the International Chamber of Commerce and on several occasions he represented The Dial, The New Republic and The Nation as Paris correspondent. He is best known as the translator of the works of Cocteau, Morand and Valery. In recent years, he has been at the Federal Reserve Bank here.
>
> Second, as to the French newspaper man. He is John Houseman. His father was French and he was born somewhere on the banks of the Danube, far, far away. He was educated in England, was a cowboy in the Argentine and once wrote for The New Statesman in London. His real name is Haussmann, like the boulevard in Paris, yet he has changed it to Houseman "because everybody insists upon spelling it that way." And he may be right. The clippings from

*London on "Women Kind" have it Houseman so as Houseman it is
likely to remain.*

*Until 1928 the two world travelers had never met nor had ever
heard of each other. Over the cold cup of coffee they discussed
France, the stage and wives. A couple of Frenchmen away from
Paris.*

"I write," said Mr. Galantière.

"So do I" replied Mr. Houseman.

"It would be fun writing a play together," said one.

*"Why not?" answered the other. "And how about another cup of
coffee?"*

*They are warm friends and at present Mr. Houseman has "moved in"
with Mr. Galantière at the latter's apartment. They have another
opus in the works.*

*"Don't think I was dumb when I took on a banker for a partner,"
says the easy-going Houseman, who knows as little about money
as Mr. Galantière knows about Broadway. "Lewis takes me down to
the Federal Reserve to look at the new banknotes and I take him
up Broadway to contemplate the sights. Neither of us knows what
the other is thinking about and we never argue over anything. A
couple of sightseers from out of town."[179]*

The reporter accepted at face value Lewis's accounts of his father, education, and army service. But Houseman had also dissembled: his father, born in Alsace, was Jewish, a fact that Houseman had deliberately concealed since his youth.[180]

Three and One received faint praise from Robert Benchley, who wrote for the *New Yorker*:

*Another comedy which rather smirks its way through the well-
trodden bowers of amorous dalliance is "Three and One." It has
been adapted from the French of Denys Amiel by Lewis Galantière
and John Houseman, so the chances are that it is well translated,
the only doubt being of the necessity of translating it at all.
As the title suggests, three men (Brian Donlevy, Paul McGrath,
and John Eldredge) circle with lecherous intent around one*

young woman (Miss Lillian Bond), with Ruth Shepley and Edith Van Cleve as referees. The play was fortunate in being hailed by the critics as very dirty, which will give it a good matinee business anyway.[181]

The play persevered through 120 performances and earned $400 each for Lewis and John.

Lee Miller

Lewis Galantière (above), Adviser on Foreign Relations to the Federal Reserve Bank of New York and a *littérateur* of some note, recently burst forth as a playwright. His *Three and One* (which he and John Houseman adapted from the French of Denys Amiel) opened at Manhattan's Longacre Theatre shortly after his original play, *Women Kind*, opened in London.

That summer, Zita applied for a Mexican divorce; her letter to John asked him to sign the papers immediately so that she could remarry. He signed. After Labor Day, John moved into Lewis's building at 125 East Fifth Street. It was an elegant apartment house, and John rented the only accommodations he could afford: a maid's quarters.

John's "breakthrough" (his word) came when Lewis introduced him to Virgil Thomson, a friend from Paris. The scene was one of Constance Askew's Sunday salons. Thomson had composed an opera for which Gertrude Stein had written the libretto. Intended for an all-Black cast, it was named *Four Saints in Three Acts* and was scheduled to premiere in Hartford. The problem was that Thomson had neither a hands-on producer nor the money with which to pay for one. Lewis told Thomson that Houseman was their man.

Thomson guided Houseman by the arm to Askew's library, and spoke to him about the production. Houseman, it seemed, possessed the three attributes Thomson was looking for in a producer: a slightly British accent (for credibility),[182] desperation (for dedication to the task), and subservience (Thomson could control him). The following day, over a period of two hours, Thomson screeched the lyrics of *Four Saints* to his own piano accompaniment[183] while Houseman "sat there trying to look intelligent and appreciative and hoping with all my soul that he would invite me to work with him."[184] Thomson offered Houseman the job and Houseman accepted "in a mood of irresistible euphoria."[185]

Four Saints in Three Acts was part opera and part dance. It had a huge cast, intricate staging, an impossibly brief gestation and a miniscule budget. It was an education by fire in casting, direction, coordination, staging, set design, costumes, scenery, and lighting. And Houseman pulled it off. The opera ran for four weeks at the Forty-Fourth Street Theater in New York and was declared an artistic triumph. Most importantly, it bestowed on Houseman the aura of being a successful theatrical director/producer.[186]

John and Lewis's *Lovers, Happy Lovers* opened in New York during the last week of January 1934, its name changed to *And Be My Love*.[187] Houseman sat through the opening performance and "hated every moment of it." He was relieved when, the next morning, Brooks Atkinson, writing in the *New York Times*, damned it with faint praise: "a flawless comedy, though dull." It closed after five performances.[188]

In December, Houseman abandoned his collaboration with Lewis in favor of one with Orson Wells, and the fellowship that Lewis and John had shared while playwriting waned as their career paths diverged. They would reunite in the Office of War Information at the onset of World War II, but never again had the intimacy of those desperate earlier days. In his autobiography, Houseman eloquently drew the curtain on that time:

> So passed another anxious, idle summer [1935] in the green, steaming heat of the Hudson Valley. Twice I drove with Lincoln Kirstein into the Berkshires and once Mina came down and spent three days with me in New York City. Defying the copperheads with which the South Mountain Road abounded that summer, other ladies paid platonic visits. Lewis Galantière came once but found the atmosphere too rustic for his taste. Walking down the center of the South Mountain Road at hours set aside "pour la promenade," in his light flannel trousers, straw hat and jacket, he surprisingly resembled photographs of Marcel Proust.[189]

Houseman settled in Hollywood after the war, but the two tried to stay in touch. When Lewis returned from a trip to Europe in early November 1953, he was not surprised to find a slim envelope containing a single sheet of letterhead with its familiar cinnabar ink on blue-gray paper:

HOUSEMAN

Dear Lewis,

We shall arrive in your city on or about December 11th and shall be there for about a month.

This is to inform you that we expect, nay, demand, frequent intercourse with you during that time. We shall be reachable at New City and, more conveniently in town, c/o Phoenix Theatre, 270 Park Avenue, New York 17, Plaza 3-7672.

Yours, JH [190]

CHAPTER 6

1931-1938:
LEWIS AT THE BANK

TWO YEARS INTO THE DEPRESSION, Burton Rascoe, former literary editor of the *New York Tribune*, was trying to make ends meet as a literary agent in California. Lewis wrote to him:

December 9, 1931

[Economic] conditions? Jesus! I swear I don't know...why the whole world shouldn't go to hell. Hoover is shooting a few hypodermics into the financial structure with his bank inventions but, apart from that, nobody seems to be doing a damned thing. Many banks are still not shaken out; Snyder looks for the stock market to break through to lower levels; I can't find anybody who dares pronounce a cheerful word...all I say is colored by my own fatigue, nerves, and fundamentally depressed state.

If only things would happen, it wouldn't matter what things, nor where: but we seem to be in a sort of treadmill; everybody waiting for something to break and nobody doing anything. As concerns the world in general, the solutions all seem to me political; with regard to the USA in particular, the only thing I can think of is a hell of a cut in workmen's wages (they haven't been hit yet the way the white-collar boys have), so that industry may make profits again and the industrialists themselves move out of their slough of despond...

Have you heard about the man who tried to buy—at Macy's—a toilet seat without a hole in it? They hadn't it in stock, would have it made up, etc...Why did he want it? 'I lost my ass in the market, but I still like to read.'

And the medical congress at Vienna? The German reports his miracle—put a pig bladder in a man and he is walking the street; Englishman his—a cow's stomach...and he is walking the streets; the American: 'We put a horse's ass in the White House and he's got us all walking the streets.'

Which is no way for a respectable central banker to be writing to a California (and therefore respectable) family man. I wish you were here.

Yr ever affectionate[191]

Lewis was fortunate to have found a home at the Bank. Many businesses had gone under. Condé Nast's *Vanity Fair* magazine would not be seen for another forty-seven years. At the Bank, Lewis had the pleasurable burden of corresponding with bankers and economists whose cultural interests and intellects sometimes matched with his own. One was the economist Thomas Balogh who, three decades later, would become a cabinet adviser to British Prime Minister Harold Wilson[192] and a Life Peer as "Baron Balogh of Hampstead in Greater London." John Maynard Keynes said of Balogh that he—Keynes—could learn more from speaking with Balogh for an hour or two than he could by spending several days in London. On the other hand, Keynes also referred to Balogh as "Oxballs" because of the combative way in which he asserted his unconventional, and yet usually prescient economic analyses.

Lewis and Thomas met in New York in 1928, while Balogh was doing research under a Rockefeller grant, and corresponded after Balogh returned to England in 1930.[193] Their letters are a mixture of economics and very personal confidences, this being an example of the latter:

September 6th 1934

10, Old Jewry

London, e.c.2.

metropolitan 8001

My dearest Louis,

... on a holiday mirabile dictu, I used the opportunity to sneak
away...

Louis my dear, I really did not believe I was capable of such
intense enjoyment in matters non-political and non-economic.
It was a revelation to me to feel young and healthy! : to be
able to look at Byzantine mosaics, passionately adoring how
the change in the light gave new and still newer life to its
glittering mystic pattern...Never shall I forget an evening in
Bologna, sipping some cool drink and looking at towers, half-
ruined and sticking up like large fingers pointing to heaven.

Louis, why did I have to be there alone? I think pleasure can be
enhanced a thousandfold if one can feel the immediate reaction
to the finest vibrations of one's soul, and I really do not know
anyone but you about whom I could say that. I have thought of
you when I saw the Galla Placida, and I thought of you when I
was descending into the bitter cold of the Rhone glacier...I
could see once more what is really important, I regained my
sense of proportions and again I could distinguish between what
agitates us and what is really important.[194]

In 1936, Baron Balogh, seeing that the economic sanctions that France and
England had placed on Germany were porous and that Hitler was hell bent
on developing the military strength to "oppose the shoe of Europe," predicted the sanctions' counterproductive effect:

June 12, 1936

Germany is able to export her more obsolete war material and
in return gets raw material and foodstuffs so as to produce
ammunition of the newest type...If Germany is successful in
increasing these exports, she can keep up her capacity for
ammunition manufacture at the cost of foreign countries, and can
feed her population at the same time, if not well at least to an

extent which prohibits actual physical deterioration, and I am
afraid that that is the only limit of the German system...

... It may well be that the old heuristic principle that the
worst and most stupid thing will happen, will remain true. That
is to say, sanctions will not be abandoned, but will be allowed
to leak and lapse (we leak nowadays on many points!) which of
course will (a) drive Mussolini a little closer to Hitler, (b)
will not re-establish collective security, (c) will not do
anything to strengthen us in the Mediterranean but will merely
prolong the present agonising trend.[195]

The same *"old heuristic principle"* was on Lewis's mind when, the following year, he deplored America's failure to enact commonsense economic
reforms:

It is hard for me to say much about recent developments here
because we have been living in such confusion of tongues that
few men have been able to hear themselves think...The Congress,
which adjourned a few days ago following a special session
dazzlingly devoid of accomplishment, ranted and wrangled without
touching any problem of importance...Our big problem has been
the decline in money coming forward for new capital investment.
If this should go on into next spring, it will of course be
serious and Government funds in volume may have to be pumped
into the economic arteries of the country.[196]

During his tenure at the Bank, letters also flowed to and from Helen Haines,
Lewis's former Los Angeles Library School teacher. In April 1936, she wrote
to thank Lewis for his admiring review, in *The Nation*, of her authoritative
library text, *Living with Books*, and to tell him that she had just dined with
Gertrude Stein, Alice B. Toklas and Janet Flanner:

I have talked of you, with two people who know you, during this
last year. The first was Gertrude Stein, who was in Pasadena
just a year ago, when I had a luncheon with her at Mrs. Gartz's,
in Altadena. It was a very intimate and quiet affair, of just
eight persons—only two of whom (one of them, me) had, I think,
the slightest idea of Gertrude Stein's work or proclivities.
Among them were Upton Sinclair and his wife: Upton, seriously,
earnestly, solemnly intent on tracking Ms. Stein's Meaning to

its Lair. I mentioned your name to her and she responded with
such animation; said she had seen you in New York, before she
came west. I don't think anyone could help liking her; she's
what one could call "a good sport;" also a person, distinctive,
rugged, with a fine mind. But also, it seems to me, in the grip
of an almost psychopathic megalomania; a complete obsession
that she is the world's greatest genius of literature. Ms.
Toklas was very interesting to me—so rather oddly witchlike. A
little creature, but gay, gentle and intelligent. The other
acquaintance of yours is Janet Flanner...She asked me about you—
where you were and what you are doing; said you were "so very
able" she wished you were able to keep up regular writing"[197]

When away from his office, when not cowriting dramas with John Houseman, Lewis continued to translate books into English. Between 1930 and
1937, there were six French and German works.[198] His most ambitious was
The Goncourt Journals, an account of mid-nineteenth-century French life
that Burton Rascoe had negotiated with Doubleday. Lewis credited his ICC
compatriot René Arnaud in the preface and footnotes,[199] for which René
expressed his appreciation:

September 9, 1937

Dear Old Pal

... I have received your beautiful book and I have read with
passion your preface...I am amazed that you named me in
your notes; me, a modest popularizer who will never have the
necessary time and money to be a real historian...

Your godson is patiently waiting to meet you. Maybe you can
finally send him a photograph as you have often promised...

... When do you come?[200]

Lewis's publisher, Reynal and Hitchcock, also induced him to translate
the latest work by Antoine de Saint-Exupéry,[201] whose earlier book about
aviation, *Vol de Nuit* (*Night Flight*), had won the 1931 Prix Femina literary
award. *Vol de Nuit* was a poetic fable that coalesced reality and abstraction
into a story of pilots as fully realized moral beings. Reynal had inferred

from Antoine de Saint-Exupéry's telegrams that, when he arrived in New York in January 1938, he would be bringing a finished manuscript ready for translation. What Reynal received was a pile of unrelated vignettes that, with apologies, he passed to Lewis to stitch into a single narrative. Reynal knew better than to ask Saint-Exupéry to do the work; the Frenchman was notoriously unreliable and, anyway, was about to leave on a 9,000-mile single-engine monoplane adventure from Newark, New Jersey, to Punta Arenas, Chile. Lewis took the materials, organized them, and set about inventing transitions to connect their disparate parts. He worked at the bank during the day and on *Wind, Sand and Stars* (Lewis's title) when he could.

It was an intense time for Lewis, made less so by the company of a new love; a woman who genuinely believed in him. Nancy Davis, like Margarett Sargent, painted canvasses in the contemporary way, albeit not as competently. Like Margarett, she had attended Miss Porter's School in Farmington, Connecticut; was wealthy, having inherited the current equivalent of almost $4 million from her grandfather, Horace Davis; and was the latest of an iconic lineage. Horace Davis had been a California U.S. Congressman from 1877 to 1881, president of the University of California from 1888 to 1890, and president of the board of trustees of Stanford University from 1885 to 1916. Horace's father, John Davis, had been governor of Massachusetts. And John's father (Nancy's great-great-grandfather), Isaac Davis, had commanded a company of minutemen at the Battle of Concord and, there, was the first American officer to die in the Revolution.

Nancy was tall and thin, with a classically beautiful face and aristocratic bearing. At thirty-one, she was eleven years younger than Lewis. They had been living together at 125 East Fifty-Seventh Street, and were married in a city hall wedding on March 19, 1938. Lewis shared the news with Sherwood Anderson:

Dear Sherwood,

... Since you and your wife were here, I have married. When you come up to New York again, you and your wife, you must come to see us. My wife's name was Nancy Davis. She comes from San Francisco and is a painter. You will both like her, I know, for the things she attaches value to are really the valuable things.

Yours ever affectionately

Lewis Galantière[202]

Saint-Exupéry missed the wedding by a week. He had crashed his plane while taking off from the Guatemala City airfield and returned to New York with head injuries and multiple fractures. Lewis and Saint-Exupéry worked on *Wind, Sand and Stars* for the rest of March and April 1938, but the book remained unfinished when Saint-Exupéry returned to France in May, leaving Lewis to continue on his own into the summer. In August, Nancy and Lewis were the guests of Sherwood and Eleanor Anderson (Sherwood's third wife) at their summer home, Ripshin Farm, in Virginia.[203]

Eleanor Anderson, Lewis and Sherwood at Ripshin.

Lewis's work on *Wind, Sand and Stars* while at Ripshin was an uneasy process, made more difficult by Saint-Exupéry's long distance collaboration, as Lewis later described in an *Atlantic Monthly* article:

> Saint-Exupéry had sailed home to France, and I had gone to work on the translation at Sherwood Anderson's, in the mountains of southwestern Virginia, when I received the first of an absolute rain of letters transmitting changes that he was then engaged in making in the French text. Later, when I started to tell this story to Pierre Lazareff, he laughed as he interrupted me:
>
>> "But you don't know the half of it. Each time that Antoine gave us a piece for Paris-Soir, it was the devil's own job to get it into the paper. There was no getting rid of the man. He would slip into the composing room at midnight to take out commas and change the order of the sentences. He would demoralize the whole shop, bribing the printer's devils with bottles of wine, in the middle of the night, to let him get at the forms."[204]

Saint-Exupéry revised several chapters, transforming action into moralizing. He suggested excising a third of the book, to change it from an adventure story into a polemic about "how the airplane, that tool of the airlines, brings man face to face with the eternal problems";[205] in other words, a variation on the theme of *Vol de Nuit*. Lewis bristled at the prospect of losing what he knew was a great story and told Saint-Exupéry that the deletions would sacrifice eloquence and evocation. Lewis prevailed, at least in the English version.[206]

Nancy, an avid equestrian, had been eager to ride in the cool mountain air of Troutdale, Virginia, where Ripshin was located. But, as had happened before, she was sidelined by severe back pain.[207] Sherwood recorded the Galantières' visit in his diary:

> August 12, 1938: In the evening...Lewis...made too much point of being an exquisite one.
>
> August 21, 1938:...We took Lewis and Nancy to town. Nancy became ill. It is very pitiful to see such a beautiful woman with an

injured back. They left on the evening train for New York. They have been among the most delightful guests we have ever had.

August 22, 1938: The house seems very empty without Lewis and Nancy.[208]

Saint-Exupéry returned to America in February 1939 and, that same month, Lewis handed in his resignation from the bank in order to give his full attention to *Wind, Sand and Stars*. Lewis had served as chief of the Foreign Information Division for a decade and, as of February, was in charge of about twenty economists and statistical clerks. In leaving the bank, he gave up an annual salary of $5,700 (the equivalent of about $100,000 in 2016). He explained that he had wanted to write for himself,[209] but he had no book projects on the table aside from *Wind, Sand and Stars*.

Ultimately, the French *Terre des Hommes* reflected Saint-Exupéry's philosophy of man's purpose on earth, while the English version, *Wind, Sand and Stars*, preserved Lewis's preference for an adventure story about aviation. Lewis Gannett's review of *Wind, Sand and Stars* in the *New York Herald Tribune* recognized Lewis's contribution:

At a time when most news of airplanes is operators in pursuit planes, of murder in the air, this French aviator [Saint-Exupéry] dares voice a faith that in the mould of his profession a new breed of man is being cast. To him this comradeship of the air transcends frontiers, and this fellowship gives the craft its dignity. But faith alone does not make literature; this book sings. Lewis Galantière's must be an extraordinary translation, so perfectly does the rhythm of the prose suggest the swift precision of an airplane flight, its healing and sinking, its capacity for disaster swifter than man's power to think. Such subtleties seldom survive the ordeal of translation.

Terre des hommes won the 1939 Grand Prize for Fiction from the French Academy (Grand Prix du Roman de l'Academie Française) and *Wind, Sand and Stars* won the U.S. National Book Award for Nonfiction. The American Booksellers Association voted *Wind, Sand and Stars* the year's best work of nonfiction and the book remained on the national bestseller list for nine months, selling over 150,000 copies. Royalties flowed to Saint-Exupéry and his fame grew, while Lewis earned a writer's fee but received no authorship credit; only credit as a translator. It was a painful lesson, one that Lewis would take to heart.

That summer, Lewis and Nancy visited with Sherwood and Eleanor Anderson at Ripshin, where Nancy's back once again had her bedridden.[210] From Ripshin, they took a train to California. After a year of marriage, Lewis was going to meet Nancy's mother. Therese Davis lived alone, in a majestic Spanish style home at 1829 Pacific Coast Highway in Santa Barbara.[211] Nancy's father, Colonel Norris K. Davis,[212] was not there; he had become estranged from the family when he divorced Therese to marry a younger woman.[213] Lewis described his time with Therese as a gently awkward pas de deux; here, in a letter to Sherwood Anderson:

July 20, 1939

Dear Sherwood,

... The mother-in-law is very sweet. She is ferociously shy, anxious to please and that everything shall be as I want it, so there goes on a constant after-you-Alphonse and anything-you-say between her and me. Last night she beat me badly at dominoes: I think that helped a lot. You know what it's like if anybody does—living between two women who (let's blush) "look up to" you. Well.[214]

Nancy's back pain returned, and then relented.

August 31, 1939

Dear Sherwood,

... things didn't go too well for a couple of weeks. Now Nancy is fine, paying no attention to her back, and is swimming, playing mild tennis, driving a car, and getting on generally better than I've ever known her. It scares her to be doing so well, and it will take a little time before she has full confidence, but you and Eleanor would be happy to see her as she is and I hope next year we may all be walking over your beautiful hills together.[215]

Near year-end, 1939, Reynal and Hitchcock introduced Lewis to another scion of French aristocracy, Gontran de Poncins. De Poncins was born at the turn of the century on an estate that had been in the family for nine hundred years. He'd studied painting in Paris but abandoned it to become the manager of a London silk company, then a freelance journalist, and then a self-invented sociologist. In this last incarnation, he lived with an Eskimo family near Pella Bay,[216] immersing himself in their society and becoming, to the extent he could, an Eskimo. His Eskimo clan referred to him, sometimes endearingly and sometimes contemptuously, as *kabloona*: "white man."

In the late 1930s, Eskimos still lived an ancient lifestyle, one attuned to seasonal ice floes, migrations, and the unforgiving cold. De Poncins's November 1939 sojourn was the last time they would be studied before modernity intruded.[217] De Poncins brought his sketches, notes and photographs to Reynal and Hitchcock, and they in turn handed them to Lewis:

> They invited me to listen with them to his story and look at his drawings and photographs, after which they laid a bet on him: they risked the cost of his keep for several months while he typed out his diaries. I, for my part, agreed that if the diaries fulfilled the promise of his story and his pictures, I would undertake to make a book of them in English—provided it was honorably possible for a man to do so who had never been in the Arctic.[218]

Lewis accepted the challenge but demanded a share of the royalties and credit as coauthor. The result, *Kabloona*, became a national best-seller:

August 31, 1940

Dear Sherwood,

... You know, I did an Eskimo book with a Frenchman—out of 1100 pages of diary and about 30 days of conversation with the fellow. The book must be readable, at least, because the book-of-the-month club has taken it (for December, I think); and there is one good reason why that pleases me: I have a third interest in it.[219]

· CHAPTER 7 ·

WAR'S APPROACH

THE EXTRAORDINARY COINCIDENCES THAT BROUGHT Lewis Galantière and René Arnaud and Antoine de Saint-Exupéry together had originated with the Treaty of Versailles, thirty years earlier. The treaty had been an exercise in aspirational revenge, retribution, and disarmament that was unworkable from the start. Like any treaty, it had been a prospective document, meaningful only to the extent that the parties remained committed to enforcing it. In practice, it became the jumping-off point from which the Great War's victors competed over reparations, tariffs, and debt repayments.[220] The Treaty of Versailles limited Germany's army to 100,000 soldiers and prohibited its having an air force, submarines or tanks. But in the two decades that followed, as Germany incrementally violated those prohibitions and the Allies failed to emphatically respond, the accumulating evidence of their passivity gave license to Germany to rearm. As French marshal Ferdinand Foch had predicted from the start, the treaty did not bring peace, but instead an armistice for twenty years.

In 1933, Germany's president, General Paul von Hindenburg, signed the Enabling Act, effectively making Hitler dictator of Germany. Hitler promised that he would be restrained in invoking the powers granted:

> *The government will make use of these powers only insofar as*
> *they are essential for carrying out vitally necessary measures...*

The number of cases in which an internal necessity exists for
having recourse to such a law is in itself a limited one.[221]

In a 1937 "Four Year Plan," Hitler made clear his intention:

the extent of the military development of our resources cannot
be too large, nor its pace too swift.[222]

Germany signed agreements with countries in southern Europe and the Balkans to supply the raw materials needed for armaments and stopped importing non-military-related items. At the Federal Reserve Bank, Lewis tracked these transfers of strategic materials for their economic and military implications, while nervous foreign bankers, governments, and journalists probed his judgment as to their meaning. One query from Dr. Paul Einzig, a British economist (then the foreign editor of the *London Financial Times*) asked whether the United States would intercede to stop these obvious preparations for war.[223] Lewis answered that it would not.[224]

When Hitler's Four-Year Plan memorandum was made known in France, René Arnaud, Lewis's ICC brother, wrote to share his premonitions of war. He said that "luckily," France was ready:

Hitler and Mussolini are hugging each other, protesting
that they want peace. Hum! Luckily, I have seen, during a
short military stint, how well we are prepared—It's great! I
understand hélas!...that you prefer staying outside the mélée.
Sadly, if it starts, it would be more difficult for you to stay
outside than it was the last time.[225]

René knew the meaning of war. On February 28, 1915, he had been in charge of a company near Albert, facing a German fortification four hundred yards away. The following is his account:

a glorious red rocket went up from the enemy lines and the
curtain-fire was unleashed on our heads...The 77s began to fall
thick and fast in front of and behind our outwork and to deafen
us with their whirrings and whinings and explosions. Shrapnel
was flying everywhere, lurid as burning coals. The pungent smell
of the cordite assailed our nostrils. My heart was thumping, I
must have been white and I was trembling with fear. I lit a

*cigarette, feeling instinctively that this would help to calm my
nerves...*

*Stepping over the men's backs I hurried to a bend I knew in the
trench, from which one had an extensive view over the lines.
From that moment my fear calmed down. Although my head was
above the parapet I took no notice of the shells which were
exploding in front and behind, nor of the shell-splinters which
were spinning off in every direction. I no longer thought of
the danger, I had eyes only for the slope that separated the
two lines. I had become completely involved in the situation. My
eyes searched no-man's-land and I behaved exactly as if I were
certain that no shell or shrapnel could touch me. There was
certainly nothing meritorious in this...my concern with what had
to be done freed me from fear. The true war hero...is the simple
soldier without any special skill, who has only the rifle in his
hand to keep his mind off the thought of death.*

*Little by little the storm of gun-fire calmed down. Two men had
been killed in the neighbouring section, five in the company on
our right. I heard later the explanation of this false alarm.
Two of our look-outs had amused themselves by shooting at a
flight of migrating birds, curlews perhaps, which were passing
over our trenches. This prank had been all that was necessary to
spark off the rifle-fire and bombardment.*

*The French communique at 2300 hrs. on 1st March 1915 gravely
announced: "At Becourt, near Albert, a German attack has been
completely checked by our fire." That is how history is written...*

*... [I]n the spring of 1915, we had to mount guard for several
weeks a few yards from a line of corpses: eight or ten French
soldiers mown down by a German machine-gun during one of those
vain and senseless unsupported attacks in the winter of 1914-15,
which had cost us so many men. They lay face downwards, a pace
apart—the interval prescribed for assault troops in the pre-war
tactical manuals.*

*I had plenty of opportunity to look at them during my rounds.
In the radiant June dawn they gave off an unwholesome stench,
against which the only recourse was a cigarette. While the
spring sap mounted the boughs and branches, where branches
and boughs still remained, the worms accelerated the work of*

decomposition and their wriggling played its part in the renewal
of nature. I became quite familiar with the nearest corpse. Its
right cheek was dissolving into a blackish liquid in the grass.
Its arm still appeared to grasp the rifle whose bayonet had
rusted. The dark blue of the greatcoat has turned to grey, and
the belt and ammunition pouch had crumpled up under the snow and
rain.[226]

On September 24, 1938, Hitler issued an ultimatum—the Godesberg Memorandum—demanding that the Sudetenland be returned to Germany.[227] A week later, British Prime minister Neville Chamberlain (without consulting the Czechs) signed the Munich Pact, acceding to Hitler's demand. Hitler promised that the Sudetenland would be his "last territorial demand" in Europe. In a letter to Sherwood Anderson, Lewis, certain of Hitler's ambitions, lamented the opportunities for concerted action that Europe's elites had chosen to ignore.

September 26, 1938

Dear Sherwood,

... God in heaven, what an imbecile criminal suicidal world. And
I have been in anguish about it. Of course I would like to see
this house painter who fancies he is Joan of Arc smacked in the
snoot. But nobody will smack him; nobody takes him by the nose
and slaps his cheeks and kicks him in the bottom. They do him
the honor to offer him fair combat, to go to war, their people
with his people. And it is extraordinary how justifiable a war
seems when it is about to begin. Emotionally, I say to myself,
"Hey, the British, French, Russians, et allies, ought to go to
war. We ought to go to war... And then what? How will it look to
us 10 years later? Who says today, about this coming war, that
it is made by bankers (except of course the Communists, who
want the war and will say it was capitalistically "inevitable"—
with Soviet Russia fighting in it!)? Of course Hitler should be
stopped. But—by war?...I swear, I don't know, I don't know. We
know how to do it without war—or thought we did in the 10 years
or so between the creation of the League and the signature of
the Kellogg-Briand anti-war pact. But none of the big fellows

let collective security have a chance—and see where we are. What
a horrible choice is before us! ...

Your ever affectionate Lewis[228]

In the aftermath of World War II, the Munich Pact brought shame to its
signers: the image of Chamberlain grasping a fluttering paper and declar-
ing "peace for our time" came to epitomize the foolhardiness of attempting
to appease tyrants.[229] Yet Chamberlain had no options. It would be June
1940 before the advanced Mk II Spitfire aircraft could be put into the field
to meet the Luftwaffe's fighters in the Battle of Britain. The Munich Pact
helped to buy that time.[230] Two weeks after the pact, René Arnaud wrote
to Lewis:

October 12, 1938

My old friend,

... I returned to Paris in mid-August to find that the situation
had become dire. On September 24th, the day after Godesberg, we
have seen the posters of mobilizations on the walls, demanding
the "immediate recall" of certain reservists.

We were, at that moment, in Ville-d'Avray, near Versailles, in a
friend's home. I immediately went to Paris and, in this scared,
hushed town, where we couldn't see a smile anywhere, I went to
buy uniform trousers. There wasn't any more military wear in the
shops, and I found only hunting trousers, in green khaki. And I
am no hunter.

On Monday, the mood was pessimistic as we waited for Hitler to
speak. I called Edith [René's wife] in Paris and, that evening,
sent the family to Royan, where my brother has a house. And I
said "ouf!" [Whew!] It was a good thing I did. The next day, a
large police officer brought my recall notice. I would have been
very worried had I left my family behind in Paris. I travelled
to Provence, where I joined my garrison and prepared the
mobilization of my regiment. At that point, the mobilization
order was countermanded, and today everything is fine. We escaped
a conflict. The poor Czechs must be very upset with us, but
if war had broken out, they would be much worse off, and all
Europe would be up in fire. Nor did we have much enthusiasm for

preventing the Sudists from becoming Bosh. What's the harm if they, themselves, don't mind?

My view of the drama is this: In 1918, we "conquered" because we had a coalition, which is a fact we have forgotten. The Treaty of Versailles's provisions, which were short-term measures, inevitably proved irrelevant. They gave us a brief military pre-eminence, and the illusion of real strength. We alone were to be armed, and Germany disarmed. We could believe that we were still the "big nation" of Louis XIV and Napoleon. And we continued the classical politics of Richelieu and the monarchy, with our alliances in Central and Oriental Europe. But now we must face the truth: we are a nation of only 40 million souls against a nation of 80 million. Our nationalists who still dream of hegemony know too much history, which is to say that they don't know enough. Their nationalism should have been to have had children.

And now, what will you say to France? Isn't Hitler a megalomaniac who dreams of hegemony? Isn't a European war inevitable the day we try to stop his crazy plans? Isn't it better to act now? I answer this way: That every delay is a good thing. I can't admit, for a minute, that there can be a preventive war. Postponing the war for six months may postpone it for six years, or for sixty years. And if, one day, Hitler should attack us, then we will go willingly.

And there is something else. Everywhere, there is a groundswell against war. Even in Italy and Germany, there was joy and relief after the Munich Pact. Europe will not likely go to war because a lot of its people have already experienced it. Nonetheless, at the end of September, I was scared for Europe. I could imagine my sons, once the war was over, begging along the roads and running after the cars of rich Americans who came to Europe to see the ruins.

A few days before Munich, a petroleum company man asked me how much compensation he would get if his company was bombed from the air. I answered coldly that, if there was a war, there would be no compensation, no indemnity. There would be no French francs. Nothing. During the Hundred Years War, the farmer who had his house destroyed did ask for écus from the King of France...He had to beg.[231]

In December, René continued:

> What do these two oddballs [Hitler and Mussolini] have in
> reserve for us in 1939? I would be very pessimistic if September
> 1938 had proven that, in the end, everyone is still scared about
> the war. There are still too many people around who have fought
> the other war of '14, or have seen it. When that generation
> will almost all disappear, nothing will stop this collective
> craziness. In the end, this is not a very joyful thought.[232]

Saint-Exupéry returned to France in March 1939, at about the time that his publisher, Gallimard, went to press with *Terre des hommes*. The author drove to Berlin to see for himself what was going on and was there when Hitler's forces occupied Czechoslovakia. What he saw convinced him that war was inevitable. On August 23, 1939, Stalin and Hitler entered into a nonaggression pact in which Stalin agreed, in substance, to participate with Hitler in the invasion of Poland. Two days later, Britain announced an alliance with France and Poland against the anticipated German attack. René Arnaud wrote to Lewis:

> My old friend,
>
> We are in crisis again. We are expecting the answer of Hitler
> to Chamberlain. When you receive this letter, the decision
> will have been made. If the answer is one thing, then, next
> month, I will be finishing my holidays in a cottage we just
> purchased in Vert, 6 kilometers from Mantes. I will be digging
> philosophically in the garden and picking pears and apples. If
> the answer is something else, then I will be in the hell of what
> I knew more than 20 years ago and that has since nourished my
> nightmares. ... [Lewis and Saint-Exupéry will soon echo these
> thoughts in Flight to Arras.]
>
> You must share my anxiety of war: Paris menaced with ruin, my
> children and wife in misery, threatened with death if a pilot
> decides to bomb the little village where our house is nestled
> and where they are at the moment. Myself, serving as a captain
> with my old pals of 22 years ago, leaving for a new campaign
> that I am certain will be horrible.

I am writing to you from Paris. We have started the regimen of bombing alerts. Not a public light glows in the street...

L'Arc de Triomphe appears splendid under the moon, against the darkness of the Place de l'Etoile. Is it all going to be destroyed?

What about your research on Nazism? Do you see how it is relevant today and may be more relevant tomorrow?

Adieu, older brother. Your godson Michel, a strange little fellow, sometimes loving and sometimes sulky, would like to know you. The other boys are fine. Thank God. They are my reason to live, and they are why I feel so sad when I think of the approach of war...

Goodbye ...

Your friend, René Arnaud

Address in peacetime: Vert

Address in wartime: Capitaine René Arnaud, Cor 83 á Auxerre (They will forward it to me wherever I am.)

P.S. Dollar at 40 francs...Adieu New York. I couldn't afford you anyway.

Three days later, Germany invaded Poland and Britain's ambassador to Germany delivered a joint French-British ultimatum to Hitler: If hostilities did not cease by 11:00 a.m., a state of war would exist between Great Britain and Germany. Germany did not respond and, at 11:15 a.m., Prime Minister Neville Chamberlain spoke to the British people:

This morning the British Ambassador in Berlin handed the German Government a final Note stating that, unless we heard from them by 11 o'clock that they were prepared at once to withdraw their troops from Poland, a state of war would exist between us.

I have to tell you now that no such undertaking has been received, and that consequently this country is at war with Germany.

The French government delivered a similar ultimatum to Germany that expired at 3:00 p.m. that same day. France, Australia, and New Zealand declared war on Germany. Saint-Exupéry reported for duty to the Tou-louse-Francazal airfield in southern France, near the Pyrénées. He was as-signed to the 2-33 Reconnaissance Group, 120 miles east of Paris.

The ensuing eight months became known as the "phony war" or, in French parlance, the "drôle de guerre," during which neither France nor Britain took military action against Germany. Churchill referred to it as the "Twilight War." On October 25, René wrote to Lewis:

> My old friend,
>
> ... The one truly useful thing I have done is to explain to my men, in a matter-of-fact way, the nature of actual combat. I have done this because the French soldier needs to understand why he has to do such things. (They are good men—not warriors, not military men, but brave. They are soldiers and ready to fight when taught how to do it. I think they will do it well, if the bosch attacks.)
>
> ... Will they attack the "Ligne Maginot" that I think is so strong or will they do as they did in 1916, and invade through Belgium and the Netherlands. I think we can expect it. Maybe an attack would be good: there is nothing worse for an army than to do nothing...
>
> ... I leave you my pal. I won't see you in Europe before the end of the war. Hitler will do bad things, and oblige us to do the same. My best regards to your wife, whom I hope to see one day.
>
> My best to you.
>
> René Arnaud, Capitaine[233]

March 7, 1940, letter from René:

> My old friend,
>
> ... In November, then in January, we thought that the Germans were invading Holland and Belgium, therefore we were ready... Now, could we see a big blow coming in the spring? A frontal attack on the Ligne Maginot would cost a lot, and would not lead farther than the attack of 1916 on Verdun...In any case, I

cannot even imagine what peace would look like. If, as I believe,
we can conquer Adolf, what will we do with Germany?[234]

Hitler invaded Denmark the morning of April 9, 1940, and moved into Holland, Belgium, and Luxembourg on May 10. The following day, Colonel Charles de Gaulle was ordered to assemble a new Fourth Armored Division and, with it, to delay the Nazi advance toward Paris until reinforcements could arrive. De Gaulle's tanks attacked German advance troops at Montcornet, France, about twenty miles from the Belgian border, killing several hundred and taking 130 prisoners while losing fewer than 200 men. De Gaulle did this despite having had no radio communications between his tanks, no air support, no artillery support and no antiaircraft guns, all of which the Germans possessed. The Germans renewed their advance two days later and de Gaulle met them at the town of Crécy-sur-Serre, twenty miles west of their first encounter. On April 26, 1940, Lewis assessed how the war would play out, which is to say, he greatly underestimated Germany's capacity for a protracted military conflict.[235]

On May 17, General Maxime Weygand was appointed Supreme Commander of French forces, and three days later, the Germans captured Abbeville. De Gaulle, now promoted to brigadier general, met the Germans on the western outskirts of the city and drove them back, taking another five hundred prisoners. Edith Arnaud wrote to Lewis on May 22, 1940.

I have received good news from René this morning and his mood is
good. Besides, all of us don't doubt victory. It will be hard,
very hard, but we will get "them."

René just came for a 5 day leave on May 5, he went back on
the eve of the invasion of Holland, Belgium, Luxemburg and
when he arrived in Paris by train at 7 am he found out the
painful news...refugees are aimlessly wandering, hunted away
from Belgium and from the North of France, and truly this view
saddens me and breaks my heart, but also revolts us. These
unfortunate people have lost their homes and are dispersed
without places to go. Despite all, there is some work to soothe
all this misery...

All my best wishes for you and your wife,

Edith Arnaud

It goes without saying with what faith and hope we need the help of the USA.[236]

Fifty miles northeast of Abbeville, at the town of Arras on the Scarpe River, a British Expeditionary Force attacked a German armored division. The heavily armored British Matilda tanks withstood the guns of the German Panzers and were pushing the German line back when Commander Erwin Rommel turned his antiaircraft guns on them. Nearby, Deputy Battalion Commander René Arnaud and his fellow ground troops faced overwhelming German fire. René wrote to Lewis:

Mon cher vieux,

... the Germans did not lack anything, not even gasoline...

My stay in the line didn't inspire me with overwhelming confidence...Out of the 20 men, 12 were elementary school teachers and the others were minor civil servants...Some were excellent, notably the commander himself, an admirable leader, at the same time firm but human, knowing how to be feared and loved at the same time...Two or three other officers were calm and energetic. But the others—repented communists—lacked... gumption, and counted on a miracle for this war to end without a battle. I don't want to complain about the school teachers, because then I would have to do the same with the bourgeois: notaries, lawyers, shop owners, etc..."hiding" [at the General Headquarters]...being messengers and scribes.

... upon these thin men [his men], tired without being trained, badly surrounded by insufficient officers and mediocre non-commissioned officers, fell the great attack that you know about. The tanks easily moved the regiments of men who were lacking heart and anti-tanks cannons. And when we were able to fight back, to block the tanks with our '75, clouds of planes would come, filling up the skies without seeing any French or English plane and reduced any resistance to silence...having fought as did we at Verdun. But those older men ignored or had forgotten the realities of war. At Verdun, when the German Fokkers were

flying over us for hours...our mood would go down several degrees. But the smallest tricolor ribbon seen up there would bring back our hopes and put our heart back in our chest! Our young ones understood very quickly that we were outclassed; that we had something like 600 planes against 6,000. In my opinion, this is enough to explain our defeat.[237]

From above the fray, in the skies over Arras, army captain Saint-Exupéry and his flight crew—an observer and a gunner—looked on as René Arnaud and his men fought below. Saint-Exupéry had taken off from Meaux, on the Marne River about a dozen miles east of Paris, to assess whether Arras had fallen. Their plane, a Bloch 174, had twin wing-mounted engines and a clear plastic nose and canopy that gave unobstructed views in most directions. Saint-Exupéry had an escort of nine single-engine fighter aircraft—Dewoitine D.520s—that, although slower than the Messerschmitt Bf 109s that pursued him, were more maneuverable. Two of the escort fighters were lost. Saint-Exupéry's Bloch was hit by ground fire but was not disabled. It returned to base, its three-man crew unscathed and exhilarated with having cheated death. For that flight, Saint-Exupéry was awarded the Croix de Guerre avec Palme, France's highest award for valor. His was one of twenty-three crews that made up his flight group at the start of May. By the end of that month, the twenty-three had been winnowed to six by German fighters and ground artillery. Saint-Exupéry told of having seen Arras in flames and of hundreds of German tanks poised to move on Paris.

Belgium surrendered on May 28, 1940, and British and French troops were driven to the northern shores of Dunkirk, about seven miles west of the Belgian border. There, between May 26 and June 4, over 330,000 British and 120,000 French troops were evacuated, in boats of all shapes, sizes, and types, to England. On June 3, René wrote to Lewis:

You will know how utterly devastating has been the French collapse. No one high or low had ever supposed it possible. There had been some ideas they were over-confident but there is no excuse—no treachery—just sheer weakness, over-confidence and

*want of foresight. It means, of course, that by the time you
read this, the first round will have gone far further than you
can imagine. Comment is useless. All I tell you is true. It is
not possible for Weygand[238] to rally the French in time.[239]*

Prime Minister Paul Reynaud recalled General de Gaulle to Paris and named him undersecretary of state for national defense. He also summoned Marshal Philippe Pétain from Spain to serve as vice premier. On June 9, 1940, with Reynaud's approval, de Gaulle traveled to London and met with Winston Churchill, whom King George VI had just named prime minister. The purpose of the meeting was to see if the British would support a French resistance government based in France or North Africa. De Gaulle returned with Churchill's commitment of additional military support.

The Germans entered Paris on June 14. That same day, de Gaulle urged Reynaud to create a government in exile in Algiers. Reynaud agreed. De Gaulle flew to London to obtain Britain's assistance in relocating the French government but, as he was en route, Reynaud resigned as prime minister and was succeeded by Pétain. The next day, Marshal Pétain broadcast to the French people:

*France is defeated, but it is not the first time that she has
been defeated and there is no reason to believe that she
will not rise again this time as she has done so successfully
before. In particular, I believe that an honest understanding
with Germany would bring us peace for a long time to come. This
quarrel of the centuries across the Rhine must be brought to an
end. If France tries to move in that direction, I believe that
she will win.*

Winston Churchill arranged for de Gaulle to speak to the French people over the BBC. His speech went out on June 18:

*The leaders who, for many years, have been at the head of
the French armies have formed a government. This government,
alleging the defeat of our armies, has made contact with the
enemy in order to stop the fighting. It is true, we were, we
are, overwhelmed by the mechanical, ground and air forces of the*

enemy. Infinitely more than their number, it is the tanks, the aeroplanes, the tactics of the Germans which are causing us to retreat. It was the tanks, the aeroplanes, the tactics of the Germans that surprised our leaders to the point of bringing them to where they are today.

But has the last word been said? Must hope disappear? Is defeat final? No!...For France is not alone! She is not alone! She is not alone! She has a vast Empire behind her. She can align with the British Empire that holds the sea and continues the fight. She can, like England, use without limit the immense industry of the United States...Vanquished today by mechanical force, in the future we will be able to overcome by a superior mechanical force. The fate of the world depends on it.

I, General de Gaulle, currently in London, invite the officers and the French soldiers who are located in British territory or who might end up here, with their weapons or without their weapons...to put themselves in contact with me.

Whatever happens, the flame of the French resistance must not be extinguished and will not be extinguished.

Tomorrow, as today, I will speak on the radio from London.

Marshal Pétain signed the armistice on June 22, 1940. It required him to disband the French army and required France to pay the cost of the German invasion and to accede to German occupation of more than half of the country. The unoccupied portion of France would become a German vassal based in the spa town of Vichy. The French Republic was voted out of existence on July 10 and Pétain became France's "Head of State," in essence, its dictator. The republican motto "Liberté, égalité, fraternité" was replaced with "Travail, famille, patrie": Work, family, fatherland.

Pétain appointed Pierre Laval the Vichy Minister of State, and Laval thereafter carried out policies dictated by Germany, turning the French Republic into a fascist regime. Pétain announced, "The government remains free; France will be administered by the French." The United States recognized the Vichy regime as the French government; it did not recognize de Gaulle's Free France. De Gaulle's remained a lone voice.

René to Lewis

*... I left the army in July and was named chief of a reserve
battalion effective June 25, which is to say from the Armistice
date...After one month spent in the depressing atmosphere of
Vichy, I went back to Paris where the rest of my family met me.*

On July 12, the *New York Herald Tribune* bore a full-page headline: "France's Spirit Only Numbed, Lewis Galantière Predicts That Its Revival Will Destroy Oppressors." Lewis condemned Marshal Pétain and Pierre Laval for their collaboration with the Germans and promised that "the lightning of the French spirit will blast Laval's Gestapo and the world will witness the reemergence of the French Phoenix from its ashes."[240] "France's Spirit Only Numbed" cheered a dismayed New York readership. But there was at least one dissenter, who voiced his opinion in a handwritten note on Waldorf Astoria stationery (verbatim):

"Personal—Germany"

Mr. Lewis Galantière—Sir

*What an ingrate you are to write an article about the treatment
that Germany gave France—I think they were fine—they should
have taken more revenge & given France much worse—You are her
[sic] in our U.S. & can therefore brag & talk rot, if all the
French people were like you, there would be no France now. I
think Pétain has good common horse sense to see that Germany
has been so lenient. Now they are building up four destroyed
bridges & other important places. You will now have a France
not dominated by the thieving, treacherous selfish who sent
France to her doom, be glad she is now in safe hands of Germany.
England would only have added her to her Empire—well she won't
have her British Empire much longer & I hope Hitler will dump
her into the English Channel same as my ancestors dumped that
English tea into Boston Harbor in 1773—Boston tea party (for
your information) since you seem such an ignoramous [sic] —Adieu
don't be an ingrate—bad business.*

J. A. Bennett, S.A.R. [Sons of the American Revolution][241]

Six years earlier, Thomas Balogh had blamed the demise of the German Republic on the character of the German people, attributing to them a masochistic, collective inferiority complex and an infatuation with simplistic phrases. He judged that Germans lacked the will to preserve representational government.[242] In 1940, Lewis applied for a Guggenheim Foundation fellowship to examine that very proposition, which he framed as follows:

> the chief tenets of the national socialist state were not
> the product of circumstances arising out of the War of 1914-
> 1918, but had their roots deep in the German past...[that] the
> Weltanschauung [philosophy of life or world-view] of the Germans
> is different from that of the English, the Dutch, and the French,
> whose social and political heirs we of America are.[243]

Lewis asked Albert Guérard, professor of comparative literature at Stanford University to recommend him to the Guggenheim Committee. Guérard obliged but cautioned Lewis that every other similar recommendation he had submitted to the committee had been for naught.[244] But this time was different: Lewis was awarded a grant of $2,500 (the equivalent of $45,000 in 2017).[245] When he received the news, Professor Guérard was as pleased for himself as he was for Lewis:

> April 1, 1940
>
> Dear Mr. Galantière,
>
> I am delighted indeed to hear of the Guggenheim Award, and I
> should like to believe that I influenced the committee to some
> degree. Your jumping from banking to the Goncourts [Lewis's
> translation of the Goncourt Journals] to German Nationalism is
> simply breathtaking. In the realm of the spirit, you are the
> original Young Man on the Flying Trapeze.[246]

Lewis told the Guggenheim committee that he would complete the project in eighteen months but, even in that spring of 1940, he knew his conclusions. In a May issue of *Forum and Century*, Lewis charged that the German people had not been the innocent victims of Hitler's madness but, rather, his enablers.[247] And, for the first time, he addressed, in print, the subject of antisemitism:

> *...Of course many Germans are shocked by excessive anti-Semitism, just as many Americans are not in the least shocked by a light touch of anti-Semitism... But to assume that the German who is shocked by a pogrom is also made miserable by the Greater Germany drive of the Nazi regime is to ignore a thousand years of German history and indoctrination...*

On May 1, 1940, nine days before Germany invaded France, Lewis told Professor Guérard that, in his opinion, war with Germany was necessary. His predictions about the postwar consequences were prescient:

> *... I am strongly anti-isolationist—not, God knows, out of any hatred of the Germans, but oft of the feeling that the world will be a much worse place to live in than it is if the Germans win. And I say that, if the Germans win, there will be few Germans unhappy over the fact, cultivated or uncultivated, Nazi or not-Nazi, even liberal or illiberal. I say further that if all Europe goes irrevocably authoritarian, our own problems will, by a process of contagion, be solved in* [an authoritarian way]...

> *The Germans have, confound them!, the bon parti,* [the good match] *without any doubt. If they win, the world is theirs (and this goes far beyond Hitler, this 'theirs'). If they lose, we shall join together to patch them up. It is as if every criminal were to know in advance that whatever his crime he would be treated as a psychiatric case in the tenderest way, not even put into a prison uniform, for it would be impossible to cure him if he were distinguishable from the rest of society. On the other hand, if we (and I mean 'we') win, some of us—the English, the French—win a barren victory, come forth ruined, like a man who has 'won' the victory of seeing the firebug Condémned (at best) who burnt down his house to the ground.*[248]

———————— ❦ ————————

· CHAPTER 8 ·

FLIGHT TO ARRAS

SAINT-EXUPÉRY WAS DEMOBILIZED ON JULY 31, 1940. Both Pétain's Vichy government and the editors of the Paris literary magazine *La Nouvelle Revue Française* (now under Nazi editorial control) invited him to work for them, but Saint-Exupéry would not subordinate his conscience to the purposes of either. On December 21, 1940, he boarded a small ship of the American Export Lines and sailed to America, arriving in New York City on New Year's Day 1941. There he was greeted by de Gaulle representatives seeking his support for the general. Saint-Exupéry demurred. He thought the general to be a divisive self-promoter:

> De Gaulle ceased to be a soldier and became a political leader.
> I should have followed him with joy against the Germans. I could
> not follow him against Frenchmen.[249]

General de Gaulle was a man who held grudges. In North Africa in 1944, he would exact his revenge.

Saint-Exupéry signed a contract with Reynal and Hitchcock to write a book about his reconnaissance flights in northeastern France. Its title for the American market would be *Flight to Arras*. Lewis was retained as a sounding board for the author and to produce the English-language version. He was not handed a portfolio of stories as he had with *Wind, Sand and Stars*; because Saint-Exupéry had not yet written the first word. Knowing the Frenchman to be both a procrastinator and a perfectionist, Lewis and Eugene Reynal's wife, Elizabeth, spent the ensuing months extracting each paragraph from him. *Flight to Arras* emerged laboriously, and usually late at night:

> My wife, who was very fond of Saint-Exupéry and loved to hear him talk, had nevertheless one subject of complaint concerning him: he telephoned me too often in the middle of the night. I was then translating Flight to Arras chapter by chapter as it came from his hands, and was therefore intimately associated with his torments of composition. Whenever he had written a particularly difficult passage, and felt that he had to read it aloud immediately, it was to me that he would telephone. And I, at two o'clock in the morning, under the half- mocking and half- furious stare of my wife, understanding not a word of what the rapid muffled voice was reciting into the telephone—for I was of course more than half asleep—would nod my head, interject an appropriate "Ah!" or "That's good, that is!" while I sought in vain to catch at the thread of his discourse; and upon his insistent demand, when he was through, that I tell him what I thought, would repeat mechanically and hypocritically, "Magnificent! Magnificent!" Generally the session ended with a long silence in which I seemed to hear Saint-Exupéry turning his ideas over in his mind, then a sudden "Good! Sorry to disturb you. Good night," and he would hang up.[250]

Flight to Arras spoke of what it meant to be French: how a particular Frenchman, epitomizing all French airmen, had flown on reconnaissance missions he knew to be futile. It told of Messerschmitt fighters shooting from above while antiaircraft guns fired at him from below.

> I was later to hear foreigners reproach France with the few bridges that were not blown up, the handful of villages we did not burn, the men who failed to die. But here on the scene, it is the contrary, it is exactly the contrary that strikes me so powerfully. It is our desperate struggle against self-evident fact. We know that nothing can do any good, yet we blow up bridges nevertheless, in order to play the game. We burn down

real villages, in order to play the game. It is in order to play the game that our men die.[251]

René Arnaud as well had urged Lewis to tell the story of the individual French soldier's heroism in the face of overwhelming force; here in a July 1, 1940, letter:

The prime thing now will be to face up to what can be said in America about the French...The facts are these...and I am going to try and get them into concrete form: We did far more, even in men, than we promised. We did infinitely more in the air than anyone thought possible. The French who said they had four thousand airplanes had really none, by which I mean they had only a small number. One or two went up once or twice and fought gallantly, but were quite useless from any point of view...

From the moment of Sedan, the French General Staff gave up. They never had a backup plan. In principle, they did not fight again, and there is endless evidence of this. (It is not made up.) Every British unit found itself in the same position, fighting against German infantry whom they never failed to beat; always having to be hauled back because the French on either side had given way. This happened again and again.

It is a stark, cruel fact. The blame is on the High Command, and no one is going to stand up at this time of day and defend Gamelin because he, of course, has no defense at all.

It is your duty to explain France, to explain the defeat to people who believe that the French did not put up a fight.[252]

Lewis impressed upon Saint-Exupéry the need to tell *that* soldier's story. *Flight to Arras* was the first time that many Americans understood how valiantly the French soldier and airman had resisted the German onslaught:

Saint-Exupéry, in *Flight to Arras*:

France accepted the war in the face of logistical truth. They told us: "It's eighty million Germans. We cannot acquire, in a single year, the forty million French that we lack. We cannot change our land from one of wheat to one of coal."

René Arnaud in a letter to Lewis:

> ... we must face the truth: we are a nation of only forty million
> souls against a nation of eighty million. Our nationalists who
> still dream of hegemony know too much history, which is to say
> that they don't know enough.[253]

Translating from French to English requires preserving the lyricism of the first while applying the greater precision of the second. That was the ability that Lewis brought to the task. Here are examples. In each case, the first paragraph is from *Pilote de guerre* (the book's French title) and the second is a verbatim translation of that text into English. The third is Lewis's translation of the same paragraph in *Flight to Arras*.

French

> Je n'opposerai pas l'été, les fruits qui mûrissent, les
> poussins qui prennent du poids, les blés qui lèvent, à la
> mort si proche. Je ne vois pas en quoi le calme de l'été
> contredirait la mort, ni en quoi la douceur des choses serait
> ironie.

Literal translation

> I would not pit summer, its ripening fruits, its chicks
> growing plump and its rippling wheat against imminent death.
> I do not see how the calm of summer could counter death, nor
> in what way life's sweetness could be only irony.

Lewis's translation

> It would be easy to write a couple of fraudulent pages out of
> the contrast between this shining spring day, the ripening
> fruit, the chicks filling plumply out in the barnyard, the
> rising wheat—and death at our elbow. I shall not write that
> couple of pages because I see no reason why the peace of a
> spring day should constitute a contradiction of the idea
> of death. Why should the sweetness of life be a matter for
> irony? [Here, recalling René Arnaud's musing that, soon, he
> would be digging in his garden or once again enveloped in
> the horrors of war.]

And

French

> *Je songe à l'absurde d'un survol d'Arras à sept cents mètres.*
> *A la vanité des renseignements souhaités de nous. A la*
> *lenteur de l'habillage qui m'apparaît comme une toilette pour*
> *le bourreau. Et puis à mes gants. Où diable trouverai-je des*
> *gants? J'ai perdu mes gants.*

Literal translation

> *I think of the absurdity of assessing Arras from an altitude*
> *of seven hundred meters. Of the conceit that we are gaining*
> *information. Of our slowly putting on our flight suits, which*
> *strikes me as men dressing for the executioner. And then my*
> *gloves. Where the hell are my gloves? I lost my gloves.*

Lewis's translation

> *I think of the absurdity of flying over German-held Arras at*
> *two thousand feet. Of the futility of the intelligence we*
> *are asked to bring back. Of the interminable time it takes*
> *to dress in these clothes that remind me of men made ready*
> *for the executioner. And I think of my gloves. Where the*
> *devil are my gloves? I have lost my gloves.*

Lewis and Saint-Exupéry spent hundreds of hours together on this endeavor, and developed a mutual respect. But the two were irreconcilably different men, and it cannot be said that they became intimate friends. Saint-Exupéry extolled the man of action, Lewis the man of knowledge and reason. Saint-Exupéry wrote to expiate and exalt, Lewis wrote to convince. Politically, Saint-Exupéry distrusted the democratic rabble, preferring leadership by a strong benevolent nobility. Lewis trusted the collective judgment of a free citizenry and distrusted the slippery machinations of consolidated power. When, in 1943, Saint-Exupéry said,

> *For the second time in this war, I have succeeded in avoiding*
> *becoming a member of a general's staff, or a propaganda*
> *writer...*[254]

the purposes that he disdained were those that Lewis would serve. The two men shared a passion for the written word, but they were not candid with each other. Each held back; each had his secrets and protected his vulnerabilities. Saint-Exupéry, speaking through the aviator in *The Little Prince*, said "Thus I lived alone, with no one I could really talk to." The same was true of Lewis. Saint-Exupéry and Lewis existed in proximity but alone. Each played the role he had written for his character.

A photograph of Lewis, Saint-Exupéry, the publisher Eugene Reynal and his wife Elizabeth sitting around a café table was among Lewis's papers at Columbia University's Butler Library. Lewis is seated at the leftmost position, visible only by his sleeve and the side of his suit jacket. *He* tore his image from the photograph, leaving the Reynals and Saint-Exupéry.

Lewis, the only one not dressed in a dark suit, wore a light gray and rumpled one. And, at five feet five inches, he was diminutive compared to the Reynals and the six foot two Saint-Exupéry. The photo suggests that he had just directed a facial expression at Saint-Exupéry, which he may have thought too undignified for posterity. Certainly, Lewis would have left the photo intact had it conformed to the public persona he had cultivated.

CHAPTER 9

THE OFFICE OF WAR INFORMATION (OWI)

THE HEADLINE ON THE *New York Herald Tribune*'s editorial page was "Pétain's Struggle to Rescue France."[255] It had been nearly a year since Lewis had rebuked Pétain in print but, in this piece, he recast the old general as a pragmatist, struggling to preserve France:

> In July, 1940...I denounced Laval, referred to Pétain as his dupe, and took it for granted that the France of the glorious device, Liberté, Fraternité, Egalité would be born again of her own ashes. It would appear that I overrated Laval and underrated Pétain...
>
> In the whole world there is not a more misleading and ridiculous concept than that of Pétain as the free-willed friend of the Germans. The idealists who pour their contempt upon Pétain forget not only how helpless he is to fight with other weapons than evasion, negotiation, delay...His first concern cannot be ideological, it must be to lighten the burden carried by the French people, to keep life going among them as far as possible...Men resist, they yield, they resist again, they yield again, in order to gain time, stay alive, gather strength—and fight another day. This, not collaboration, is the case of the French.

But a year later, Pétain announced that the Vichy government would henceforth be, in substance, fascist:

> Authority no longer emanates from below.
>
> The only authority is that which I entrust or delegate.

Vichy France, he said, would devote itself to Nazi Germany's "defense of civilization."[256] That summer of 1941, Lewis described, in an unpublished memorandum, the conditions then existing in Vichy, alluding to a confidential source that was probably René Arnaud:

> In unoccupied France it is forbidden to turn a radio on to a foreign station in a public place. Radios are therefore set just inside the open door of the cafe-owner's back room, and the public collect and listen in silence to London, chiefly, Boston when it comes through clearly.
>
> Darlan has retained his place by agreeing to out-Laval Laval. Had it been otherwise, the Germans would have forced Pétain to bring Laval back.
>
> Pétain is still liked. Laval is the most hated and feared. Darlan is detested, but is looked upon as a man who might any day, at the will of the Germans, be replaced by Laval.[257]

The memorandum said that the Germans were purchasing food and goods and paying cash to the farmers and shopkeepers, the payments lending a patina of correctness and fairness to the dealings. But it was a farce because the Germans were obtaining the money, in the first place, from the indemnity payments that Germany was extracting from the French government. Lewis wired Edith Arnaud in Royan $100 for her subsistence and that of her sons, Dominique, Philippe, and Lewis's godson, Michel.[258]

In January 1942, the Roosevelt administration consolidated war-related government information and propaganda within a single agency: the Office of War Information, or OWI. The Pulitzer prize–winning playwright Robert Sherwood was tapped to be director of its Overseas Branch, and he asked Lewis to head the French Section.[259] Lewis completed a preemployment security disclosure form—a "declaration of appointee"—that asked for his prior employment, affiliations, education, and family. He answered the latter two categories—education and family—untruthfully.[260]

He identified his high school as the Lycée Condorcet in Paris (1908–1912) and his college and university education (1912–1915) as the École Normale Supérieure and the University of Paris (simultaneously), from which he received credits in history, philosophy, political science and economics. He said that he graduated from the university in 1915 with the degree *licencié-ès-lettres*. In fact, the year of Lewis's putative graduation from the University of Paris—1915—was the year he graduated from the Los Angeles Library School. Lewis furnished this information knowing that the U.S. Civil Service Commission could not communicate with any educational institution in Nazi-occupied France and that even if, beyond all odds, the French institutions received and accurately responded to an inquiry, their responses would be disbelieved as German disinformation. He safely assumed that his education claims would be unverifiable until after the war's end, at which time further inquiry would likely not be made.

He recast his Jewish Latvian parents (Joseph Galantière and Cecile Lurie Galantière) as Joseph Marie Galantière, born in Cérons, France, and Cécile (maiden Pourtalès) Galantière, born in Fribourg, Switzerland. The Civil Service form contained a closing attestation: "I hereby certify that the answers to the foregoing questions are true in every particular." Lewis signed the form. The Civil Service Commission attached a photo.[261]

Lewis. National Archives,
Military Personnel Records Center, St. Louis, MO.

Robert Sherwood recruited John Houseman to lead the radio broad-cast operation. Houseman was fluent in French and German and had a basic knowledge of Spanish. He came to the office from David Selznick Productions in Culver City, California, where he was a vice president. The newspaperman Nelson Poynter had recommended him:

January 11, 1942, Poynter memo to Robert E. Sherwood, with a
copy to Colonel Donovan

Re: the hiring of John Houseman as Radio Program advisor.

There is a crying need to invent a new technique in
international propaganda broadcasting. The ordinary American
commercial program is not the answer. We are fighting a religious,
fanatical crusade. In turn, we must sell the "religion of
democracy." It is a different, tougher assignment than to sell
a cereal or a toothpaste. Houseman has been recommended as the
man who has the professional craftsmanship, the imagination, the
personality to do this.

He is giving up a job at $1,000 a week to work for $150.[262]

Robert Sherwood endorsed Poynter's suggestion:

> *I agree with the conception of John Houseman's job as outlined in your memorandum of January 11. I talked to him yesterday at considerable length and also talked to him and Ernst Lubitsch together and I am sure that Houseman will be intensely valuable to us.*
>
> *He will start work in about two weeks and I hope that he will be able to begin operations here in New York immediately... It seems to me that Houseman should have at the beginning the job of producing the four daily programs to England for rebroadcast which I hope will have been started by then*[263]

The OWI's broadcast entity was the Voice of America, or VOA. Its offices were at 270 Madison Avenue in New York City. In his autobiography, *Unfinished Business*, Houseman described his surprise at discovering Lewis already ensconced there:

> [Robert Sherwood's deputy, Joseph Barnes] *led me on a tour of the half-finished premises and introduced me to some of the people with whom I would be working. Some were old friends; among them, in a dark corner next to the men's room, bent myopically over a yellow legal-sized pad, I found my former roommate and co-author, Lewis Galantière, who had left the Federal Reserve Bank to join Sherwood as an expert on French affairs.*[264]

John Houseman. National Archives,
Military Personnel Records Center, St. Louis, MO.

OWI programming consisted of news stories and opinion (cleared through the State Department) in the native tongues of their intended listeners: the subjugated peoples of Europe and the German soldiers who were their occupiers. The VOA radio signal was beamed to Europe by shortwave radio from New York (if urgent) or sent via transatlantic cable to London for rebroadcast. The first broadcast went out February 1, 1942, and these were its first words:

> *Attention! This is the Voice of America!*
>
> *The Voice of America at War.*
>
> *Our voices come to you from New York across the Atlantic Ocean.*
>
> *America is today in its sixty-sixth day of the war.*

*Today and every day from now on we shall be speaking to you
about America and the War. Here in America we receive news from
all over the world. This news may be favorable or unfavorable.
Every day we shall bring you this news. The truth.*[265]

The VOA dealt in drama, news, and opinion. At the start of 1942, Lewis's French programming denounced the Vichy government as Germany's quisling and laid the responsibility upon Laval and not Pétain. Here is an extract from Lewis's March 28, 1942, script for the people of France:

*Berlin announces that the Marshal had a conversation with
Laval in the Forest of Randon, south of Vichy...[and] Admiral
Darlan visited Laval at Chateldon. The purpose of their
meeting is clear: it is to define the conditions of the sale of
France to the Germans and the conditions which will govern the
installation of a Quisling-style Nazi government in France...*

*It goes without saying that the American government could not
have any more consideration for a Laval Government in France
than it has for a Quisling Government in Norway or for the
Mussolini Government in Italy. The feeling of the American
people for the French people is unchangeable: it is one of
affection and confidence. But we are sure that the French people
itself, if it were able to egress itself freely, would insist
that we do not confuse it with Pierre Laval and would ask us to
protect it against this gangster in the pay of Germany.*

*You know Laval better than we do. There is no need for us to
remind you of the foul career of this man—a career of crooked
intrigue, of profiteering, of heartlessness, cowardice, and
double-dealing.*[266]

Lewis described his work and its importance to Helen Haines:

March 30, 1942

Dear Ms. Haines,

*... I have been organizing broadcasts to France (from New York)
and we are putting on seven 15-minute shows (they are called
shows) a day...my special pride, is more "political warfare"
than news...I love what I do, and I know that it may be useful.
If, by what we do, we can keep the French fleet from falling into*

> German hands; if, by what we do, we can secure that American
> troops will one day be welcome in French Africa instead of being
> fought there by the French as the English were in Syria—the work
> will have been worth doing.[267]

In July 1942, Saint-Exupéry gave Lewis a chance to do more. General Henri Giraud, a hero of the First and Second World Wars, had escaped from a German prison camp, and Saint-Exupéry, believing that Giraud, rather than the hard-to-handle de Gaulle, should lead the free French troops, asked Lewis to tell the War Department of his (Saint-Exupéry's) willingness to travel to France, find General Giraud, and persuade him to fly—in a plane that Saint-Exupéry would somehow obtain—to rendez-vous with an American cruiser. The vessel would bring General Giraud to Washington, DC, where the general and the U.S. Combined Chiefs of Staff would strategize a North African invasion. Since the French forces in North Africa were with the Vichy regime and would attempt to repel an Allied invasion, General Giraud's presence would be needed to tell them to hold their fire.

Lewis thought well enough of the plan that he went to Washington and proposed it to a member of the Combined Chiefs and a member of the OSS. He expected at least polite interest but what he received was a severe dressing-down:

> Never have I been the object of such a rebuff...frankly, a
> bawling-out—as at the end of my little speech. My friend Saint-
> Exupéry might perhaps be a genius, but he was certainly a
> complete idiot. As for me, what right had I to intervene in
> matters that did not concern me and about which I could not be
> more ignorant? If they ever heard that I had repeated a single
> word of this grotesque pipe-dream to anybody at all, they would
> take personal and particular pleasure in seeing that I was put
> away in a Federal penitentiary for a dozen years. And my friend
> Saint-Exupéry the same.[268]

When Lewis returned with the news, Saint-Exupéry said, "Ah? So that's how it is! They're cleverer than I had imagined." Lewis had not comprehended, as had Saint-Exupéry, that a variation of the proposal was already in the works: President Roosevelt and Prime Minister Churchill had just approved plans for Operation Torch—the British and American invasion of Morocco, Algeria, and Tunisia—with the expectation that if General Giraud (under the *nom de guerre* "Kingpin")[269] gave the order to stand down, the North African French forces would obey.[270]

When Operation Torch was put into motion the Allies extracted General Giraud from Vichy, brought him to the HMS *Seraph*, and offered him the post of commander in chief of the North African French forces, the appointment to take place *after* the military campaign succeeded. General Giraud counteroffered: he would accept the appointment if he was immediately made commander in chief of the Allied invading forces (the position Eisenhower held). The Allies refused and placed Giraud on Gibraltar, where he sat out the invasion.[271]

That fall, Lewis was appointed the OWI's principal field representative, Overseas Operations Branch, Outpost Bureau.[272] His base of operations was to be London. On Saturday evening, October 3, 1942, he boarded a twenty-seven-ton American export flying boat, the *Excalibur*, for the trip from New York to Botwood Harbor, Newfoundland, an intermediate fueling stop.

Excalibur

The aircraft arrived in Botwood at sunset. The passengers disembarked for dinner as the aircraft was refueled and cargo was off-loaded and on-loaded. Those who finished eating early and were milling about on the pier heard the lapping of waves against the *Excalibur*'s hull and saw the Milky Way, unusually brilliant in the remote harbor, whose lights were protectively darkened against enemy detection. The air was clear and cold. When the last passengers had entered the plane and settled into their seats for the overnight flight, the gangplank was withdrawn. The fuselage door was shut tight and the *Excalibur* lumbered back into the harbor for takeoff. The pilot ran through the takeoff checklist, and then slowly pushed the throttle levers forward to full power. The throbbing of the *Excalibur*'s four radial engines filled the cabin as the aircraft gathered speed, its hull splashing along the water's surface and then lifting off. But, once airborne, the plane transmitted the shuddering vibrations that indicated an imminent stall. The pilot lowered the nose, to trade altitude for airspeed and, when the aircraft was just above the surface, pulled back on the wheel. The *Excalibur* rose but once again signaled her intention to stall. Struggling to remain airborne, the pilot entered into a series of porpoising arcs and dives until the aircraft slammed, nose-first, into the icy water, its engines roaring. Upon impact, the fuselage broke away at the tail and the cabin immediately flooded. Lewis, struck unconscious, was submerged. When the divers got to him, his lungs were water-filled and he was not breathing. His was one of twenty-six cold bodies removed from the aircraft and taken to the hospital. Three of the hospitalized died and American newspapers announced that Lewis was one of them. They were wrong.

Lewis's submersion in the frigid salt water of Botwood Harbor had slowed his metabolic processes through a phenomenon known as the "mammalian diving reflex." His body had reflexively conserved the oxygen it needed for his brain and other vital organs to survive. The medical staff drained the sea water from his lungs and gave him forced respiration. And it worked.

Attending physician's notes:

Patient's condition precarious on admission. Superficial laceration of forehead and right lower leg. Latter shows some redness about it accompanied by bruises. No evidence of infection present. This patient was under water for some time before being recovered, and artificial respiration was practiced on him before admission to hospital. In severe shock, lungs filled with rales—coarse and moist.[273]

Over the next several days, Lewis pulled himself back from the edge. The reports of his death had been premature.[274]

1942-10-03 Patient...treated for shock on admission = 1000 cc's human plasma. Oxygen inhalations...force fluids, short wave therapy to chest ...

1942-10-04 Is somewhat improved today, but still quite confused...Is able to take some fluids by mouth. Complains of pain in right upper anterior chest. A clicking sensation can be palpated in this region—possibly fractured 2nd and 3rd ribs.

1942-10-05 Improvement continues. Patient much brighter. Still pain in right anterior chest, especially on coughing and breathing. Rales less.[275]

1942-10-07 No rales today. Patient feeling fine except for pain in region of fractured ribs when he moves.

By October 8, Lewis was able to write an account of what he could remember:

It was at the take-off from the place in Newfoundland. [Aircraft] seemed okay. Was not overloaded. But she nose-dived, crashed—and I was one of 37 suddenly in the water. I was knocked unconscious instantly (even before being in water, I believe). I know nothing except that at some time in the 18 to 24 hours during which I was unconscious, I certainly had—but only for an instant—the sensation of being in water.

Actually I was picked up in no more than 2 minutes, treated in the crash boat and on the dock, and kept in an oxygen mask for some hours and given shots of blood plasma. My life was saved by the quick work of the airline crash-boat crew and the equally wonderful devotion of the Canadian Army hospital staff. A very sympathetic padre, questioning me in my delirium, gave me extreme unction—but I'm not going to need it yet for a bit.

The crash took place at about 7:30 PM Saturday. We had every result—from instant death to getting off with a scratch. All things considered, I was very lucky. They thought Saturday night that I'd go, but I didn't. I'm tough...

... as soon as my ribs are sound, my chest void of seawater, and my bruises reduced, I'll have myself carried by plane back to [New York].[276]

Lewis celebrated his forty-seventh birthday in the Botwood hospital. The many letters he received included these:

From his publisher, Curtice Hitchcock:

October 8, 1942

Dear Lewis:

... You may not have realized what an important guy you are but our telephone has been ringing steadily about you ever since the news appeared in the paper Monday morning about the crash. Yesterday we had a wire from Mike who is out in the Middle West and Saint-Ex and all kinds of other people have inquired and would want to send their best if they knew I was writing...Curtice[277]

From his old friend Burton Rascoe:

October 8, 1942

Dear Lewis:

... While you are taking a forced rest maybe you'd like to tackle a job that was offered me the other day. A publisher asked me if I could, and would, condense The Decline and Fall of the Roman Empire into one volume of about 450 pages...[278]

Always, Burton [279]

From his wife, Nancy:

> *October 12, 1942*
>
> *Dear Snooky:—*
>
> *... That nice man from the office of Strategic Services chatted with me by telephone Friday, & believe me his wide and open conversation was as near akin to champagne as conversation can be to a woman used these last days to imbibing stagnant air bubbles...*
>
> *I know that you will be pleased to hear a little story circulating from Woodstock— "Mrs. Galantière's husband speaks nine languages fluently; his specialty is Japanese. He is going abroad to set up an international radio station from which he will address the world but he will of course concentrate on the Japanese..."*
>
> *I do so hope, my love, that you will come back. Please write me when you can—with all my love.*
>
> *Nancy.*[280]

Lewis was flown back to New York City at the end of October. An attempt to haul the *Excalibur* aboard a Navy vessel failed and she remains, today, at the bottom of Botwood Harbor.

That winter, Lewis contracted pneumonia—the effects of submersion exacerbated by earlier chronic lung scarring. He had been and would remain a smoker of Turkish tobacco cigarettes. Hospitalized for four weeks (two in an oxygen tent), he lost twenty pounds, and his leg muscles atrophied. But the events of March 8, 1943, brought him back to his microphone. That Sunday night, two hundred British aircraft obliterated the lightly defended Renault factory in Billancourt, a western suburb of Paris, taking 350 French lives. Renault had been manufacturing Nazi light tanks, aircraft engines, and trucks. In a radio broadcast, Pétain condemned the raid as "criminal aggression" and placed the blame for France's fate on the Free French rather than the Nazis. He also asserted that the primary role of higher education was to imbue students with a "new conscience":

My friends, I have just heard that the Paris suburbs were the object of another Anglo-Saxon attack this afternoon. [Pétain spoke of an "Anglo-Saxon" attack, rather than a "British" attack, in order to lump the Americans with the British.] Again there are dead and wounded, and ruined homes to be added to the long and painful list of victims of our northern towns, of Brittany, Normandy and Tunisia. While protesting against actions that nothing can justify, I address to the families of these innocent victims my deep grief and affectionate condolences.

Rebel commanders [de Gaulle] have chosen emigration and return to the past—I have chosen France and her future.

It would be in vain to expect the end of our decadence, as long as children had not received a new conscience from their teachers. Is this not the great mission of those who are entrusted with education?[281]

The next day, Lewis broadcast to France via short wave from New York:

The speech made by Pétain at Vichy last Sunday constitutes such a string of false pearls that I cannot refrain from referring to them and commenting upon them...

The Marshal of France, the man who was once known as the Hero of Verdun, the man who calls himself the Chief of the French State—Pétain—exonerates the Germans from all responsibility for this war! Pétain accuses France, accuses his own comrades in arms of yesterday, of the responsibility for the war of 1939! ...

If it is your wish that the criminals responsible for this war, responsible too for the ills you are now suffering, be punished—do not count upon Pétain to procure you this satisfaction. Pétain has said loudly and unmistakably that for him the Germans are innocent; that for him only the French are guilty.[282]

In the spring of 1943, Saint-Exupéry left New York to rejoin his reconnaissance squadron in Algiers. No doubt he and Lewis promised to meet again, in Paris.

General Giraud was then commanding the North African French military. He had been promoted to the post when the tenure of his predecessor, Admiral Darlan, was cut short by an assassin's bullets. But Giraud was himself soon maneuvered out of power by General de Gaulle, the far abler politician. Saint-Exupéry asked de Gaulle for a meeting; the General refused. When de Gaulle gave a speech praising French writers who had chosen exile over collaboration—identifying each by name—he conspicuously omitted Saint-Exupéry. When the crew of the Free French warship *Curie* asked if Saint-Exupéry could join them on patrol, the admiralty curtly replied: "Saint-Ex is not a Gaullist!" And when a French soldier wanted to read a Saint-Exupéry book, he found that there were none to be had because the General had banned them from North Africa.

Back in New York, Lewis's doctors declared him fit for field duty, even though, since the crash, he had lost an inch of height and weighed 137 lbs.[283] His new assignment was as OWI's chief French regional specialist, working under his old friend John Houseman.[284] Lewis wrote to Helen Haines with the news:

> January 2, 1944:
>
> Dear Miss Haines...
>
> I had...spent an unsatisfactory summer in New York,[285] lacking the good sense to go away and rest properly, feeling myself overwhelmed by the quantity of work that came to my desk, and showing myself as an irritable and disagreeable person in most of my relationships. But I rather think I have worked out of most of that, following a couple of explosions of temper which cleared the air (at the office, I mean)...
>
> I shall be crossing again to London in a few weeks, and I expect to see something of the big push [D-day] when it comes off. Our own part in it is an interesting thing to plan and prepare for.[286]

Lewis arrived in London on February 19 and two months later began the first of his broadcasts to the French with these words:

> This is the American Broadcasting Station in Europe [ABSIE]... In this historic year, 1944, the allied radio will bring you tremendous news.

Lewis and Ernest Hemingway reunited at the Dorchester Hotel in London.[287] Hemingway had just displaced his wife, Martha Gellhorn, as *Colliers Magazine*'s western front reporter[288] and was hoping to accompany the troops in a landing craft on D-day. Lewis would not make the crossing until August 1, 1944. For now, his job was to remain in London and mold French public opinion to Roosevelt's purpose: to prevent a de Gaulle dictatorship on the one hand or a French civil war on the other. Lewis was tasked with persuading the French that a non-Gaullist government would be in France's best interest;[289] Roosevelt and his secretary of state, Cordell Hull, planned to impose an allied military government, to exist until a representative French government could be established. The name they gave the undertaking was the Allied Military Government of Occupied Territories, or AMGOT. But just as Roosevelt and Hull were laying plans for a post-liberated France, so too was de Gaulle and his Committee of National Liberation. De Gaulle's strategy was to divide France into ten governing regions, each headed by a Gaullist commissioner—a *commissaire régional de la république*—with broad authority to enforce law, maintain order, purge the existing civil administrators (including police and judges), and replace them with de Gaulle loyalists who would report directly to the general.

Lewis's task was made more difficult by the patronage appointment of George Backer as the OWI director of propaganda. Backer had, at various times, been a real estate developer, movie producer, aspiring playwright, and failed newspaperman. He had neither experience nor demonstrable competence in international affairs or propaganda;[290] his qualification was that, during the 1930s, he had been a New York City councilman and a supporter of Franklin Roosevelt, and Backer's wife, Dorothy Schiff, and Roosevelt were thought to have been romantically involved. Or so Backer boasted.[291]

On the eve of D-Day, Lewis told Backer that the French needed to be convinced of four things: that the United States and Britain were opposed to the Vichy regime and to its collaborators; that they wanted to see the restoration of France as a world power; that they intended that the French people would choose their post-war form of government; and that the choice had to be made by *all* of its citizens, meaning that the choice had to be deferred until the residents of metropolitan France were once again able to vote. Lewis cautioned Backer that, until that day, American and British recognition of the Free French as the Provisional Government of France would be premature. (The Provisional Government of the French Republic was the successor to the joint de Gaulle–Giraud French Committee of National Liberation.) In short, Lewis advised Backer that the OWI had to impress on the people of France that, at that moment, de Gaulle could not legitimately form a French government from a base in North Africa. There could be no French government until all of France was liberated.[292]

In late June 1944, Backer suggested a strategy for assessing whether the French would accept an interim AMGOT regime, as opposed to one headed by de Gaulle: it was to interview the residents of liberated Normandy and ask them how they felt about the Americans, the British, and the Allied Expeditionary Force.[293] Lewis told Backer that the answers to those questions would not only be unreliable but, worse, that when word of the inquiries got out, as it certainly would, even the neutral press would protest the Unites States' intrusion into French affairs. He warned Backer that it would be "exceedingly dangerous to add this fuel to the campaign of vilification and misrepresentation of the American people and their Government" and that

> no approach made to the French people prior to the recognition
> of de Gaulle will be considered to be...devoid of political
> significance by any press in the world, including our own...
> [A]lthough the interrogatory would be made in the name of the
> Anglo-American Forces...it would be construed as a purely
> American measure.
>
> The Gaullists (outside of France)...have always known that...it
> must be the Allies and not themselves who physically liberate

France...[The Gaullists'] primary aim...has been the seizure of power and the carrying out of a revolution. Everything that they have said—from their point of view quite properly—has been... intended to promote these aims.

The following month, Lewis quashed another self-injurious "good idea"; not one of Backer's, but from the bureaucracy that had bred him:

July 18, 1944

To: Mr. Backer

From: Lewis Galantière

Last week Mr. Brennan, of Mr. Guinzburg's division, sent me the text of President Roosevelt's prayer for the success of the assault in the West, for translation into French, with a message to say that he was planning to do a series of posters to contain excerpts from great speeches or great statements by United Nations leaders.

I sent back the President's prayer with the statement that it would not do for France—a country where nobody except a priest offers public prayer, where no ceremony except a church service involves public prayer, where there is a distaste for the association of religion with government, and where it is considered indecorous to wish to write one's own prayers or to recite other prayers than those prescribed by the church.

All this is merely preliminary to the suggestion that the operating divisions should submit their plans formally to the Planning Board before beginning to execute them...If you will let me have a copy of the ABSIE job, I will undertake the revision for you.[294]

Lewis spent a good deal of his time suppressing the wrong-headed ideas that spilled from the minds of dilettantes in the OWI.[295]

Three weeks after D-day, Lewis crossed the English Channel—from Southampton to Normandy—with General Philippe Leclerc's Second French Armored Division. It was his first time in France after more than a decade. Lewis shared the experience with his friends Peter and Sonia Colefax.

August 18, 1944

Dear Peter and Sonia ...

...It was dark when we dropped anchor. My party—four Americans and four Frenchman—were taken off very quietly in a Coast Guard cutter, transferred to an LC5, run up to the beach, transferred to a truck, run up to a base camp where there was no room for us. It was then nighttime under a great moon, a soft summer night. We thought we would sleep in the church of a neighboring village, but it was full of GIs who had arrived an hour before and were in all the chairs and all over the floor. We walked through the moonlit village knocking on the doors of empty houses and finally, in a farmyard, we knocked on the door and woke up a farmer. He gave us a room—not a loft—over his stable; it had U.S. Army bunks in it with thin fresh straw mattresses. He brought us a candle and a couple of bottles of cider, and there I spent my first night in France.[296]

The day that Lewis made that channel crossing, the flight crews of the French air base on Corsica spread the word that a Lockheed P-38 Lightning reconnaissance aircraft bound for southern France had not returned. The twin-engine Lockheed was one of the fastest aircraft in the sky, but was not a forgiving machine or one that invited sensory communion. It was a plane flown by proxy, through electromechanical systems that demanded a pilot's subservience; the very kind of flying that was anathema to Antoine de Saint-Exupéry, who may have been overcome by the plane's technical complexity. Or he might have been recklessly indifferent to a life burdened by the pain of past aviation accidents and surgeries, by the loss of his beloved flying companions—all now gone[297]—and by de Gaulle's suppression of his writing. Or he may have been downed by the guns of a German Messerschmitt.[298]

Whatever the cause, Saint-Exupéry's passing marked the end of an era. In the early days of flying, a cadre of men had risked their lives for aviation. Piloting by magnetic compass, altimeter, speed indicator, and an engine gauge or two but—primarily—by sight, they had flown through cold spiking rain and billowing heat. They had flown, it was said, *by the seat of their pants.* Saint-Exupéry had thought himself fortunate to have been counted among them. But by the summer of 1944, the era of those days and those planes and those men had passed. Saint-Exupéry's plane vanished somewhere south of Marseilles on July 31, 1944. It would remain undiscovered for the next sixty years.[299]

As Generals Patton and Leclerc began their push to Paris, Lewis entered the areas they liberated. He gives this account:

> I went out on the following day with a P.A. truck which carries news round the country to the communities where radios had been confiscated, where there is no power in the towns, where no newspapers are printed, and where the people have been cut off from the outside world.

> We went through St. Lô to Canisy ...and Cerisy. It was particularly interesting, as in two of these towns the truck had never entered before. The truck stops on the main square and a march is put on the playing machine. As soon as the music sounds, people move in from every direction. First the kids come running, then a few old women whose emotion is the deepest, then the rest of the population, including the mayor, the postmaster, the largest farmer...and others. They stand round the truck, and the news which you people provide to the P.W. post in the field is read to them through a microphone and the loudspeaker. After the news, La Marseillaise is played. In two of these places, La Marseillaise is heard for the first time since June 1940. The gendarme stands at attention and the population stands round with their arms at their sides, and you stand there...saluting them...and you begin to see tears rolling down their cheeks. These people are so filled with happiness, with delight at your coming...

> The old women want to kiss you, but don't dare; they want to touch you...You look at them and then they grab your hand and begin to shake it...

> The next day I went on ...a reconnaissance and intelligence tour...We got into Percy two hours after the Germans have left. We found a considerable number of refugees from regions

round...In Canisy, one of the most badly destroyed towns, I talked to a couple of boys 15 and 16. During the conversation I said, pointing to the ruins, "You have a job to do; you have to rebuild France." The kid said that was okay; but they only hoped there were no more bodies under the rubble. These kids have the impression everywhere of being able to take care of the future. They were most curious about America, asking "how do you get all these trucks and tanks?" I told him about the motorcar industry which produced 5 million cars a year and could therefore do this kind of thing. And then they said, "Oh, then it is not so hard."

Going up and down the peninsula there was this contrast: there is one route from Cherbourg down towards La Haye-du-Puits where nothing has been touched: Les Pieux, Briquebec. Along that route you scarcely get greeted by anybody. The little kids make a "V" sign. When you followed the route to the east where there has been more destruction than you can imagine (St. Lô has been razed flat), and when you go through those destroyed towns...Everybody greets you, everybody waves at you, everybody smiles at you. The kids take off their caps if they think you are an officer. The spirit of those people is amazing, and their capacity for perceiving the reality of the situation, their moral capacity for seeing that all this seemed to be necessary in order to be liberated, is something that simply melts one.

The destruction takes place where the Germans resist, where they are on the run it is at a minimum. I understand that St. Malo is being destroyed, because the Germans are resisting.

Wherever our people go, they begin by introducing themselves to the Civilian Affairs officer, who is an American officer in American territory. They are extraordinarily good fellows. I have seen all different types. I saw a first lieutenant, a North Carolina boy who had never been in Europe before. He was of a patience—and human wisdom—and a sweetness with those people that was wonderful to see. It makes you happy that a fellow like that should be representing you...

About towns. As you doubtless know, all towns are out of bounds to troops other than...Labor battalions...The relations with the local population seem to be actually of the best. Neither chewing gum nor cigarettes are lacking among the civilian population. The boys are giving them away, and they also dispose of a helluva lot of their rations...

It is a place where you are proud of Americans and where the reception given to Americans in 1944 belies everything that was published in the American press between December 1942 and June 5, 1944. It is the reception of 1917 all over again. For these people, liberation comes first, and friendship with their Anglo-American Allies is something that is absolutely unquestioned.[300]

Lewis in an unidentified French town.

Our troops behave well, on the whole. As one civil affairs officer said..."There's a little rape, a bit of looting, a certain amount of drunkenness." As to the Germans, these people tell me the officers were "correct," the troops were not to be trusted when their officers were not around. The S.S. troops were really vicious and except [for] their own officers nobody kept them in order. When they wanted food and drink, they thrust a gun into the belly of whoever opened the door. All Germans started looting indiscriminately once the retreat began.—There is considerable curiosity about America: I was asked many questions. The passage of the convoys, so grim and powerful, so endlessly flowing by, aroused the deepest respect. Here, at any rate, where the American stuff has been seen, nobody will ever again think it worthwhile to go to war without the U.S.A. on their side—which is in a sense the measure of our responsibility. And now that the Third Army, indeed the whole 12th Army Group, has performed such a brilliant maneuver advancing with such truly American speed, these people respect us as fighters and not only as builders...I am on duty tonight. It is midnight and my phone is ringing.[301]

On August 21, de Gaulle entered the newly liberated town of Laval. As with each town he visited, he met with the town leaders, shook their hands, and spoke of continuing the fight to liberate France:

I promise you that we shall continue to fight till sovereignty is re-established over every inch of our soil. No one shall prevent our doing that. We shall fight beside the Allies, with the Allies, as an ally. And the victory we shall win will be the victory of liberty and the victory of France.[302]

De Gaulle led the Laval townsfolk in singing *La Marseillaise*. Many wept, with relief and with pride.

Four days later, as the Second French Armored Division and the Fourth U.S. Infantry Division advanced from the outskirts of Paris, the commander of the German garrison, Dietrich von Choltitz, surrendered.[303] General Leclerc's Second Division paraded down the Champs-Élysées and a million French citizens lined the streets. De Gaulle, starting at the Arc de Triomphe, walked the mile and a half to the Place de la Concorde and was then driven in a slow procession to the Cathedral of Notre Dame. He did not flinch when the snap of snipers' rifles drove the crowd to flatten themselves on the sidewalks and take shelter. He later wrote,

I went on, touched and yet tranquil amid the inexpressible exultation of the crowd, beneath the storm of voices echoing my name, trying, as I advanced, to look at every person in all that multitude in order that every eye might register my presence, raising and lowering my arms to reply to the cheers. This was one of those miracles of national consciousness, one of those gestures which sometimes in the course of centuries light up the history of France...And at the center of this outburst, I felt

I was fulfilling a function which far transcended my personality,
for I was serving as an instrument of destiny.[304]

When de Gaulle announced the formation of a new provisional government, Lewis reported to Wallace Carroll—director of the OWI in London and an adviser to General Eisenhower on psychological warfare—that the prospects for a smooth transition to a civilian government were good, notwithstanding de Gaulle's attempt to muzzle the press.[305] It seemed to Lewis inevitable that de Gaulle would lead the interim government:

Unless he makes shocking blunders, Gaulle is certain to
remain in power. No one is attempting to get along without
him...There is no fear of dictatorship nor shred of idolatry
because the very thought is ridiculous. With a complete spirit
of free criticism, Gaulle is judged, examined, and discussed
by Parisians, although they accept the idea of his immediate
leadership.[306]

Director Carroll replied with a cable to OWI Special Operations director Philip Hamblet:

We are doing what we can to help the State Department, which is
still urging the recognition of the Provisional Government of
France...

Until [Seldin] *Chapin* [U.S. State Department counselor of
mission, Paris, France] *arrived in Paris, the State Department*
had been without any intelligence from there and so they have
appreciated to the utmost the cables and memos that Galantière
has been sending, as have we ourselves.[307]

Given popular sentiment, Roosevelt had no alternative but to recognize de Gaulle's provisional government, but he fretted that de Gaulle was a fascist who aspired to a "one-man government in France."[308] After another three months of dealing with de Gaulle's political machinations, Lewis started to suspect the same. He was particularly alarmed by de Gaulle's attempt to choke off the supply of newsprint for dissenting papers and warned OWI Director Carroll of it:

*Within the next few weeks—unless the newsprint situation makes
this impossible—the entourage of General de Gaulle plans to
bring out seven additional dailies as hereunder (this will
bring the total up to twenty-nine for the city of Paris)...it is
assumed that all will be subservient to the Gaullist will...*

*... my informants say de Gaulle has allowed the internal policies
of the Government to be formulated by men who are fascist in
inclination and capitalist in tendency and training, and whose
aim is not democracy but a demagogic dictatorship...it is
noteworthy that the Resistance press refused to follow de Gaulle
in his blame for internal conditions upon the severity of the
winter and the "miscalculations" of the Allies. The Resistance
press will, it appears, not again accept the idea that "les
Américains" may be made the whipping boys for whatever goes
wrong in France...*

*... [De Gaulle's] mode of attack upon the Resistance press
is likely to be the following. By the manipulation of press
regulations and manipulation of the newsprint supply, the
subservient press would succeed in putting their rivals out of
business. Since the radio is already a Government instrument,
and since there is but one French news agency in the field... the
controlling group would have at their disposal all organs of
opinion...*

*... elections...will give the Government (controlled by the de
Gaulle entourage) a considerable majority...[and] the Government
will then proceed to create a scarcely veiled dictatorship in
the style of that of Napoleon III. My informants believe that
the nation is politically apathetic...*

*These considerations require a re-examination of our position
vis-á-vis the Provisional Government. If all that has been
related in this memorandum should turn out to be fact, then
clearly the determination of the American attitude to the
Provisional Government is one which must be made at Washington
in the highest quarters.*[309]

This assessment, marked "secret," resulted in Lewis receiving authorization to do whatever he thought necessary to supply the resistance press
with newsprint. How Lewis achieved his objective is unknown but that he

achieved it is certain. On April 9, 1945, Aristide Blank, the secretary-general of the French National Press Federation, sent Lewis this note:

> Dear Lewis,
>
> Before you leave Paris I want to thank you, on my own behalf and on behalf of the officers of this Federation, for the help you have never ceased to give us from the moment of your arrival in Paris. You, better than anyone else, knew the difficulties which the Resistance Press was encountering daily, and my colleagues and I are fully aware of your efforts to help this press, born during the war and of the war. Even more than your efforts, we appreciate the sympathetic understanding which you displayed. Numerous are my fellow newspaper publishers who felt that what you were really expressing was the sympathetic understanding of the United States in the matter of France and of the Resistance.[310]

Lewis returned to the United States, but it was a short sojourn. Six months later, he was handed another OWI assignment. Relieved of Nazi occupation and with the surrender of Germany imminent, many French had come to resent the continuing presence of American military personnel on their soil. American soldiers had responded with their own resentment over the ingratitude of the people they had just liberated. Lewis was asked to return to France, identify the forces at work and recommend solutions. The assignment came with a new title: Special Advisor on French Affairs to the Commanding General, Assembly Area Command.[311] Lewis's investigation revealed that German and Gaullist propaganda and "the blundering tactics of the State Department in their dealings with General de Gaulle"[312] had led "urban populations" to believe that the that United States had entered the war in order to seize France's foreign markets; especially those of its colonies. But Lewis also found that the rural French did not share that opinion. They were less concerned about the continuing U.S. presence than that America might withdraw from the international scene. Lewis submitted these observations and his recommendation—to institute an educational campaign—to Philip Hamblet, director of the OWI's European Theater of Operations. Hamblet responded with two letters, both dated September 13, 1945. The first went to OWI executive director Thurman L. Barnard:

> September 13, 1945
>
> Dear Barney:
>
> Thanks so much for sending us Lewis Galantière. Much more than anything I can say about the importance of his being here is the enclosed series of memoranda which Lewis prepared after approximately a week back in the theatre. I think it is perhaps the best exposition of the redeployment problem in our relations with the French which I have ever seen. I knew that Lewis would get the feel of the situation soon after his return, but I had no idea that it could be so quickly summarized. I sincerely hope that the program which he has outlined can be carried through, and I think that it might well be useful if your French sections in New York and Washington could have access to Lewis's comments on the problem which is immediately ahead here.
>
> Sincerely,
>
> Philip C. Hamblet[313]

The second was to Lewis:

> Dear Lewis,
>
> ... you have so far surpassed in your September 10 memoranda what I was sure you would be able to do. I think it is remarkable that after you have been away from France for six months that you could so quickly get back into the feel of the present situation, on the other hand, I must admit that had I not felt that you would be able to do so I would not have asked you to come back.
>
> ... I just want you to know how much I appreciated personally your willingness to make this additional sacrifice in carrying through on the job on which we have all been working. I salute you, sire.
>
> Sincerely
>
> Philip C. Hamblet[314]

France's Constituent Assembly unanimously elected de Gaulle head of the government, giving Communists positions in five of the twenty-two ministries. When the Communists demanded a 20 percent reduction in the military budget, de Gaulle refused and threatened to resign. A compromise budget was adopted, but de Gaulle saw that he was not going to have the unconditional authority to govern that he thought essential and, on January 20, 1946, he resigned from the government.

*Colonel Louis Dio and Lewis at a propaganda
recording session for broadcast to France.*

After the war, René Arnaud joined the French commission of the International Chamber of Commerce, in the same building at 33 Rue Jean Gaujon where he and Lewis had worked so long ago. Writing to Lewis, René commented, "I go back 20 years, as Dumas would say."[315] In those earlier days René had written a memoir about his time as a foot soldier on the Somme during the First World War, but a traumatized French public then had no appetite for another war journal.[316] It was not until after the Second World War that Éditions France-Empire printed *La Guerre, 1914–1918: Tragédie Bouffe*. René sent Lewis an inscribed copy:

To Lewis Galantière and his charming wife

In memory, Lewis, of the 20s and of these long talks at the "Rendez-vous des Mariniers" where our friendship was born.

A sincere homage,

René Arnaud [317]

The *Rendez-vous des Mariniers* was the restaurant at 33 Quai d'Anjou where René and Lewis and Hemingway sometimes dined. Nearly all signs of the neighborhood dining place are now gone.[318]

Ezra Pound had spent the war in Italy from where, in hundreds of radio broadcasts, he praised Mussolini and Hitler, condemned Roosevelt, and blamed Jewish capitalists for having caused the two wars. American armed forces arrested and detained him in Pisa where, after three weeks of incarceration in a small outdoor cage, he suffered a mental breakdown. Brought back to the United States to be tried for treason, Pound was declared mentally incapable of defending himself and then confined at St. Elizabeth's psychiatric hospital in Washington, D.C. where, for the next thirteen years, he awaited trial.[319]

In 1958, Lewis was serving as a director of the American Civil Liberties Union, but he had little enthusiasm for defending the anti-Semitic Pound, especially given the freshness of the holocaust's scourge. In an April 14, 1958 letter to his friend, E.E. Cummings, Lewis described the ACLU's position on Pound's confinement in a tone that can best be described as clinical:

Dear Cummings,

I think I can finally write an intelligible statement on the position of the American Civil Liberties Union in re Pound.

The ACLU is not concerned solely with the Pound Case. It is interested in the fate of many thousands of people who are in Pound's situation vis-a-vis the law; that is, people who are charged with a crime, cannot be tried to ascertain their guilt or innocence because of their mental state, and appear to have to spend the whole of their lives in institutions without an opportunity to clear their names.

There is a provision of law under which the Department of Health, Education and Welfare (which I think governs St. Elizabeth's Hospital) has discretion to release into private custody, or to recommend such release to the Department of Justice, a person so circumstanced even though he be not "restored to sanity." The ACLU would like to see relief of this kind obtained by all those to whom it can be granted. It has hoped for several years that Pound's well-known and energetic lawyers may bring an action of this kind as a test case, from a favorable issue of which others might profit. If such an action were brought, the ACLU would issue a statement supporting Pound's lawyers….

I wonder if you saw a short letter from E.P. to the (London) Times Literary Supplement of April 4? Quite incoherent.

Ever yours,

Lewis Galantière[320]

The month that Lewis sent this letter, Pound was released on a motion to dismiss on the grounds of permanent insanity. He returned to Italy that summer, where he resided until his death in 1972.

CHAPTER 10

ANTIGONE

T<small>HE WEEK BEFORE</small> C<small>HRISTMAS</small> 1945, Lewis wrote to his former teacher, Helen Haines, addressing her, as always, with deferential formality:

> Dear Miss Haines,
>
> ... I've been home from Europe about six weeks. All of my time abroad—two years—was almost equally divided between England and France, with weeks out here and there for work elsewhere. It was a rewarding couple of years, 'specially the time spent working with the military...
>
> ... I am at the moment immersed in theater affairs. I have made an adaptation of a play by a French writer called Jean Anouilh on the theme of Antigone. We call it, for American purposes, "Antigone and the Tyrant"; the subject of the play being the clash of two wills, two ideals, one might say—Antigone's and Creon's. Katharine Cornell is doing Antigone; Cedric Hardwicke is doing Creon: the rest of the cast, alas, is mediocre; but Cornell's husband, Guthrie McClintic, is an admirable director, and he may get sufficiently good performances out of them. We open in Detroit on 5 January; in New York on the 28th or the week after, I am not sure. It's a very powerful, eloquent play: but there are lots of words in it, and I can't say how the theater reviewers will take it.[321]

Lewis's premonition that the theatergoers would think his *Antigone* had "lots of words in it" was prophetic. The reviewer for *Billboard* magazine said that the play might appeal to a "sprinkling of intellectuals":

Katharine Cornell...may be awarded a sincere salute for an
arresting theatrical experiment. Antigone, as translated from
the French of Jean Anouilh by Lewis Galantière, is all of
that. Viewed as such, this modern dress version of Sophocles'
tragedy demands respect on the score of some fine acting, expert
staging and interesting treatment. However, as a full evening's
entertainment in the theater—certainly in the commercial
theater—Antigone is unsatisfying. Its customers will likely
be limited to Cornell and Hardwicke fans and the sprinkling of
intellectuals...Antigone sums to a fine and courageous experiment,
but it looks doubtful to exceed the limited run for which it is
skedded. [sic]

It did not help that Ms. Cornell was fifty-three years old when she played the lead—King Creon's younger daughter—a miscasting for which the fault lay with Ms. Cornell, who was also the play's producer. Ms. Cornell had seen the play in Paris a year earlier, while on a USO camp tour, and had purchased the American rights.[322] Lewis addressed the predicament in a March 11, 1946 letter:

Antigone...is not, I believe, a New York success, despite the
fact that I have Katharine Cornell and Cedric Hardwick. The
actual fate of the play is unknown to me, for I left New York
[for Mexico] sometime before it opened there. I have received
the notices, which are respectful, but not of the sort to send
the public scurrying to enjoy 'a great evening in the theater'.
In considerable part, the fault is mine. Unlike any French
actress, Cornell, who is about 50 years old, was afraid to
play the part of a young girl (about 20). Anouilh's Antigone
is not only 20, she is delineated as a stubborn, childish 20...
Well, not to go into tiresome detail, what is suitable and
acceptable as motivation for the act of a child is, of course,
not necessarily so in respect of an adult. Cornell playing
Antigone as a mature young woman, I thought to furnish her with
better motives than those which Anouilh had lent to his child-
Antigone...I have no further news since the play opened in New
York on the 18th February: it may have closed: on the other hand
it may be doing what they call "good business."[323]

Antigone ran for sixty-four performances.[324] For a while, the minor role of the messenger was played by Marlon Brando, in his second appearance on a New York stage. When Lewis wrote to Helen Haines on June 25, 1946, he was resigned to the production's fate:

> I wish you had seen Antigone. Hardwick was wonderful, and that seriously limited, middle-class (and very sweet, very generous) Cornell ended by playing magnificently. Strange, though, how long it took her to get fully into the part—months. I shall send you the book. It is a failure, but a decent one—my part in it, I mean.[325]

Lewis's *Antigone* did better at the Old Vic Theatre in London, where Laurence Olivier directed a thirty-six-year-old Vivien Leigh in the title role and cast himself in the lesser role of the single-person chorus.[326] The only commercial movie made of Lewis's play was released in 1974, with Geneviève Bujold ably portraying Antigone as a waif with a spine of steel. Stacy Keach, Fritz Weaver, Leah Chandler and James Naughton also starred.[327]

During those postwar years, Lewis wrote book introductions and also articles for *Town & Country, Glamour,* and *Atlantic Monthly* magazines. And he continued to translate the writing of great French authors, including Voltaire and Jacques Maritain, translations that drew raves from his publishers:

THE INNER SANCTUM
OF SIMON AND SCHUSTER

> October 22, 1947

> Dear Lewis,

> Your own new translation of gems from the <u>Wit and Wisdom of Voltaire</u> is magnificent...Your work on <u>A Basic Voltaire</u> is so masterly and so creative that a new dimension has been added to the editorial approach.

> At our next session, let's review again the other Galantière books...When we agree on one or more that excite you most and to which you would like to give priority...we will be

glad to work out a contract agreement and propose a royalty advance...

Max Schuster[328]

December 16, 1947, letter from Kurt Wolff of Pantheon Books:

I have just received a letter from Maritain in Rome from which I would like to quote:

> *"Thank you ever so much for your kind letter of December 3. I hasten to tell you that I am delighted that the translation of my Court Traité will be made by Lewis Galantière. Of course he is the most brilliant translator for any French text into English. Please convey my warmest thanks and heartfelt regards to him."*

I am now waiting for the agreement for the English rights which we have asked for in Paris and as soon as we have them we shall get together.[329]

Morris G. Bishop, professor of romance literature at Cornell University, offered Lewis the chance to teach three courses in French during the 1948–1949 academic year: twentieth-century literature, sixteenth-century literature, and civilisation Française.[330] Lewis would have loved to have been able to accept: living in the manicured campus setting of an esteemed university, conversing with scholars in any discipline he wished with libraries and source materials at hand, holding forth at academic sherry hours and at dinners with visiting speakers, and cultivating the young minds of students who would be awed by his knowledge and experience. How tantalizing it must have been. And sadly out of reach. Accepting the offer might have required Lewis to furnish Cornell with documentation of his invented academic credentials. It was too late in his life, and too humiliating a prospect, to start offering explanations.

CHAPTER 11

THE COLD WAR

For the first time since the threat of Islam a thousand years ago,
Western civilization is on the defensive.
—**John Foster Dulles on communism, May 6, 1948**[331]

AT FIFTY-FOUR, LEWIS'S DESIRE TO be consequential had not dimin-
ished. In March 1949, he joined the staff of a new biweekly magazine, the
Reporter, which identified itself as "liberal." (At the time, the term connot-
ed advocating liberty and opposing communism.) Lewis was one of four
full-time staff writers, all former OSS or OWI members.

The *Reporter* dealt with politics, economics, and societal issues.[332] It
advocated democracy, capitalism and international engagement and denounced fascism, communism, racial segregation, and McCarthyism. Max
Ascoli and James Reston founded it, but it was probably funded by the CIA.
(Its financial records have since been lost, destroyed, or suppressed.) Ascoli's second in command was Irving Kristol, and the magazine's contributors
included John F. Kennedy, John Kenneth Galbraith, Ray Bradbury, Dean
Acheson, James Baldwin, J. William Fulbright, Henry Kissinger, Malcolm
Cowley, Bernard Malamud, Vladimir Nabokov, Daniel Patrick Moynihan,
and Mary McCarthy.[333] Arthur Schlesinger Jr. agreed to serve as an advisor
and, as his first piece of wisdom, he criticized Ascoli's staffing choices:

I hope you will not think that I am going nationalist on you,
but the pattern of appointments from the point of view of
running a magazine in America is a bit weighted on the non-
American side. [David] Wills is an Englishman, [and] Galantière
has spent most of his life in France. [334]

Schlesinger's insight became moot when Lewis resigned after four months (although he continued to contribute articles to the *Reporter* on a freelance basis). Lewis explained his resignation to Helen Haines:

I can't work with a man [Ascoli] who asks your views and then
grows furious and even insulting when they don't coincide with
his. [335]

The man is a maniac; if he weren't, I should have had a really
interesting time. [336]

After the *Reporter*, Lewis wrote for other publications. Hamilton Armstrong, the editor of *Foreign Affairs*, the journal of the Council on Foreign Relations, printed one of his pieces in the October 1949 issue[337] titled "Through the Russian Looking-Glass—the Future in Retrospect," in which Lewis compared nineteenth-century Russia and America as seen, respectively, by le Marquis de Custine and by Custine's contemporary countryman Alexis de Tocqueville. Lewis offered Custine's conclusions and also his own:

Custine

> *... despotism is never so fearsome as when it claims to be*
> *doing good, for then it assumes the right to explain away*
> *its most revolting acts by its good intentions, and to offer*
> *ills endlessly in the guise of remedies.*

Lewis

> *The lessons to be learnt from a reading of Custine are*
> *obvious. One is that...the notion of planting the seeds*
> *of constitutional democracy in the soil of an ancient land*
> *without democratic traditions is an idle dream.*

Lewis

> ... in a country where the governors have not yet learnt the
> advantages of liberty, even for themselves, the governed are
> obliged to recoil from the instant punishment that is the
> reward of honest expression.

Lewis made his sentiments about capitalism and socialism clear in a letter to Helen Haines:

> I consider state-owned and state-managed bigness (ironic that it
> had been instituted by those who were ethically the enemies of
> bigness) are more horrid than private bigness if only because
> the management of the former are above the law, make their own
> law, are answerable to no control, and the latter are, with all
> their power, nevertheless subject to law and to the pressure of
> public opinion...Well, I won't go on, but my mind is well made
> up: no blueprint society for me![338]

Lewis's second article for *Foreign Affairs*—the one that appeared in its July 1, 1950, edition—was the most favorably reviewed and most consequential writing of his career. Titled "America Today: A Freehand Sketch," it explained the virtues of American democracy and capitalism. He wrote the piece out of concern that the Soviet people did not know America except through communist propaganda that had impugned her motives, morality, and stability. The following are excerpts:

> When a nation...attains to world leadership, it preserves that
> rank only so long as its culture—which is to say not merely
> its achievements in the humanities but also its manners and
> beliefs and civil institutions—commands respect and some degree
> of emulation. For although leadership is [attained] by power it
> is maintained over a significant span of time only with the free
> assent of the led; and free assent is given only to moral and
> not to material authority...These are the conditions of world
> leadership. Without them wealth and might lead only to hatred,
> conspiracy, and revolt against the physically dominant power...
>
> [Western Europeans] are doctrinaire because they are in search
> of security on the most modest standard; and security is not
> something which is promised by God when He sends a babe into

the world, it is not a natural condition of life—wherefore they believe it must be planned and blueprinted...

That, in a world of centralization of political power, we [Americans] have preserved not only the self-reliance of the individual but also the autonomy of the local community is a fact which we may proudly acclaim. This is our highest moral contribution to the present age. Secondly, in a world in which economic concentration is absolutely inescapable—because without it the wants of millions cannot to any extent be economically satisfied—we have come nearest to accomplishing the separation of economic power and political power...And this too presents a moral aspect, since it has required that our economic leaders adjust themselves to the fact that those who conduct great affairs have a responsibility to the people which transcends whatever selfish interest ownership may inspire and whatever lure power may dangle before the eyes of the managers of enterprise.

It was the Reverend Samuel Webster, of Salisbury, Massachusetts, who warned from his pulpit in 1777 that "encroachments on the people's liberties are not generally made all at once, but so gradually as hardly to be perceived by the less watchful."

I think of our exaggeratedly reviled pressure groups—economic, religious, racial, professional, regional, ideological—this non-authoritarian but regulated substitute for a chamber of corporations; and I reflect how these hundreds of minority representations contribute to the annulment of the greatest danger inherent in democracy, which is the tyranny of the majority—that tyranny exercised today in Russia and yesterday in Hitlerian Germany.

The ideal of self-government has sunk so profoundly into the American being that Europeans, who imagine it means merely freedom from monarchical absolutism, have scarcely the faintest notion how different our democracy is from theirs. A Frenchman is aware that we are a federation of states; but when you point out to him what this means—that we have no European-style ministry of the interior, with its nationwide police and its prefects and sub-prefects ruling over the geographic divisions and subdivisions of the nation, he is...astonished...

Despite farm-price support, despite tariff protection, despite public pensions and free services, the American stubbornly retains his habit of looking after himself...

Our Constitution is the only fixed point in our society, revered as if Heaven-sent; yet even it is a kind of set of chess rules allowing all the permutations essential to democratic free play...

Our weakest sector has been in government...the right of disposal over a $40 billion budget offers immense temptations; the federal tax power has become so great as to corrupt men's intellects and imaginations even when it does not corrupt their morals...

America pulses with life. It may, like a tree, have its rotten branches, its dead wood; but when those branches are cut away— as happens again and again—the tree goes on nourishing. This is something which cannot be said for any blueprint society, of the Left or Right, bureaucratic or theocratic. Contrary to what was taught by the Fascists 20 years ago, it is the democratic society that is dynamic and the doctrinaire society that is static. Our society is not doctrinaire, is not all of a piece; its existence does not depend upon the quiescence and subservience of each tiniest part to the whole. Its moral nature is not imposed upon it by external authority, but inheres in it as the soul in the body...[339]

"Freehand Sketch," described American capitalism as Lewis saw it: a nonauthoritarian and decentralized system in which individual entrepreneurial endeavor was permitted to thrive.[340] The monograph was praised by American intellectuals.

M. Lincoln "Max" Schuster of Simon and Schuster wrote to Dewitt Wallace, publisher of *Reader's Digest* (and a director of the Free Europe Committee, the parent of what would become Radio Free Europe).

July 13, 1950

Dear Wally,

... You might have someone look up an article in the July 1950 issue of "Foreign Affairs" published by the Foreign Policy

Association: I refer specifically, to an essay entitled "America Today—A Freehand Sketch" by Lewis Galantière.

Ordinarily this is a rather technical and specialized magazine for scholars. But this particular essay is so brilliant, so affirmative, and so truly inspiring in demolishing the popular myths about American Life, culture, and civilization, that it would be a salutary thing if you could see your way clear to excerpting it in the "Reader's Digest," and thus bringing it to millions of readers all over the world. The Galantière article is the sort that makes you proud to be an American. I am advancing this suggestion purely on my own, without any instigation by Galantière. In the present state of the world the theme of this essay seems deeply urgent and timely.[341]

From Eugene Rostow, professor of American history and institutions at Cambridge University and future dean of the Yale Law School.

EUROPEAN OFFICE OF THE UNITED NATIONS

Palais des Nations, Geneve

4 August 1950

My dear Galantière, I have just come back to find your extraordinarily good article on America To-day in "Foreign Affairs." I hope that it will be re-printed in the overseas editions of the "Reader's Digest" and spread very far. I think it strikes exactly the right note and with real depth, power and feeling...

Yours cordially,

Gene Rostow[342]

Jean-Jacques Servan-Schreiber, a French politician and journalist and founder of the weekly news magazine *L'Express*, sent a letter to Lewis at the offices of the *Reporter*:

I ...congratulate you on your admirable Foreign Affairs piece. Not only is that my opinion, but a widely shared one among French journalists and editors. Your article has become (this is by no means an exaggeration) their basic instrument for understanding present day America. Beyond any doubt you have accomplished by this piece a political act of proven importance.

To give you an example: The editors of the socialist paper
"Franc-Tireur" have shown a much greater sympathy to American
problems since they have had your "free-hand sketch."

... I hope to have the opportunity of meeting you again and I
shall take the liberty of calling on you when we are in New
York...

Yours sincerely,

J. J. Servan-Schreiber[343]

Frank Altschul, a Senior Partner of Lazard Freres and head of the newly formed Radio Free Europe, wrote,

My warm congratulations on a brilliantly conceived piece!

Yours sincerely, Frank

But when Lewis's friend, Alfred Knopf, suggested that Lewis expand the theme into a book-length dissertation, Lewis demurred.[344]

Lewis had just completed *Freehand Sketch* when, on June 25, 1950, seventy-five thousand soldiers of the North Korean People's Army crossed the 38th parallel, starting the Korean War. At about that same time, several prominent Americans including Allen Dulles, *Readers Digest* owner DeWitt Wallace, Ambassador Joseph Grew, and investment banker Frank Altschul created an anti-communist organization called the "National Committee for a Free Europe," soon renamed, more concisely, the "Free Europe Committee" or "FEC." The FEC in turn created a radio broadcast service for the Eastern-bloc countries that it named "Radio Free Europe" or "RFE." When Lewis expressed an interest in the fledgling organizations, Altschul put Lewis on retainer as a part-time advisor. Funding for FEC and RFE came covertly from the CIA, which asked Lewis to complete a "Personal History Statement," a background disclosure form similar to the one he had furnished to the OWI in 1942. Once again, there were questions about his family and education. Lewis wrote that he had lived in Azerbaijan from 1895 to 1901; in Paris from 1901 to 1917; and that, while in Paris, he had received degrees in economic theory and research:

Elementary school: 1901 to 1908, Ste. Marie-de-Monceau, Paris,
France and Downside Abbey, Bath, England (a Roman Catholic
monastery that is home to a community of Benedictine monks).

High school: 1908-1912, Lycée Condorcet, Paris, France.

College: 1912-1915, University of Paris, graduating with a
bachelor of arts degree in letters, arts and sciences—a licencié
es lettres—at age nineteen.

Lewis wrote that his father, Joseph-Marie Galantière, had been born May 30, 1860, in é-Cérons, France (just north of Toulouse) and was French by birth. His father's residence at death (in January 1920) was given as 20 Quai de Béthune, on the Île Saint Louis, Paris France (the address being between Lewis's 1924 apartment and that of his friends William "Bie" and Jenny Bradley).[345] He reported that his father had owned an "oil extraction" company the name of which Lewis could not recall, the company having been dissolved in 1909. His mother, Cécile Pourtalès Galantière, was born in Fribourg, Switzerland, and acquired French citizenship when she married Joseph in 1888. She had died in May 1931 at a hospital (the name of which Lewis could not recall) in Freiburg im Breisgau, in Baden-Württemberg, Germany, about forty miles north of Basel, Switzerland. Lewis's sole relative "by Blood, Marriage or Adoption" who was not a U.S. citizen was given as René Arnaud, a cousin, age fifty-six, who lived at 15 Rue d'Orléans, Neuilly-Sur-Seine, Paris, France.[346]

Once again, these fabrications appear to have passed without consequence. It is possible that the CIA assumed that Lewis's PERSONAL HISTORY STATEMENT entries were accurate and did not require further confirmation. Or the agency may have relied on his 1942 OWI filing under the assumption that its contents had been verified. Or, if Lewis's deceptions were uncovered, they might have been buried for the good of RFE or by Lewis's friends with the power to do so. Or Lewis's deceptions might have been held in reserve as a means of coercion, or might have been used for that purpose. No evidence has come to light to support or discard any of these possibilities. An FOIA request to the CIA yields this reply:

> To the extent that your request...seeks records that would
> reveal a classified association between the CIA and the subject,
> if any exist, we can neither confirm nor deny having such
> records...If a classified association between the subject and
> this organization were to exist, records revealing such a
> relationship would be properly classified and require continued
> safeguards against unauthorized disclosure. You may consider
> this finding a denial of this portion of your request...

One other entry on the form departed from the literal truth. Lewis gave the grounds for his divorce from Dorothy as "incompatibility," whereas the divorce decree had been granted based upon Dorothy's uncontested claim of desertion. Of course, Lewis's reason was the more accurate.

In August 1950, Lewis joined the Council on Foreign Relations as an academic member. Hamilton Armstrong, editor of *Foreign Affairs*, the organization's journal, had recommended him.[347] Lewis also continued his freelance writing. The front cover of the January 13, 1951, *Saturday Review of Literature* announced its theme: "AMERICA and the MIND OF EUROPE, Mid-Century." Lewis was the issue's "guest editor."[348] A book based on that issue would become a European best seller.

On January 10, 1951, the State Department put Lewis on retainer as a consultant[349] and, on November 28, placed him on its "Executive Reserve" of persons that the department would call upon to handle various undefined "key assignments."[350] Lewis then ostensibly served four masters: RFE, the Free Europe Committee (FEC, RFE's parent organization, which in the ensuing years would often disagree with senior RFE staff on policy), the State Department (which sometimes disagreed with FEC policies), and the CIA.

Lewis's first major assignment for RFE was to assess its Munich and Paris transmitting operations and hire broadcasters and journalists for the

Polish, Hungarian, Rumanian, and Bulgarian desks.[351] His means of travel was the MS *Vulcania*, with first-class accommodations both ways.[352] When Lewis returned, FEC president C.D. Jackson announced that Lewis was coming on board full time as "Counsellor to Radio Free Europe."[353]

RFE's propaganda strategy was for Eastern Bloc émigrés to broadcast their personal stories of daily hardship and secret police intrusion into their private lives. Broadcasters reminded their listeners of the tyranny, ineptitude, and corruption of their governments in the expectation that resentment would lead to dissent, and dissent lead to self-liberation. RFE furnished the studio facilities and broadcasting equipment and paid the émigré staff. The émigrés wrote and broadcast programs (referred to as "scripts") that were expected to adhere to RFE's written general principles as to content, referred to as written "guidances." As Lewis described it,

> RFE is not an American "voice," it is an American management of...European exile voices.[354]

Lewis wrote the *Radio Free Europe Policy Handbook*, a sixty-two-page document that set overall policy for the issuance of *guidances*. It echoed a promise made by Frank Altschul to those trapped behind the Iron Curtain:

> We assure militant anticommunists that they will be given the means to fight for the liberation of their country when the time comes.

It was a commitment on which the United States would renege.

Initially, the émigré/broadcasters' scripts were reviewed and approved by the RFE managers—Americans—prior to broadcast. But that precaution was shelved when it became evident that the number of American managers at the Freedom Radio desks who were fluent in the languages of the broadcasting staff was insufficient to keep up with the task. Other reasons (rationalizations) given were that prior review decreased the spontaneity and thus the authenticity of the speakers' voices, and that preapproval constituted "pre-broadcast censorship."[355] Broadcasters were soon trusted to conform their scripts to the guidances. At the start, the practice had few adverse consequences.[356]

During the 1950s, RFE's emphasis shifted from émigrés' personal stories to hard news from within the Eastern Bloc countries, supplied by covert contacts; communist radio broadcasts; and teletypes that were monitored. RFE ultimately established a network of fifteen news and information bureaus that interviewed Eastern European travelers.

After the spring of 1951, Lewis drafted RFE's guidances in consultation with William E. Griffith and Paul Henze, with Lewis based in New York and Griffith and Henze in Munich, RFE's European base of operations. Input also came from RFE satellite country service directors including Jan Nowak for Poland and Nöel Bernard for Romania. Griffith and Henze furnished Lewis with information about events in Eastern Europe, including political infighting; abuses of power by factory heads, party leaders, and secret police; and data such as production rates and shortages. (The CIA and State Department relied on the Griffith/Henze reports as a primary source of their Eastern Europe intelligence.)[357] Lewis furnished the State Department and the CIA with advance drafts of his special guidances, and those agencies routinely approved them. It was the kind of political-military-propaganda coordination that Lewis had advocated in a September 4, 1951, article in the *Reporter*.[358]

With McCarthyism in full fever during the 1952 U.S. presidential election, the candidates—General Eisenhower and Senator Stevenson—each insisted that the Eastern Bloc citizens must be freed from Soviet domination. John Foster Dulles growled, in a *Life* magazine article, that the United States "wants and expects liberation to occur," provided, he said *sotto voce*, it can be done without bloodshed or reprisals. Republicans accused Roosevelt and Truman of having sold out Eastern Europe at Yalta.

Lewis cautioned RFE's émigré broadcasters to give little credence to campaign promises of U.S. military assistance in overthrowing a Soviet-controlled regime:

> Gen. Eisenhower and his chief advisor on international affairs, Mr. John Foster Dulles, have spoken with great firmness... [W]e of RFE...cannot comment upon these statements with unqualified optimism, for to do so would be to deceive our listeners by inspiring in them exaggerated hope of a Western intervention of which there is as yet no sign.[359]

Nonetheless, when Eisenhower took office the following year and C. D. Jackson departed the FEC to become his special assistant, Lewis was constrained to communicate the Eisenhower-Jackson promise of *liberation*[360] as opposed to the mere *containment* of the USSR.[361] Soviet captivity, RFE promised, was not to become a "permanent fact of history."[362]

These sentiments, which were repeated by RFE commentators, became imprinted in the minds of Eastern Europeans who awaited their release from tyranny. Many formed the impression that if they organized an armed revolt, the United States would come to their aid. Stalin reinforced that perception by repeatedly asserting that the threat of a U.S. invasion was why Eastern Bloc subservience to the USSR was necessary.[363]

The U.S. policy of *liberation* faced its first test in June 1953. The USSR drew upon its Eastern Bloc satellites to help finance the Korean War, but the economies of those countries were failing under the weight of corruption, unrealistic agricultural and industrial policies, and the dissipation of worker motivation under collectivism.[364] To squeeze more and cheaper production from Czechoslovakia and East Germany, Moscow instructed the regimes to adopt harsh measures, which, in turn, ignited worker protests, notably in Plzen, Czechoslovakia, and East Berlin. When the protesters were quickly and bloodily suppressed, President Eisenhower did nothing. His promises of liberation were refuted by his inaction. Lewis feeling betrayed, wrote Special Guidance no. 12-A, "On the Situation in

East Berlin." In it, he advised the RFE staff that neither the United States nor NATO could be expected to act on the election-year platform of *liberation*. In Guidance 12-A, he warned RFE broadcasters to refrain from encouraging armed resistance by their listeners:

> We do not advise other Eastern European workers to follow the example of the workers of East Berlin. We advise them only to take heart from what has happened there and to make note of it for the future...They should always be careful not to resort yet to overt acts which might only result in defeat, further suppression and enslavement.

> RFE...Must avoid inciting the populations of its target countries to similar actions at this time. We must remind our audiences that premature demonstrations of resistance will lead only to ruin and despair, for they are sure to be put down ruthlessly by the Soviets and their puppet stooges...[W]e do not want them to endanger themselves needlessly at this point.

The Free Europe Committee quashed Lewis's Guidance 12-A and replaced it with a different Guidance 12-A, one created two days later by FEC political advisor Reuben Nathan with input from a "Friend" (meaning the CIA) and from FEC officials.[365] Titled "The Opening of a New Phase," the guidance proclaimed that the people of Eastern Europe should prepare for "effective resistance"; that it was time "to call Moscow's bluff"; and that "nothing less than the freedom of the captive peoples is acceptable."[366]

William Griffith and Paul Henze (RFE's frontline directors) were furious when they saw Reuben Nathan's Guidance 12-A, and ridiculed it for what it was: "the 'stupid' 'hare-brained' advice of U.S. government and FEC 'psy'warriors.'" RFE Director Lang threatened to resign over it, and RFE's political realists dismissed it an exercise in self-delusion.[367] For Lewis, it was a clear sign that he, Griffith, and Henze stood in one faction of RFE—the frontline pragmatists[368]—against the policy theorists and remote bureaucrats who imagined that their "big picture" perspectives would, ipso facto, change things on the ground.[369]

Neither NATO nor the United States came to the aid of protesting Czechs or East Germans. Eisenhower's policy of *liberation* was shown to have been election-year bravado. The United States had called its own bluff: *Liberation* was not and would not become U.S. foreign policy.[370] Lewis's RFE broadcast guidances thereafter advocated evolutionary rather than revolutionary changes, the goal being self-liberation through evolution of the Eastern Bloc countries.[371]

The Free Europe Committee had a print operation—the Free Europe Press—that dropped tens of thousands of propaganda leaflets from balloons over Czechoslovakia, Poland, and Hungary. Lewis was primarily responsible for the content of the Hungarian campaign, titled "Operation FOCUS." The Free Europe Press base of operations, like that of RFE, was Germany; its primary target was Budapest; and rising between the two was the barrier of the Austrian Alps. A launch site was selected that would achieve the shortest possible flight path: Berchtesgaden, in the vicinity of Hitler's former mountain retreat, three hundred miles due west of Budapest. The prevailing winds were favorable, the U.S. military offered up its war surplus inventory of large weather balloons and helium, and the skies over Hungary rained paper.

In his Operation FOCUS leaflets, Lewis identified twelve reforms with which he believed all Hungarians would agree. More than agree, he thought they might be a credo about which Hungarians would coalesce into a spontaneous movement—one without an organizational structure beyond the consensus of the Hungarian people that they were entitled to these basic improvements in their lives:

1. Real autonomy for the local councils.

2. Free speech; free assembly.

3. The rule of law, not the reign of the party.

4. The land belongs to those who till it.

5. Free trade unions and free workers.

6. An end to industrial slavery.

7. Production for Hungary's well-being.

8. Living standards must be raised.

9. Services for the people in the hands of the people.

10. Homes, not barracks.

11. Equality of education; free intellectual life.

12. Freedom of worship and of conscience.

The reforms were printed on colorful glue-backed stickers that Lewis thought the free-spirited Hungarian young would enjoy plastering on the Communist Party propaganda posters that blighted the city. He was right. The stickers' demands soon buried the propaganda in counterpoint, and resulted in Imre Nagy's Hungarian puppet government[372] filing written protests with the State Department. When that didn't work (after all, RFE was a private and not a governmental operation) the regime attempted to shoot down the balloons with ground and aircraft fire. And when that failed, they spread the word that the pamphlets harbored infectious germs, or explosive charges, or incendiary devices, all of which claims were popularly derided.[373] The U.S. press carried stories about the balloon drops, and the publicity increased the contributions to the Crusade for Freedom, RFE's public fund-raising arm. But the *National Opposition Movement*, Lewis's name for the twelve-point program he had hoped would spontaneously emerge, did not. Instead, Hungarians, coping with the daily difficulties of living in a police state and knowing of the Czech and East German experiences, enjoyed the distraction of the print campaign but went about their daily lives, still disunited.

In the mid-1950s, three events changed the Eastern Bloc political landscape. The first was a June 1955 compromise reached between Nikita Khrushchev and Yugoslav leader Josip Broz Tito ("Marshal Tito"). Khrushchev agreed to not interfere with Tito's governance of Yugoslavia's internal affairs, and Tito agreed to remain putatively nonaligned but to generally favor the Soviet camp in international matters. The arrangement came to be known as "Titoism" or "national communism."[374] In the deal they struck— the "Belgrade Declaration"—Khrushchev expansively announced that there were "different forms of socialism" (implicitly equating Soviet communism with socialism) and that Soviet-Yugoslav relations would thereafter be based upon "mutual respect and non-interference in one another's internal affairs." Khrushchev's statement—a face-saving and gratuitous rationalization of the compromise that Tito had forced from him—was one that he soon regretted, as it raised the expectation in the other Eastern Bloc countries that they might have the right to become "different forms of socialism." Khrushchev would later disabuse them of that hope, but the words having been spoken, Lewis determined to make the most of them.

The second event was Khrushchev's denunciation of Stalin at the twentieth All-Union Party Congress in February 1956 (the "Secret Speech"), coupled with the purging of Stalin supporters from positions of power in the satellite governments.[375] Although framed as an attack on Stalin's cult of personality, communist orthodoxy was not the subject. Rather, the denunciation and purges were driven by economic and political necessity. Khrushchev needed to both consolidate power and keep the creaky machinery of the Eastern Bloc economies productive by allowing real reforms of their corrupt command structures.[376]

The third event was another U.S. presidential election. During the 1956 campaign, President Eisenhower and his Democratic challenger, Adlai Stevenson, once again promised that the United States was "with" those living behind the Iron Curtain, including the Hungarian people. Eisenhower decried an "eagerness to avoid war" in the face of Soviet injustice.[377]

Lewis perceived Titoism and the "Secret Speech" to be a shift in the Soviet economic treatment of its satellites, from inflexibility to gradual accommodation. He incorporated that thought into his March 24, 1956, Guidance no. 26, titled "The De-Canonization of Stalin,"[378] which instructed RFE broadcasters to advocate reforms within the Eastern Bloc governments, but not their overthrow. Among the goals Lewis thought attainable with "de-Stalinization" were the purging of Stalin's collaborators, the purging of the secret police, and the recognition of explicit citizen's rights. Lewis cautioned that the reforms would have to be advocated without communicating any expectation of U.S. backing. He warned his RFE broadcasters that America would not lend military assistance to armed resistance movements and emphasized that talk of "self-liberation" by force was "self-deception"; only "liberalization" and "gradualism" could be hoped for.[379]

Guidance no. 26 was greeted with scalding criticism by an RFE policy official, John Dunning, who argued that anything less than the overthrow of the Eastern Bloc satellite countries would "provoke debate and disrespect for RFE policy thinking among the working staffs." He described Lewis's Guidance no. 26 as "delusory and unproductive propaganda and thinking," and condemned it as "uncomprehending and defeatist." Dunning wanted it immediately withdrawn and repudiated,[380] an opinion he expressed in an April 2, 1956, letter to RFE director William J. Convery "Connie" Egan.[381] As usual, William Griffith and Paul Henze agreed with Lewis that Dunning's bellicosity was unrealistic. With Griffith and Henze's support, Lewis prevailed.[382] But, as of that spring of 1956, the sides were drawn at RFE. One faction—Dunning, Nathan, and RFE director Egan—lined up with Eisenhower's election-year bombast and favored broadcasts that agitated for the immediate democratization of the Eastern Bloc countries. A second faction—Griffith, Henze, Jan Nowak, and Lewis—advocated a strategy of liberalization and gradualism.[383] For Lewis, this was more than a philosophical or even a strategic divide. It was personal. He loathed Dunning and Egan for their lethal combination of dull-wittedness and arrogance:

- In a May 26, 1956, critique of an Egan memorandum, Lewis derided political objectives that were manifestly unrealistic and unattainable. He pointed out that Egan was taking positions inconsistent with those of the FEC, the State Department, the CIA, and also statements that Egan himself had recently made; that Egan's memorandum was "too angrily written to go down with anybody"; and that what Egan was saying was "dangerous—You never seem to have your Exile staff in mind: this is a mistake." He essentially scolded Egan:

  > I am sorry that you continue to consult me after the fact, and not before...You are aware that this memo contains fundamental matter which is in conflict with the successive analyses of events, and the lines laid down, in papers I have written in the past (CS Guidance number 14, Special Guidances 24, 25, 26, etc.). Those analyses and those lines were checked (as was always my practice) with Griffith, and by him with the desk chiefs at Munich. Not only have the responsible members of your Munich staff agreed with them, but they have made them the basis of the RFE Munich output. To some extent, also, despite the mute rejection of my papers by your immediate assistants, they have been followed by the operating staff in New York.[384]

- Lewis decried a "deep gulf" between RFE Munich and New York and placed a good part of the blame on Egan:

  > Egan...has taken RFE policy into his own hands for many months...
  >
  > Whereas Munich is in the stream of the wise and tactful tradition built up these past six years, and handles East European problems with a judicious mixture of regard

> *for the American interest, RFE/New York is deserting RFE*
> *traditions and turning the organization into a shrill-*
> *voiced USIA [U.S. Information Agency].*[385]

- And Lewis described Dunning as

> *... a fool. His thesis is that it is the mission of RFE*
> *to sell democracy and the American way of life: "We owe*
> *this to the people who support us; that is what we are*
> *here to do."*[386]

The liberalizing events in Yugoslavia created hair-trigger expectations of revolution in the Eastern Bloc, making it crucial that RFE's émigré broadcast staff be informed, intelligent, and, above all, circumspect.[387] Of special concern was the Voice of Free Hungary, or VFH. William Griffith had been warning that the VFH desk suffered from a "lack of translation and summarizing facilities [that] seriously handicapped [it]" and that

> *There were...too few Hungarian-speaking Americans in RFE/Munich*
> *capable of listening to and to some degree judging policy*
> *compliance and programming technique of programs in... a crisis*
> *period.*[388]

Griffith instructed Andor Gellért, the head of VFH, to cull his broadcast staff and hire more competent replacements. But Gellért, who was frequently disabled by illness, did not carry through. The existing Hungarian staff remained intact and, without adequate oversight, some staff members made policy decisions that were beyond their competence.[389]

In June, RFE eliminated the job of the Hungarian language summarizer-analyst, which further degraded Gellért and Griffith's abilities to timely learn of errors of judgment or of mischief at VFH.[390] Sensing jeopardy, Griffith told RFE director Egan that New York should instruct its émigré broadcasters to curb their support for reform leaders who advocated violence. Egan did not heed him.[391]

On June 28, 1956, communist workers in Poznan, Poland, rioted over demands for increased production output. Fifty-three workers were killed by government militia, an event that the Polish regime tried to keep secret by instituting a news blackout and jamming RFE's Poland broadcasts. Protesters broke into the building housing the jamming equipment, threw the equipment onto the street and crushed it. With Polish radio stations silent, RFE's Voice of Free Poland's broadcasts went out unimpeded. It was the only news heard. Lewis's guidance advised restraint,[392] a policy that Novak and his Polish Service had independently concluded was prudent. The Voice of Free Poland broadcast this message:

> Incidents like [the Poznan protests] *play into the hands of...* [the] *Stalinist clique, who want the return of terror and oppression. The struggle for freedom must end in victory, for no regime based on repression can last. But in that struggle prudence is necessary. And therefore in the name of the ardent desire, common to us all, for Poland's freedom, we must call on the people to preserve calm and refrain from acts of despair.*[393]

Tempers cooled, and the stage was set for subsequent reforms.

On July 18, 1956, Griffith wrote to Lewis—for his eyes only—to report that some of the Hungarian broadcasters were not adhering to Lewis's guidances prescribing gradualism: a change of broadcast staff and greater American control was needed.[394] Lewis warned Whitney Shepardson, then president of the Free Europe Committee, that the Hungarian desk required a contingency plan in the event of a popular uprising and, importantly, urged Shepardson to let *him* develop one. Shepardson both denied Lewis's request and removed him from the operational arena:

> August 1, 1956
>
> To: Mr. Galantière
>
> From: Mr. Shepardson
>
> Beginning today, August 1, 1956, your status within Free Europe Committee changes from that of "Consultant-Advisor to Directors RFE-FEC for Policy and Plans" to "Consultant-Advisor to the President."

The engagement is for three months,—August, September and October 1956...As "Consultant-Advisor to the President" I hope that you will be able to... [prepare a] new statement of the mission of the Committee as a whole, redefining its function in terms of the situation behind the Iron Curtain as we see it today.

Fatefully, Shepardson denied Lewis's proposal to develop a plan for how RFE would respond to a popular armed insurrection by Hungarians:

... As for the further matter, i.e., that of a planned and coordinated approach to various captive countries—beginning with Hungary, we have made a beginning, among ourselves, and we will have a plan. That, however, is a separate matter. [395]

The self-delusion of Shepardson's statement that "we have made a beginning, among ourselves, and we will have a plan" would soon cost lives.

In October 1956, the Polish government put Khrushchev's policy of Titoism to the test when, without Moscow's approval, it raised workers' standard of living, granted peasants concessions, removed Moscow-appointed Stalinists from the government, and elected Władysław Gomułka (a reformist) first secretary of the Polish Communist Party. With Soviet troops already stationed in Poland, Gomułka might have been removed by force but, instead, Khrushchev agreed that he would remain in power and, in return, Gomułka agreed to remain loyal to Moscow. Throughout the negotiation process, the Voice of Free Poland, under the leadership of Jan Nowak, urged Poles to avoid bloodshed and to support Gomułka, explaining that, although a communist, Gomułka represented the best hope for further internal reforms. The Voice of Free Poland broadcasts were dispassionate while nonetheless reporting that the Soviets were interfering in the internal affairs of a putatively independent Poland.

News of the events in Poland reached Hungarians over the Voice of Free Hungary. Two days after Gomułka's election, twenty thousand citizens of Budapest spontaneously gathered in the city and demanded independence from the USSR. That evening, a member of the secret police killed a student demonstrator, igniting long-dormant resentments. Hungarians banded into ad hoc militias, thousands strong, that freed political prisoners, executed procommunist officials and battled Soviet troops. The country's former chairman of the Council of Ministers, Imre Nagy, removed from power a year earlier for advocating reforms, was called back to form a new government. The Soviets negotiated a troop withdrawal and, by November 4, it seemed that the Hungarian uprising had succeeded. Then three members of the Nagy government defected and requested Soviet intervention. The Soviets reneged on their agreement with Nagy, their tanks reentered Budapest, and the Soviets removed him and reasserted control over the government.

At the start of the invasion of the city, the Soviets imposed a news blackout and jammed local news broadcasts. Protesters destroyed the Soviet's jamming equipment. Militias that had seized hundreds of local radio transmitters went on the air throughout Hungary and broadcast the news that they had raided secret police offices and freed political prisoners. Although the transmissions were weak, they were picked up by RFE monitors in Germany, relayed to VFH Munich, and reported on by RFE announcers in moderated programs.[396] Those hundreds of local transmitters soon became known as "freedom stations."

VFH director Andor Gellért, when not out sick, met with his senior staff and issued instructions for the day's programming. They assured him that they would comply.[397] Some did not. Several VFH broadcasters issued passionate statements that, in some instances, encouraged armed revolt. Three VFH broadcasters offered military advice under the identity of "Armed Forces Specials." On October 27, a fictitious "Colonel Bell"[398] broadcast that the local Hungarian authorities should secure weapons stores with which freedom fighters and partisans could sabotage telephone and rail lines and implied that foreign assistance would arrive once a revolutionary central military command was established. The next day, the same Colonel Bell explained resistance methods and stated that

Hungarians must continue to fight vigorously because this will have a great effect on the handling of the Hungarian question by the Security Council.[399]

The statement was both untrue and impossible in view of the veto power of the USSR in the Security Council.

When these transmissions went out, the only American on staff who spoke Hungarian, Bill Rademaekers, tried to keep Washington and New York apprised of events. He did not have the time or authority to take remedial action.[400] RFE's practice of having permitted radio scripts to be broadcast without prior clearance became toxic. As reported after the fact by Griffith,

Program distinctions tended to become meaningless and writers who would not ordinarily have been permitted to write political commentary apparently did so, at least during the period 23 October to 4 November, with very little supervision by those in charge of the desk.[401]

Compounding the harm, after October 23, 1956, Hungarian guidances were written by Lewis's nemesis, Reuben Nathan.[402] He exhorted the VFH broadcasters to demand the immediate withdrawal of Soviet forces, to unify the insurgent forces, and to demand the "maintenance of the power and authority of the revolutionary councils." One of Nathan's guidances was so belligerent that a distraught Griffith sent this message to New York:

To Egan and Galantière

URGENT STRICTLY CONFIDENTIAL

Re Nathan guidance received late last night, paragraph 2, quote

"But the very possibility of a major international conflict (for which so many people behind the Iron Curtain have been hoping for so long) should have an encouraging rather than a discouraging effect."

Considering its effect on our exile staffs and on our audiences
[and] in view *[of its]* probable result—thermonuclear conflict—
consider this paragraph directly, flagrantly contrary [to]...
Government and RFE POLICY, raising questions whether writers
[of] this guidance *[should]* implement policy during this crucial
period. Urgent action *[to]* avoid such statements in *[the]* future.
Instructing desks to disregard this passage. Please advise.

Radio Free Europe's handling of the Hungarian Revolution was a debacle. Sixteen radio transmissions disregarded, distorted or misapplied Lewis's earlier guidances prohibiting encouragement of armed resistance. Having implied to Hungarians for years that the West would support them in organized resistance to Soviet domination—but having never explicitly promised military assistance—the Voice of Free Hungary had persuaded Hungarians that they had a military ally in the United States. It had been bravado, indulged in by the Eisenhower administration and promulgated by Nathan and his RFE faction. When asked about his "liberation position" on November 15, 1956, President Eisenhower squirmed:

Now, we have never asked, as I pointed out before, and never
believed that, never asked for a people to rise up against a
ruthless military force and, of course, we think, on the other
hand, that the employment of such force is the negation of all
justice and right in the world....

But what I do say is the policy is correct in that we simply
insist upon the right of all people to be free to live under
governments of their own choosing....

Among the peoples of the Eastern Bloc, the acronym "NATO" came to be derided as "No Action, Talk Only."[403] Or, as Zbigniew Brzezinski later described it, "the impotent futility of U.S. posturing which masqueraded as the policy of liberation."[404] As described by Charles Gati in his book *Failed Illusions,*

*After years of preaching "liberation" and "rollback," now, with
the moment of truth at hand, the United States did not know what
else to do.*

There were no plans whatsoever on the shelves.[405]

By November 20, 1956, twenty-five hundred Hungarians lay dead, two hundred thousand had fled the country, and the revolution had been crushed. Shepardson had stopped Lewis and Griffith from developing an operational plan for VFH. His dismissive rejoinder "... we will have a plan" was of a piece with his bureaucratic grandiosity. RFE's leaders had imagined themselves players in a game of global chess. They had, in fact, been self-deluding bureaucrats, in over their heads.

As of the Hungarian Revolution, RFE had ceased to perform the function for which it had been created—propaganda as a tool of foreign policy—and had become instead a bureaucracy for its own sake: a career medium in which political appointees and administrative staffs took root and became comfortably planted. To those careerists, Lewis's presence was a goad, an admonition. Rather than have to cope with him, they reassigned him to matters that would not impede or reflect upon their own sclerotic inconsequentiality.[406] It was a time of entropy:

*With the crushing of the Hungarian Revolution and reassertion
of Soviet control over Eastern Europe, RFE fell into an
institutional crisis that lasted nearly five years...FEC and RFE
management turned over and its competence declined, staff morale
worsened, the State Department's influence over RFE operations
increased, and CIA officials themselves began to express doubts
about the future of the autonomous influence project they had
spawned and nurtured.*[407]

A. Ross Johnson, *Radio Free Europe and Radio Liberty*

Shepardson's successor as president of the FEC was General Willis D. Crittenberger, described as one of President Eisenhower's "golfing buddies."[408] Crittenberger's successor was Archibald "Archie" S. Alexander, whom Lewis kindly described as "not intelligent." Lewis submitted successive letters of resignation but, each time, was made promises that persuaded him to stay on.[409] On December 8, 1960, he proposed to Archie Alexander that Bill Griffith and Zbigniew Brzezinski (then thirty-two years old) and he assess RFE's target countries and prepare background country papers that would include recommendations for RFE guidances and programming.[410] It is likely that Alexander did not agree to the proposal because Brzezinski and Griffith went on, without Lewis, to coauthor an article that they submitted to "Ham" Armstrong for publication in *Foreign Affairs*. On March 9, 1961, Lewis wrote to Ham, urging him to publish the Brzezinski/Griffith piece:

Dear Ham,

Zbig Brzezinski and Bill Griffith tell me that they are doing a piece on Soviet Europe which they hope you will print. They say it will include proposals for US policy. Except for this, I would not be writing you, for on other grounds I feel confident that you and Quigg [Philip W. Quigg, managing editor of Foreign Affairs] will find their [piece] first class. I write, however out of fear that you may think them perhaps not "distinguished" or "authoritative" enough to suggest policy. Their authority as scholars and analysts, in their field, is in my view as great as, say, Kissinger's in his. Brzezinski, besides, has this personal authority, that he wrote the joint Harvard-Columbia papers, one on East Europe; the other on ideology, commissioned by the Senate Foreign Relations Committee, and wrote also Kennedy's Chicago speech to the Polish-American Congress, and has lately testified before the Senate Committee. Griffith (who is doing a history of E. European events since the beginning of "the Saw" (at M.I.T. he is), is constantly consulted by CIA and well-known in the State Department. Both have been discussion leaders in your own shop. (Coincidentally, I recently put up both for academic membership in the Council.)[411]

The Brzezinski/Griffith article appeared in the July 1961 issue. Its first sentence likely gave Lewis a sense of validation:

The United States has never had a realistic and effective foreign policy toward Eastern Europe.[412]

Drs. Brzezinski and Griffith observed that Eisenhower's policy of "containment" had been ineffective in the countries already under Soviet control and that the policy of "liberation" had been unserious. They recommended "peaceful engagement" with the Soviet satellite countries, with the aim of encouraging independence from Moscow in domestic affairs while not expecting that they could extricate themselves from Moscow in international affairs. And they recommended that RFE continue broadcasting to those countries:

> The Communist regimes naturally seek to maintain their monopoly
> on the means of communication in these countries, because
> otherwise they cannot transform them into totalitarian
> societies. In broadcasting to the captive peoples, the West is
> performing one of the roles of a free democratic opposition
> which the Soviet Union and the East European Communist regimes
> deny to their peoples. We should not consider stopping these
> broadcasts.[413]

In February, Lewis learned that Archie Alexander's RFE reign was about to end. An RFE staffer, Ernest A. Gudridge, leaked the news. Lewis was, once again, hopeful:

> February 19, 1961
>
> Dear Ernest,
>
> It goes without saying that the thought of Archie Alexander
> Payne continued in office has been much on my mind.
>
> I find the pretext [for having Archie serve as long as he did]
> that "we can't go on changing presidents every two years"
> frivolous. I can think of three presidents you wouldn't want
> back; and though it may be their luck, staff morale and general
> disorganization were not so low in [the prior president's] terms
> of office as in Archie's.
>
> The reason to get rid of him is the same as the reason was to
> get rid of his three predecessors: it's simply a case of the
> leopard and his spots...
>
> The day your news is officially confirmed, I shall cheer up. Yours,
> Lewis[414]

That same month, Lewis wrote a critique of Archibald Alexander and his senior staff. It is unlikely that he intended it for eyes other than his own:

> Archie...is a fascinating case. The unbelievable thing about
> him is that he is not intelligent. He can't see beyond his own
> nose...Being incapable of thought, of real reflection, he spends
> his time calculating. He concentrates on administrative problems
> because he loves to play with building blocks. This, behind the
> façade of patience, courtesy, "liberalism" and humanitarianism,
> is the character of our Archie. A weakling whose strength is
> wholly in secretiveness and stubbornness.[415]

On Allen Dulles's recommendation, John Richardson Jr., a New York investment banker, took over the FEC presidency. Richardson was a gifted administrator who, during the ensuing seven years of his FEC tenure, restructured the organization, revitalized the Munich operations (a process ably begun in 1960 by Major General C. Rodney Smith), and established clear lines of communication between those personnel and the New York office. Richardson quelled the factionalism that had plagued the New York offices, oversaw the departure of Reuben Nathan, and reinstated Lewis, then sixty-five years old, to the central role of formulating policy and restoring international lines of communications. Here a December 14, 1962, itinerary from Lewis arranged for that purpose:

> To FEC President Richardson,
>
> If you approve, I shall leave for Munich Saturday evening, 5
> January, stay two days after the Symposium (13th and 14th), go
> to Paris for 15th to 17th, to London 18th through 20th, and
> return on the 21st.
>
> In Paris, I want to talk to Alfred Grosser (Sorbonne) on Germany,
> to Paul Rist of the Morgan Bank on the Common Market, and to
> Jelenski (Congress for Cultural Freedom)...on how East Europe
> looks...
>
> In London, I shall talk to Delgado about the public relations
> job he and Minton have been working up in West Europe (helpful
> in drafting WEAC agenda) and I shall try to see Labetz and
> Laqueur of Survey, to try to interest them in a special number

on the communist position today (the "Trends" line). I'll spend
Sunday with Leonard Miall, a BBC-TV friend who would be called
"vice president for public affairs" in an American network, to
try to get him to do a show on East Europe—of the right kind.[416]

For another five years, Lewis furnished Richardson with accurate firsthand reports of the political lay of the land in Eastern and Western Europe while also preparing guidances and broadcast scripts. At RFE and the FEC, the judgment of Lewis Galantière was, once again, respected.[417] RFE regained the State Department and the CIA's trust: they again deferred to the FEC in matters of broadcast policy.[418]

In early 1965, approaching seventy, Lewis tendered his resignation a final time. He also resigned from the ACLU's board of directors, on which he had served for more than a decade as an advocate of freedom of expression.[419] And he resigned his membership on the Council on Foreign Relations. That last evoked an appeal from the CFR's executive director:

Dear Lewis:

Thank you for your letter of January 25th even though I am
disappointed by its message. We would all really hate to have
you resign from the Council after these many years but I suppose
you have thought it over carefully from your own point of view.
Is there any chance you might reconsider?

It would mean a lot if you would.

Very sincerely, George S. Franklin, Jr[420]

Lewis did not reconsider. He left each of these organizations at the peak of his career, and for the best possible of reasons. He was returning to his first love. He was returning to the world of writers.[421]

· CHAPTER 12 ·

THE INTERNATIONAL PEN CONGRESS

SINCE THE WAR, THE SOVIET Union and its Eastern Bloc satellites had dictated what its individual citizens could do, where they could travel, and what they could say, write, and read. The secret police clandestinely scrutinized every element of its citizens' lives. At Radio Free Europe, Lewis had contrasted that authoritarian model with the freedoms of the Western democracies. But for many writers worldwide, those Western freedoms had been illusory. American authors had been blacklisted by timorous publishers and film studios for having associated with communists or for having refused to capitulate under questioning by the House Un-American Activities Committee. And foreign authors whom the U.S. State Department had considered too sympathetic to communism had been denied visas to enter the United States under an "ideological exclusion clause."[422] Ironically, the exclusionary policies of the State Department often alienated the very authors that the CIA was trying to win over from communism through its covert financial support of Western cultural organizations. This was the case with Latin American writers.

Latin America had parallels to the Soviet Bloc countries in that the peoples of both endured poverty and political repression at the hands of dictators who pursued or perpetuated power in the name of communism.[423] Standing outside of these ideological polarities and largely untouched by the realpolitik and commercial opportunism of each was an association that advocated freedom of expression for authors. PEN International (PEN being a loose acronym for poets, playwrights, essayists and novelists) was founded in 1921 and, by the mid-1960s, had over seventy chapters in fifty-eight countries that met annually to confront the persecution of writers and the censorship of their work.[424] Its annual meetings, termed "congresses," had taken place mainly on the European continent. The first Asian congress had been held in Japan in 1957[425] but, as of 1963, no international PEN congress had taken place in the United States. In that year, the Farfield Foundation donated $2,000 in seed money to PEN America to host the congress in New York City. It is reasonable to infer that Lewis had long known, from his many communications with the CIA and the State Department, that the Farfield Foundation was a CIA front.[426] The New York Congress was set for June 1966.

To lead the international effort, PEN needed someone—an American—who was known and respected in the world of literature and the arts and would be an effective fund-raiser, who had demonstrated managerial abilities, and who had credibility with the State Department and could handle the visa problems. Lewis was elected president of PEN America, to serve a two-year term. In 1965, the National Council on the Arts and the National Endowment for the Arts were both too newly created to be financial supporters of the New York Congress, and so Lewis had to turn to private sources. He obtained contributions from U.S. publishers, corporations, and PEN members, but mainly from the organizations with names that he had dealt with while at the Federal Reserve Bank and at the Free Europe Committee: the Ford Foundation, the Rockefeller Brothers Fund, John D. Rockefeller III, and the CIA (through the Asia Foundation and the Free Europe Committee). The Ford Foundation's grant of $75,000 was the single largest and was conditioned on the State Department endorsing New York's hosting the International Congress. In February 1966, Lewis obtained Secretary of State Dean Rusk's agreement to serve as an honorary sponsor, and the State Department fell in line.[427]

The visa application and approval process was lengthy, humiliating to the applicant, and often futile.[428] If you were on the State Department's blacklist (as most foreign left-leaning authors were), a visa application would be approved only if, in any particular case, the State Department and the Department of Justice agreed that your presence in the United States was "in the public interest." If Lewis sent PEN Congress invitations to blacklisted authors and if the State Department then vetoed their applications, it would prove to the world that the United States was no better than the Soviets: so fearful of free speech that it forbade authors to travel, so uncertain of its ability to persuade that it tried to silence those with opposing opinions. But Lewis could not wait to see what visa approvals the State Department might grant or withhold, because the processing times were indeterminable. He could not delay mailing the invitations and urging the authors to start the application process.

In early 1965, Lewis met with various bureaus of the State Department[429] and persuaded Assistant Secretary of State Harland Cleveland[430] to issue visas to attendees from Eastern Europe and Cuba. But that still left impediments for authors from other countries, including the Chilean Pablo Neruda, who was then the world's most celebrated poet. Neruda was a visible proponent of communism, whose presence at the 1966 congress would be the litmus test of whether the United States truly stood for freedom of expression. If Neruda came, it would be tacit permission to other died-in-the-wool communist authors to come.

The International PEN Congress that preceded New York's was held in the Alpine lakeside town of Bled, Yugoslavia. There, Lewis and the playwright Arthur Miller implored Neruda to attend the U.S. congress, to which Naruda pointed out that every one of the visa applications he had completed since visiting the United States in 1943 had been denied.[431] Lewis promised that he would do all he could to assure that, this time, it would be approved. (Neruda did not know it but, one year before the Bled Congress, the Congress for Cultural Freedom—a CIA-funded anti-communist advocacy group—had covertly worked to deny Neruda the Nobel Prize.)

At the Bled Congress, Arthur Miller was nominated for the presidency of International PEN, a position that no American had yet held. Miller had garnered admirers in the East and West. He had criticized the suppression of free expression under Soviet totalitarianism but had also condemned McCarthyism, the latter having been the subject of his play *The Crucible*. When called before the House Un-American Activities Committee, he had refused to name names and was cited for contempt, which earned him a place on the entertainment industry's writers' blacklist. In Bled, when the vote of the PEN executive committee was taken, Miller was elected unanimously.

As international president, Miller was not obliged to be nonpolitical in matters unrelated to the organization. In September 1965, he declined President Lyndon Johnson's invitation to see the Arts and Humanities Act signed, and gave his reasons in a much-publicized cable:

> [The Bill] *surely begins a new and fruitful relationship between American artists and their government. But the occasion is so darkened for me by the Vietnam tragedy that I could not join in with a clear conscience...*
>
> *... American casualties are mounting daily. Our Air Force is carrying out gigantic bombardments through thick cloud cover which can only mean immense civilian suffering in Vietnam and death for innocent women and children.*
>
> *When the guns boom, the arts die and this law of life is far stronger than any law man may devise.*

Morris Ernst, a prominent New York lawyer and a member of PEN America, asked Lewis to "[clear] the air on this social and political item of tawdry confusion created by Miller." But Lewis reminded Ernst that, since Miller had acted in his personal capacity and had made no allusion to PEN, the organization's hands were tied.[432] After all, the organization's raison d'être was the toleration of freedom of expression.

Lewis was denied that discretion the following month, when Miller agreed to sponsor a peace march on Washington and John Chamberlain, a syndicated columnist, presumed that Miller was doing it in PEN's name. Chamberlain scolded Miller and PEN in a *Washington Post* article that was reprinted nationwide.

> Arthur Miller, the playwright who heads the international association of writers known as the PEN, is playing to the gallery again. Along with Dr. Benjamin Spock, he is sponsoring a peace march on Washington scheduled for November. This is Miller's follow-up to his September rejection of an invitation to the White House to witness the signing of the bill providing Federal support of the arts...
>
> What is Arthur Miller, as president of the PEN writers association, doing about the fate of some of his fellow artists and intellectuals in Moscow and Peking?...Even as Miller was joining some of his fellow writers in protesting against the Johnson foreign policy in South Vietnam, Soviet Premier Kosygin and Party Chief Brezhnev were continuing to silence Soviet writers by arresting them or declaring them insane...
>
> This is what is done to writers under the sort of government that the Communists hope to impose on South Vietnam. Yet Arthur Miller, the head of the PEN, tees off on a U.S. foreign policy that would prevent a Communist takeover in Southeast Asia.[433]

Lewis's damage-control response appeared in the November 11 *Washington Post*:

> I have read John Chamberlain's column...Mr. Miller is well able to defend his personal position—which, incidentally, though it seems to be that of some millions of Americans, is not mine. But politics are not my subject. I am concerned only with the fact that, unable to attack Mr. Miller's right to a personal position,

> *Mr. Chamberlain savages him as the president of an international organization of poets, playwrights, essayists and novelists (hence "PEN") which allegedly refrains from protest against Communist persecution of writers. I beg space to set forth the bare facts...*
>
> *... PEN's record of successful protest against the persecution of writers is carried on through a standing Writers-in-Prison Committee and goes back more than 40 years. It has intervened in recent years, and often brought about mitigation of sentence and even liberation, in the U.S.S.R. (Ivinskaya, Brodsky, Tarsis), Yugoslavia (Djilas, later Mihajlov), Poland (the famous "Letter of the 34" case and Wankowicz), East Germany (Harich et al.), Korea (Minjok Ilbo), Indonesia (Mochtar Lubis), Portugal (the book prize jury), etc., etc...[O]ur ambition is to achieve results, not to show that we are capable of moral indignation...*
>
> *The executive committee that elected Mr. Miller knows that what results from Mr. Chamberlain's charge is fantasy as regards him, just as it is a false picture of PEN.*[434]

Miller's antiwar agitation had been the very kind of political expression that the State Department's visa blacklist had been intended to forestall, at least from foreign writers. Miller's demonstration against the war undoubtedly gave pause to those in the State Department who were weighing Lewis's requests for blacklist waivers.

In February 1966, President Johnson declared that the United States should host more international meetings and directed the secretary of state and the attorney general to "remove [the] unnecessary hindrances" posed by the ideology exclusion clause.[435] And yet, a month later, Neruda's application remained in limbo. Lewis appealed to Charles Frankel, assistant secretary of state for educational and cultural affairs:

> *To disarm the most widely read of all living poets in this manner, and to let him see for himself that Americans are not ogres would, I think, be in the American national interest.*[436]

Lewis noted that even under the worst outcome—if Neruda were granted a visa to the June congress but refused to attend—at least he would no longer be able to claim that the United States suppressed voices with which it disagreed. But April came and went with no decision. In May, some authors who had been invited to the Congress but had not yet been issued visas notified Lewis that, due to the lateness of the hour and the uncertainty about their ability to enter the country, they would not be making travel arrangements. Lewis passed this on to the State Department.

> ...the delays and embarrassment involved in obtaining permission to enter the United States...under the present procedure have caused some guests to abandon plans to attend conferences...and have marred this country's image as a free and open society. [437]

Finally, in May, with a sudden recognition of the propaganda field day the Soviets were about to have, the State and Justice Departments instituted a policy of automatically granting blanket group waivers to persons traveling to international conferences in the United States whenever

> the national interest requires a group waiver of the provision of law which would otherwise automatically exclude all persons invited to the conference who had at any time been associated with a Communist party. [438]

The chokehold was released and Neruda and every other New York Congress invitee were immediately issued visas to attend the first PEN International Congress hosted in the United States.

On the Saturday night before the formal Congress, Pablo Neruda held a reading in the New York YMCA-YWCA. A crowd filled the large meeting room and overflowed into the hallways. Archibald MacLeish introduced Neruda as the world's greatest living poet. Translators took turns reading Neruda's poems, after which Neruda read the original. The audience "applauded wildly" after each Neruda reading and, at the end, hundreds gathered around the author to get his autograph.

> On Sunday, picnic baskets and wine were handed to guests as they boarded a New York harbor tour boat. In Lewis's parlance, it was a "pique-nique sur l'eau." When the boat reached capacity, delegates who had not signed up were turned away, and Lewis

assigned the author Sidney Offit, a PEN America member, to deal
with the disenfranchised:

Along with Frank Reeve, poet, translator with the physique of a
fullback and Charles Bracelen Flood, best-selling novelist and
historian, blessed with manner for all seasons, I helped clear
the deck...of non-subscribers. With his characteristic French
flourish Lewis [Galantière] expressed his gratitude.[439]

The International Congress featured panel discussions and monographs, but Lewis also scheduled group discussions among regional authors, the most productive of which was thought to be the Wednesday session for Latin American authors. It was attended by Victoria Ocampo of Argentina; Pablo Neruda, Nicanor Parra, and Manuel Balbontin of Chile; Carlos Fuentes, Marco A. Montes de Oca, and Homero Aridjis of Mexico; Mario Vargas Llosa of Peru; Juan Liscano of Venezuela; Haroldo de Campos of Brazil; and Carlos Martinez Moreno and Rodriguez Monegal of Uruguay. They spoke of the problems common to southern hemisphere authors: government censorship, customs barriers, and widespread illiteracy. Lewis and the State Department took satisfaction in the fact that those same panel members derided Castro for having prevented the writer and musicologist Alejo Carpentier from attending.

The Congress closed with a speech by Arthur Miller, the international president. Rodriguez Monegal spoke of the fortitude required of Miller that morning, and the impact of his example upon those who attended:

The closing session took place amid an inevitable sadness.
Miller is to deliver the closing speech. And although this
has not been made public, last night, his father died. The
news spreads and lengthens the faces of many. Miller has won
our hearts with his natural charm and slight gawkiness. In his
speech, he says that the Latin American delegation was the most
brilliant of the Congress, and he commends us for our round
table discussion on Wednesday...After the speech, the Latin
Americans were invited to lunch at an Italian restaurant in
the Village. We started to eat, but thought that the day had
been despoiled. Then Miller arrived, and it was as if nothing

had happened. He sat down to eat, and talked about things that interested us all. We do not know how to thank him for the friendship that this gesture revealed. He tells us that the single most important achievement of the Congress had been the revelation of Latin American literature, and promises that he will learn Spanish...Miller represents the best kind of American writer. He is a man who struggled as a writer under McCarthyism when he was a communist sympathizer, and who was persecuted by the Communists when he denounced the crushing of Hungary. He is now in the best position to preach rapprochement, concord, dialogue. The presence of Pablo Neruda in Congress is due to him. It was he who invited him on the occasion of the Congress held last year in Bled; it was he who, with the cooperation of PEN American Club, made it possible for freelance writers from all over the world to come to New York. Speaking with him, one does not feel any need to pay homage to the fame or excellence. He naturally and immediately treats you as an equal. That is his most admirable quality.[440]

That evening, eight hundred PEN attendees showed up at the Congress's dinner in the grand ballroom of the Plaza Hotel; five hundred people had been expected. Lewis enlisted volunteers to help the hotel's serving staff, but small emergencies abounded:

At night, all was harmony in the great farewell dinner PEN American Club offered its colleagues from all over the world in the traditional Hotel Plaza. Unfortunately, the spirit of agreeability provided a pretext for some of the sillier speeches...A Nobel Prize winner (who will remain anonymous) regaled us mercilessly with his travels in the East...But his was not the only unfortunate speech. There were others. Many. Only Lewis Galantière's savoir faire and his friendly occasional interventions saved the public from total torpor.[441]

The Congress was a success. Carlos Fuentes noted that authors of all political stripes had discussed their differences in an atmosphere of comity.[442] Monegal thought that the congress helped to end McCarthyism.[443] And Pablo Neruda came away pleased with the generosity of spirit that had permeated the event, but with his politics unchanged: he remained a cold warrior against American foreign policy and blind to the injustices wrought by the Soviet Union.[444]

The participation of Latin American writers and, especially, of Neruda at the New York Congress and the later publication of Gabriel Garcia Marquez's best-selling *One Hundred Years of Solitude*[445] heralded the "Latin American literary boom": the popularization of Latin American works worldwide. So said Monegal:

> the Congress was justified by many things but especially...
> [for showing] that at this time there is a Latin American
> literature that operates above the national separations and has,
> increasingly, international strength and vigor.[446]

In the September 1, 1966, PEN Club bulletin, Lewis gave his assessment:

> The New York Congress of International PEN (June 1966) was
> attended by 23 Latin American writers. With rare exceptions
> (notably Alfred Knopf's personal interest in the Brazilians)
> American publishers had paid them little heed. Their special
> session, attended by most of the 260 writers and editors present
> from 59 countries, was the outstanding event of the Congress.[447]

Lewis should rightly have credited Blanche Knopf more than her husband for the nurturing of South American writers. In June 1942, Blanche had gone to Brazil at the request of Sumner Wells, FDR's undersecretary of state, as part of a "Good Neighbors" program. There she found authors whose ability to get into print had been hobbled by widespread illiteracy and a corresponding paucity of publishers. Blanche brought their works back to the United States and had them translated and published, notwithstanding that the miniscule readership meant that the books lost money.[448] Alfred and Blanche Knopf's success came from trusting their literary judgments. In time, the world came around. For her efforts, in 1949, Blanche received Brazil's National Order of the Southern Cross. Additional honors followed. A little more than a week before the opening of the New York PEN Congress, Blanche Knopf died following months of pain from cancers that invaded her abdomen and liver. It appears that, in the end, when her doctor refused to do so, Blanche ended her life. Lewis wrote to Alfred:

> June 8, 1966
>
> Dear Alfred,
>
> What can I say? Is it a bad thing to die at the moment of one's fulfillment, when the rewards of a lifetime of work are pouring in unsolicited and both character and years make the rewards agreeable without making them extravagantly important?
>
> Nancy and I hope that Blanche's death was easy. We imagine that she would've been unhappy not for herself, but for you, who are left without her. We offer you all our sympathy.
>
> Affectionately,
>
> Lewis[449]

On the eve of the PEN Congress, Alfred wrote back. Although he had been traveling at the time of Blanche's death, his letter reveals that he knew that the way that Blanch ended her life had been easier than the pain she had endured:

> June 13, 1966
>
> Dear Lewis:
>
> My best thanks for your letter. Yes, Blanche's death was easy—far easier than her life had been for some time. You and Nancy were the last persons to have a meal with her at 24 West Fifty-fifth, and I can assure you that she got the most enormous kick out of your company that evening. She seemed pretty well to me, too, so much so that I didn't see her again after breakfast the next morning, as I had to go to Adelphi University then to take my degree and accept hers in absentia—then to Purchase to pack a bag and fly to Boston next morning to join the Henry Laughlins in their celebration of their fiftieth wedding anniversary, an

affair to which Blanche had been greatly looking forward but which she couldn't attend. Before I got back Saturday morning she had died.

Best to you and Nancy,

Yours affectionately,

Alfred[450]

Blanche Knopf had kindled America's interest in modern Latin American writers. The New York PEN Congress stoked the emergence of their literature into a worldwide phenomenon.[451]

Lewis continued as president of PEN America until May 8, 1967. In his farewell address, he shared credit for the success of the 1966 congress with Arthur Miller.[452] His seconds in command for the PEN Congress had been the sisters Marchette Chute, a Shakespeare biographer, and Beatrice Joy Chute, a novelist and teacher at Barnard College. Joy Chute wrote to Lewis two days after he resigned:

Dear Lewis,

This is just to say thank you from a grateful member for all you have done for PEN in the two years of your presidency—not only as architect of the Congress, but in all ways.

Listening to you at the Monday dinner (and it was a marvelous speech that you gave), I kept thinking how much of PEN's forward leap these past two years was owing to your standards of excellence and your unbelievable donation of time and effort. I wished for a large gold banner to unfurl itself right over your head, acclaiming you. And then I thought of that lovely phrase of Chief Justice Holmes—"the unadvertised first-rate"—and I decided that your banners will be private ones, waved by all those who know and appreciate what you have done during your presidency.

So, with a waving banner and my love. Joy[453]

The New York Congress marked the birth of the modern PEN America Center. Its success elicited a contribution from the National Council on the Arts for the establishment of a permanent PEN headquarters. One year later, the permanent headquarters were opened.

Foreign delegates to International P.E.N. Congress

Günter Grass (Germany)

Pablo Neruda (Chile)

Muriel Spark (England)

Ignazio Silone (Italy)

U. S. Authors at
P. E. N. Conference

—Pix.
John Steinbeck

—Karger (Pix).
William Shirer

—Martin Schiman (Pix).
Arthur Miller

—Stefan Congrat-Butlar.
John Farrar

—Truman Moore (Pix).
Saul Bellow

—Camera Press (Pix).
Norman Mailer

Joy Chute

Ralph Ellison

—Blackstone.
Barbara Tuchman

*Lewis, photographed at New York University during the
1966 PEN International Congress. All PEN Congress photographs
appeared in the Saturday Review of June 4, 1966*

CHAPTER 13

NANCY

FOLLOWING HIS PLANE CRASH AND near drowning in Botwood Harbor, Lewis had spent the summer of 1943 recuperating and working in New York while Nancy stayed with her mother in California.[454] This kind of separation would become their norm because, in addition to her back pain, Nancy experienced intervals of depression during which the two found it better to live apart.[455] Winters were Nancy's nadir but, in January 1944, she marshalled the strength to spend a week with Lewis at Chatham on Cape Cod before his flight to London. Nancy wrote to Eleanor Anderson that spring:

April 7, 1944

Dear Eleanor,

Lewis has been in London for almost 2 months. I believe he will remain for a long time. Probably for the duration. I miss him most terribly and often feel like a little puppy who was lost in the woods without his master.

You asked me about going to Ripshin this summer. I would like to go if it is possible...You know how much I love Ripshin and what lovely memories I have of the two summers we visited you [August 1938 and July 1939] and I would like nothing better than to spend a few weeks there this summer if it were possible and if you have not already given the home to someone else.

Nancy[456]

It was not to be. That spring, back pain reclaimed Nancy's attention, and she underwent an operation that left her bedridden throughout the fall.[457]

To the extent that she could, Nancy focused her attention on painting, which she did in a small artist's studio that she rented at Carnegie Hall. Her medium was oil, her approach was abstraction, and her works, when exhibited, were noted for their "freedom" and "spontaneity." In 1948, she exhibited in Los Angeles, San Francisco, Portland, and Seattle and, in 1953, at the Grand Central Moderns art show, the last drawing these words of praise:

ART DIGEST

These paintings attest to an ability to organize intricate statements of design harmoniously. The relation of spatial intervals contributes markedly to the expressive freedom of the canvases...Freshness of vision and approach are discernible in the work.[458]

NEW YORK HERALD-TRIBUNE, review by Carlyle Burrows

The artist manages to obtain in her work a personal note of her own...She has a very free and spontaneous style of painting; her color is quite vivid and her form dynamic; she is imaginatively and poetically inclined.[459]

NANCY DAVIS GALLANTIERE, noted artist (left) and Mrs. William R. McKeen, golf and tennis champion came to the opening of Lyla Marshall Harcoff's exhibition of oil paintings at the Santa Barbara Museum of Art.—News-Press Photo.

Image courtesy of the Santa-Barbara News Press.

Nancy's professional aspiration was to have her work displayed in a major New York gallery. That chance came in 1964, but it came with strings. Lewis had learned that Rose Fried, the owner of the eponymous gallery, was looking for someone to write the story of her career and told her that he might be able to find a doctoral candidate at Columbia willing do the job. In return, Rose scheduled an exhibition of Nancy's paintings that ran from September 15th to October 10th. It was to be, Nancy thought, the triumphal culmination of her artistic career. But when Lewis's doctoral candidate didn't materialize, Rose took out her displeasure on Nancy, treating her with open contempt.[461] Only a single painting sold, no art journal or newspaper critic gave the exhibition a word of notice, and Rose closed the book on the event with a curt note to Nancy:

Memorandum Nancy Galantière

Enclosed please find a check covering the MIT sale, less one-third on the work sold by the gallery and already paid to you. I think this is the easiest way of carrying this item.

Of course, I am sorry that there was so little in this for either of us, but at least you did get back what you put in. This is one reason I cannot put on exhibitions—no matter how good—unless I am assured of at least something for my efforts, cost of operation, and the myriad other expenses involved in gallery operation which is very high in New York

Best regards,

Sincerely,

Rose

In the weeks following the exhibition, Nancy's mood darkened. She was easily provoked by imagined personal slights and would not leave unmentioned any interaction that did not meet her impossible expectations. Waiters and cab drivers received the worst of her vitriol.[462]

Lewis recognized these as symptoms of Nancy's depression and tried to soften the causes of her irascibility. He prepared breakfast for her each morning and turned down her bed at night. He bought her small gifts and paid most of the household bills. And he reassured her of his love. But there was no immunization against Nancy's temper once she latched on to a grievance. And because Lewis and she were then living together, he was a ready target. He spent his days in an exhausting state of alert circumspection, lest he use a word or intonation that would trigger her fury. In the worst of her attacks, Nancy ransacked the apartment, breaking furniture and scattering his papers.

An especially bitter argument erupted when Lewis revealed that he was leaving Radio Free Europe to take the unpaid position of president of PEN America. Nancy fumed about the loss of income, and Lewis pushed back:

> What I do with my life is, I know, materially unprofitable (at this moment); yet it does not seem to me that it ought to be the object of her scorn and carping.[463]

Still, Lewis knew that Nancy would not relent until he acquired some other source of funds. He found his solution at the Phoenix Book Shop in Greenwich Village. Phoenix was then the city's leading dealer in rare books and first editions, and Lewis sold them his first edition of *Ulysses*. The price he got is unknown but, fifty years later, Bonhams in London posted an auction notice for the same book:

> Lewis Galantière was an American translator of French literature, writer, playwright and journalist and was, from 1920 to 1927, secretary of the International Chamber of Commerce in Paris. His is the earliest known presentation copy of Ulysses apart from the one given by Joyce to his wife Nora on the day of publication and it last appeared at auction in Christie's, New York in 2002 where it sold for $119,500.

In 1967, Nancy traveled alone to Crete.[464] Lewis met her there and accompanied her back to New York. It may have been upon their return that Nancy and Lewis were guests at the Connecticut home of Robert Penn Warren and his wife, Eleanor Clark. Their daughter, Rosanna,[465] recalls,

> I do remember him quite vividly, from parties at our family house in Fairfield: I recall his always gentlemanly appearance, and his charm—a feeling of presence he exuded. I believe he was married: I have a recollection of his wife...becoming exuberant after dinner one night, and thrusting out her leg in a manner that knocked over all the demitasses of coffee from the low table by the sofa.[466]

*Lewis, Eleanor Clark Warren and Katherine Ann Porter,
in the Warrens' back yard. Image courtesy of Library Special Collections,
Western Kentucky University.*

Nancy and Lewis spent the fall of 1968 at the Hotel Al-Jazira on the island of Djerba off the coast of Tunisia. The Hotel Al-Jazira was then, as now, a haven of white walls, blond beach sand, and iridescent blue sky and sea. Nancy was at the hotel "to recover [her] strength" (her words, by which she meant recovering her state of mind far from inquisitive eyes)[467] and Lewis hired the hotel's lifeguard, Brahim Ben Marzouk, to serve as her personal aide, at a wage of fifty dinars a month. The job was a promotion for Brahim, who, at fifty years of age, had been earning twelve dinars a month and living in his sister's home. When Lewis returned to New York, Nancy wrote to him several times a week, introducing each letter with a nom d'amour: "Dearest Lamb Pie," "Handsome One," "Little Angel," "Bo-Peep," or "Honey Bear."[468]

The following summer, the couple returned to North Africa, and a less salutary experience. Nancy slipped and fell on the marble floor of the Hotel Mamounia in Marrakesh, breaking her left femur. The surgery that ensued was done inexpertly, leaving her hobbled. Nancy lapsed into a deep depression, blamed Lewis for all that happened, and banished him. She spent thirty-five days at the medical clinic of L'Hivernage on the western outskirts of Marrakesh. There, her persistent cries of distress disturbed the other patients and provoked a staff doctor to draw up the papers for her transfer to the municipal psychiatric ward, about a block away. The doctor placed Nancy in an ambulance and instructed the driver to deliver her, with the commitment papers, to the head of the psychiatric ward. Lewis interceded and persuaded the ambulance company to instead take Nancy to the Hotel Menarah, also about a block from the medical clinic.

Although Lewis remained nearby, Nancy would not see him. And there was no room available in the Hotel Menarah for Brahim so, at night, Nancy had to get in and out of bed on her own in order to use the bathroom. The process, each time, was excruciating. Lewis arranged for a cot for Brahim to be placed in Nancy's room or, alternatively, for her to be relocated to the Tazi Hotel, in downtown Marrakesh, where Brahim could have the adjacent room:

January 17, 1969

Nancy ...

Director, Monsieur Martin, talked to me with some understanding, after phoning yesterday while I was in Casablanca getting the crutches. He said he would have a camp bed put in your room for Brahim. Anything you want except to lock yourself in and keep your neighbors awake.

Brahim suggests, as an alternative, that I move out of the TAZI [hotel] and you move into a room next to this one where he will be on call day and night.

I agree, if that is your choice.

I don't know if you can move in a big taxi or would have to go in an ambulance again. Here, you would be carried one flight up.

> *You might have to wait a day or two for a room. The Tazi is full.*
> *Brahim and I share a room.*[469]

Nancy came to believe that Lewis had taken her from the comfort of the
medical clinic in order to imprison her in the Hotel Menarah. Lewis tried
to tell her otherwise:

> *January 19, 1969*
>
> *Nancy:*
>
> *Read this carefully ...*
>
> *... I <u>saved you</u> from going into the psychiatric ward by*
> *persuading the ambulance man to tell the driver to go to the*
> *Hotel...When we arrived at the hotel, the <u>ambulance man</u> gave me*
> *those [commitment] papers. I gave them to Brahim to slip under*
> *your door on Wednesday morning.*
>
> *You were thrown out of the Clinic, yes. But you are not*
> *"kidnapped." You were taken to the freedom of the hotel and <u>not</u>*
> *to the <u>prison</u> of the ward...*[470]

Lewis's attempts to shepherd Nancy through her depression ended when
Brahim was called to Djerba to look after his sick son. Lewis had Nancy
admitted to the Ibn Nafis Psychiatric Hospital in Marrakesh, where she
spent the next five weeks.[471] As usual, he explained these things to her from
a distance and in writing:

> *Nancy:*
>
> *... Brahim had a telegram on Friday night saying his son was*
> *ill...he left on Sunday...Again you won't believe me: I had*
> *nothing to do with his leaving.*
>
> *... with Brahim gone, and me undesirable, there was no one to*
> *stay with you at the hotel. I had to take the responsibility of*
> *sending you to the hospital where you are.*[472]

Lewis and Nancy returned to New York in early March, and he arranged
for her to be voluntarily admitted to the Payne Whitney Psychiatric Clinic.[473] Writing to his friend Paul Henze,[474] Lewis made it seem as if Nancy
and he had been on vacation:

13 March 1969

Dear Paul,

Nancy and I are just back from three months in Morocco, mostly with Marrakesh as our base, and I am delighted to have the Henze family greetings.[475]

The following summer, Nancy and Lewis returned to the Hotel Al-Jazira, and again retained Brahim to bring Nancy her meals, walk with her into the sea to the depth where she could swim, and run errands. When Lewis discovered that expenditures for which Brahim had claimed reimbursement had likely been fraudulent, he told Nancy about it. She dismissed his concerns and he dropped the subject, unwilling to invest the exertion required to budge her from her opinions. And besides, he had no one else to replace Brahim, no one else that Nancy trusted.

Lewis left Djerba in mid-August but returned a month later and relocated Nancy to the Hotel Cercina on the island of Kerkennah, near the city of Sfax. Lewis may have intended to linger only a day or two, but the weather turned. Kerkennah, with an average annual rainfall of 9 inches, was deluged for the next thirty-eight consecutive days. A foot of rain fell in September and almost two feet in early October. Rivers on the mainland overflowed, 80 percent of the country was inundated, crops and livestock were destroyed, and hundreds of people were killed.[476] Guests abandoned the Hotel Cercina, and most of its staff departed for to the mainland to help their families.

When the rain stopped on October 13, Lewis left the island and returned to New York. Nancy stayed behind, a decision that was assuredly hers. During their five weeks of confinement on Kerkennah, she had grown resentful of Lewis's hovering and deaf to his concerns that Brahim was a danger. As she saw it, Lewis's admonitions impugned her competence and insulted her dignity. Nancy's disdain made Lewis indifferent: she could stay if she wanted.

In Lewis's absence, Brahim made his move and demanded that Nancy give him $2,000. When she refused, he became surly and uncooperative. Nancy's illusions about Brahim dissolved, and she was left isolated, in pain, and desperate. She wrote to Lewis on November 26:

> You said to me, when you returned from Menton last September, that you came back to Djerba partly because you were worried about Brahim, and that you could not take out of your mind the idea that he was a con artist (a fake person) who could be dangerous...Now it is too late, and I can see that you were right...Since I told him I could not give him this money, his attitude has changed 100%. He has become very upset, stubborn, shows bad manners, and even though he has very little to do to take care of me, he does it grudgingly, muttering things, moaning, complaining all the way...And now, that I have been in bed for the past two weeks, with pain in my back (along my spine) and in my leg, unable to leave my room, he is talking about going back to Djerba for the festivities marking the end of Ramadan, and to leave me alone here, the only client left at the Hotel where the only personnel left are the cook and the server...God knows I hate to have to write to you this, but I hope that you will come soon and take me somewhere else in another climate and where you will stay for a little time with me.[477]

Lewis received Nancy's letter on December 5 and immediately sent a telegram to the Consul of Social Affairs at the United States embassy in Tunis:

> Dear Sir or Madam,
>
> I am writing to you about my wife, Nancy D. Galantière, who is currently at the Hotel Cercina...on the island of Kerkennah... Today, December 5, I have received a letter from her that has really frightened me.
>
> We had taken along with us in Kerkennah...Ben Marzouk Brahim. He is intelligent, he usually displays good manners, and what French people would consider "helpful." I had, however, noticed that he had dark moods, felt that he was superior to any task he was given in life...Not only has this Mr. Brahim stopped helping her out, but she writes to me in her letter dated November 26,

which I have just received, that he is trying to put pressure on
her in some kind of blackmailing situation, asking her to give
him 2,000 dollars...As she is bedridden, in a hotel where only
the cook and a server are left behind, harassed as she is by
this man who (in his words: "has abandoned everything he had to
devote himself to you, Madame, whom I love as my mother"). Her
situation is miserable, morally and physically—and she is alone.
What this Brahim person could be able to do to her, is sufficient
cause of worries.

I am asking you...to immediately do two things. First: to call
my wife in the hotel Cercina...to assure her of your protection
in case of an emergency. Secondly, if there is a United States
consulate in Sfax...arrange that she be transported to Sfax
(Hotel des Oliviers, preferably).

You will surely understand that I would like for her to feel
more secure and happier, so that, when I arrive, she physically
will feel up to come back with me...I am planning to leave in
three days.[478]

As Lewis was writing this telegram, the police on Kerkennah were already on the scene. Earlier that morning, Brahim had knocked on Nancy's hotel room door and, receiving no response, had gone back to his room. An hour later, the hotel bellman, carrying Nancy's breakfast tray, again knocked on her door. No answer. He tested the door; it was locked from the inside. The bellman fetched Brahim and the two pounded on the door. Nothing. Brahim called the police, who arrived later that morning, with court authorization to break into the room. Inside, they saw Nancy lying on her bed, the mattress sodden with her blood. The medical examiner was called. He concluded that Nancy had slashed her left wrist and bled out during the night. He noted the official cause of death as "Massive external hemorrhage due to cuts of big blood vessels in left wrist."[479] Brahim telegraphed Lewis with the news of Nancy's passing.

Lewis flew to Sfax and gathered Nancy's belongings. They included canceled checks she had given Brahim: payment for his services during October and November. Lewis had Nancy's body placed in a zinc casket and sent to a Davis family crypt near San Francisco. Then he returned to New York and wrote her obituary:

The New York Times, December 20, 1969:

Mrs. Nancy Galantière Dies; Expressionist Painter, 62

Mrs. Nancy Davis Galantière, a painter of the abstract expressionist school, died on Dec. 5 of a cerebral hemorrhage on the island of Kerkennah, Tunisia. She was 62 years old and lived at 1 West 72d Street.

Mrs. Galantière had an exhibition in 1964 at the Rose Fried Gallery here.

A student of Hans Hofmann and Kuniyoshi, she began painting soon after leaving Miss Porter's School in Farmington, Conn. Her first New York show was held at the Downtown Gallery and her pictures hang in the Santa Barbara Museum and the Legion of Honor in San Francisco.

She is survived by her husband, Lewis Galantière, the writer and former president of the American P. E. N. Center, and a sister, Mrs. Margery Warner of San Francisco.[480]

On December 19, Brahim sent Lewis a condolence letter in which he said that Nancy had not paid him for three months—October, November, and December—that he needed the money, and that he also wanted payment for his hotel and restaurant expenses during a week's stay in Sfax:

Since your wife's passing, I have been very sad by her loss, and I am currently unemployed. While waiting for your answer and your money in the best time, please receive, Mr. Galantière the assurance of my highest regards...Don't delay the sending of this money which I terribly need.[481]

A second letter came a month later:

Oh, Mr. Galantière, I am certainly not lucky at all! From June 1968, when I had met Nancy Galantière and you Mr. Galantière, to the 3rd day of December 1969, I was like a family, I was from Morocco, Tunisia. And then this friendship between me and your wife, like an only son and his mother, your wife, and one father, you, Lewis Galantière. And the last day, I even gave my *resignation [as the lifeguard] from the Hotel Al-Jazira because of this friendship between Nancy Galantière, Mr. Galantière and now, now, I have lost my whole future, and I left behind my family and my children to live hungry.*

The day I gave my resignation at the hotel Al-Jazira, I thought I would become very Rich, from your darling wife's saying. But now, my work, my taking care of a sick person, has been lost, my salary is lost along with Nancy Galantière. But please, sir, you cannot forget me, and everything I did.

... now your darling wife is dead, you cannot think too much about her, and you cannot forget me.[482]

And a third letter, the month after that:

I have the honor to write this little letter, respectfully and seriously and to ask you to make me understand why I have written you two letters in December and in January, and until now I have not received any letter from you...

... We are like friends or brothers New Yorkers and Tunisians, and the friendship between us; that's why I left Djerba and went to Kerkennah with you and with your wife. Everything that has happened is not my fault, you have a contract signed by myself and your wife.

... As for me, I am not even thinking about this sum of money, I am thinking about your health. You have been too sad. It is not worth thinking too much about what has happened, it is necessary now to think about your health.

If you are truly my friend, please write me a letter.[483]

Lewis wrote to Brahim on March 1, 1970:

Ben Marzouk Brahim

I have received your three letters. As far as your wages for the months of October, November and December, I am reminding you that my wife had given you a check of $100 dollars (50 dinars) dated October 31, paying your wages for that month.

Four days before her tragic death, on December 1st, she gave you two checks of $50 dollars each paying you for November.

As far as the 50 dinars you are asking me for the month of December, please read the translation of some extracts of the [November 26, 1969] letter, I am enclosing here, that my wife sent me, and you will surely understand why I am refusing to pay this money to you.

This letter from my wife, please read it out loud, to your respectable sister, so that she will get to know you better as you really are, you and your nephew. [Brahim's nephew had asked Nancy to lend him $2,000. She had refused.]

You both are—but above all, you—jackals, vampires and you both bear a part of responsibility in the death of a sick woman, unhappy, who had trusted you for two years, given you her entire, and cruelly undeserved, confidence. You think you are skillful, subtle, but you are a hypocrite and a deceiving person. May Allah punish you on earth and in hell.

Don't answer me back, I will tear up your letter without opening its envelope.[484]

On New Year's Eve 1969, Lewis wrote to his friend Alfred Knopf:

Dear Alfred,

I had a letter from you around Thanksgiving Day. Before I could thank you for it, I had a cable from the American Embassy in Tunis to say that my wife had died suddenly. The cause, I learned when I got there, was a cerebral hemorrhage, which struck her in the night. She was alone (with a personal servant), and not discovered till morning, a small hotel on an island 18 km off the city of Sfax, where the authorities took care of my poor darling. The embassy turned over to me a young Consul who, most efficiently, took everything off my hands. My Nancy now rests in a family mausoleum outside of San Francisco, where a great-grandfather founded the first Unitarian Church in the 1850s.

Forgive me for running on like this. Nancy retained the happiest memory of her lunch at Purchase [the Knopfs' home] and dinner at 55th St. [their publishing offices].

Happy New Year and all the best to you and your lady.

Affectionately, Lewis[485]

Lewis made these entries in his diary:

Saturday...I prayed for the first time in my life to God to preserve her, be good to her, to keep her till I could visit her. She was already dead...

This way of missing Nancy will continue...I have for more than 30 years talked silently to Nancy. We were of the same mind about the world, the arts, the nature of people.[486]

"Talked silently." The terrible loneliness Lewis must have known. Five years later, in writing to his friend, Peter Colefax, he said, "I had an *Angel*, but we loved without fitting."[487]

· CHAPTER 14 ·

TWILIGHT

IN THE 1960S, LEWIS AND Nancy had moved into a two-bedroom apartment in the Dakota, then Manhattan's most prestigious co-op. Built in the 1880s, the Dakota occupies the block between West 72nd and West 73rd Streets on Central Park West. After Nancy's death in 1969, Lewis sold that unit and moved into a single-bedroom apartment with a view of Central Park West. It was on the top (ninth) floor and he referred to it as "the attic."[488] That same year, the residents of the Dakota began what would become an annual tradition: a potluck picnic held in the expansive central courtyard, in the cool of October.[489] Contributions included lemon icebox pies that Rex Reed made, Lauren Bacall's brownies, John Lennon and Yoko Ono's sushi, and Eugenia Shephard's spinach salad. Lewis brought one hundred of the Century Association's fresh oysters.[490]

The Century Association is an elite New York private club of authors and artists. The association has been, in different incarnations, a New York institution for nearly 200 years. Lewis was a member for at least two decades and was instrumental in obtaining the membership of others, including the publisher William Jovanovich. Lewis often ate lunch at the club, where he found comfortable friendship. On February 10, 1971, his dining mate was Dan Lacy, a senior vice president of McGraw-Hill Book Company. Appreciative of Lewis's repartee, Lacy sent him these handwritten couplets:

Lewis Galantière,

Bearing himself with a jaunty air,

Beguiles these knotty, darker

Times with quips of Dorothy Parker

And tells his own tales, of the species

Rivaled only by Archie MacLeish's—

But I'm glad disdains the hordes

who in a lemming way

Rush to peddle the gossip of Hemingway.

Thanks

D[491]

The Century Association had always excluded women from its premises and, of course, its membership. At an association board meeting on March 5, 1970, Lewis rose to advocate the preservation of that exclusion:

Mr. President,

... Let me put my cards on the table...this arrangement is in violation of the Association's by-laws...[on] "Ladies in the Clubhouse." ...

... A men's club is sui generis...A men's club is a sanctuary, a haven from the confusion and turmoil of the world...A men's club is supremely a place where a man can get away from women. Women in the plural.

... The aura generated by women talking together is whatever it may be. My own conviction is that it is incomplete. The aura generated by men talking together is wholly different...A woman entering the library is a disruptive, a foreign element. A man entering the drawing room is a welcome relief.

It is on these facts that the raison d'être of a men's club is founded.[492]

The effect of Lewis's address is known only to the members of the association. But the exclusion of women members ended in 1989, under compulsion of the courts.

Lewis last traveled abroad in 1971, as PEN's emissary to the world for the translation and dissemination of authors' works. He is pictured here, at right, in Ethiopia in late October. He was seventy-six.[493]

Lewis (right) with H. E. Ato Tekle Tsadik Mekuria (left), minister of state for antiquities, and Dr. A. Samaan-Hanna.

Lewis stayed on in Europe, spending a few days in London in June, a week in the "dirty, torn-up (streets) Paris, the motor-noisiest streets (without horn-blowing) anywhere," and then three weeks in south central France. He returned to the United States for surgery on a hernia.[494] It was probably about then that a young author in training, Jonathan Carroll, spent an afternoon with Lewis.[495] Jonathan's parents lived at the Dakota and Jonathan's father had made the introduction in the elevator. Lewis invited the student and his father to visit. Here are Jonathan's recollections:

My parents lived in New York for many years. A very small old man lived on the top floor of their building. I used to bump into him now and then when I visited the folks. He was always dressed in a perfectly tailored three-piece suit, thick silk tie, and white shirt with cuff links. We smiled and nodded at each other but never spoke. One day when I was with my father we ran into him in the hall and were introduced. His name was Lewis Galantière and from the way he dressed and spoke, he was elegance personified. For some reason I didn't understand then, my father told this stranger that I was studying literature in university and hoped someday to be a writer. Galantière lit up and said, "Well, we should talk about that—why don't you come for tea sometime?" When he was gone, my father told me Galantière was one of the greatest French to English translators. His Proust translations especially were world renowned and used in many universities. But even more interesting, this man had lived in Paris in the 1920s and knew everyone who was there then—Hemingway, Fitzgerald, Gertrude Stein, Picasso—the whole starry sky of talent that lit up that glittery city in those days.

A week later we went to visit him. The apartment was small but beautiful. Oriental carpets on the floors, substantial leather and wood furniture, and artwork covered the walls. My father spent much of the visit studying the pictures and later told me there were original Matisse and Cézanne sketches, a Picasso, photographs by Man Ray, a handwritten recipe by Alice Toklas, on and on. We spent a couple of hours with Galantière and I think he was glad for the company. In his quiet ironic voice he spoke casually of having picnics with the Fitzgeralds, going to the horse races with Hemingway, arguing with the irascible Ms. Stein. He was not showing off—just talking about the early days of his life.

His stories were amazing, as close as I will ever come to knowing or being with those gods. One thing I remember vividly came at the end of the afternoon. When he was obviously tired and winding down, Galantière paused and, deep in thought, stared at his hands. Then he said, "The one thing biographers of these people rarely talk about is how hard they all worked. Most biographies just go on and on about Fitzgerald's drunkenness or

*Hemingway's bullying and carousing. But they give little credit
to how hard they worked and at least in those days, the complete
dedication to their craft. I have never seen harder-working
people; they were like ditch diggers. When they finished for the
day, their hands were always dirty."*

On March 14, 1972, in New York, Lewis was awarded France's Ordre des
Arts et des Lettres for distinguished service in the cause of international
cultural relations. French Cultural Counselor Jean Hervé Donnard spoke
these words:

*[Y]ou always were a great friend of France and have always
worked to strengthen the ties uniting both countries. Through
your writing and your works you were and are a vital link in
our cultural relations. As a member of the Fulbright Selection
Committee for France, and as President of the International
PEN Congress in New York, as a Member of the study group of
democratic leadership and European capitalism, you were in the
forefront of cultural life in the United States and Europe...A
member [and former National Secretary] of the American
Translators Association, you have translated many French works
into English, and reading them, one gets the impression that
Maupassant or the Brothers Goncourt wrote their works originally
in English. You have conveyed every nuance; every detail stands
out clearly ...[and] you were the most loyal friend of the
authors whose works you translated.*[496]

The 1970s were trying times. Cataract surgeries performed in December
1967 had not gone well: the lenses inserted to replace his own had wan-
dered. Reading had become toilsome.[497] Lewis had emphysema, the genetic weakness of his lungs having been exacerbated by his near drowning in Botwood Harbor and a lifetime of Turkish cigarettes. And his teeth
were failing:

*I must lower myself to speak of doctors: I never was treated
by so many, in so many successive months, of such variety, and
at one end of the scale for so much money. The dentist is, it
appears, the boldest robber of our country. He gets more opening
a mouth than his son does opening a safe. Proof? His six visits
of pre-examination, $2,850.00.*[498]

As his body disappointed him, so did the America he had imagined and lauded and loved. The Pentagon Papers, published by the *New York Times* in 1971, disclosed that President Johnson had contrived the reasons for escalating military intervention in Vietnam and had concealed the bombing of Cambodia and Laos. Under Nixon, the bombing had continued until Congress forbade it. G. Gordon Liddy and James W. McCord Jr., officials of Nixon's reelection committee, were convicted of burglarizing and bugging the Democratic Party's Watergate headquarters. Nixon's advisors Haldeman and Ehrlichman, Attorney General Kleindienst, and presidential counsel John Dean resigned, and Nixon solemnly declared, "There can be no whitewash at the White House." When the White House tapings were revealed, Nixon refused to turn over the transcripts to the Senate Watergate Committee. He ordered Attorney General Elliot Richardson to dismiss Watergate Special Prosecutor Archibald Cox. Richardson refused and resigned, as did his successor, William Ruckelshaus. Spiro T. Agnew pled no contest to charges of income tax evasion and resigned as Nixon's vice president. Arab countries began an oil embargo of those that supported Israel, doubling the price of oil. And the dollar was devalued against other currencies.

Lewis stopped venturing outside of Manhattan and spent more time in his apartment and at the Century Association. Occasionally, a letter from an old friend would spark memories of some earlier adventure or an accomplishment or a pleasurable event. Or would bring sad news of loss or ill health. The voluminous body of work Lewis had created, the lives he had touched, the regrets he had borne—they were becoming less immediate, like a history of some other person. And then some chance article would revive him and make him feel engaged. That is what happened in the spring of 1973, when a *Publishers Weekly* article reminded him that, in the scheme of things, he had mattered. The article appears below; the underlinings, made in black pen, are Lewis's:

April 9, 1973 Publishers Weekly

Onward and Upward with American P.E.N.

> *Once the ugly duckling of the international writers'*
> *brotherhood, the U.S. branch has grown into one of its*
> *more dynamic members*

... International P.E.N. throughout its history has been a
staunch opponent of censorship...In the 1930s, it was one
of the first international organizations to speak out against
the Nazi book-burnings...The American Center, during its first
decades, compiled a rather dreary record as an international
participant...Unlike its counterparts in many other
countries, it had no official standing with the government,
and it was chronically broke...It was not until the mid-
1960s that America PEN moved into its current renaissance—a
period of concerted activity that shows no sign of abating...
In 1966 the American Center finally hosted an International
P.E.N. Congress in New York, and it was a roaring success,
with over 800 registrants...

If the 1966 International Congress New York marked a
coming-of-age for America P.E.N., more than any one person
it was Lewis Galantière, president of American P.E.N. in
1965–67, who "got it all together," securing financing from
foundations and government cultural agencies, arranging for
meeting rooms and accommodations for delegates in and around
New York University's Washington Square campus, assuring
through the State Department that foreign delegates would
have no visa problems, and so on, he was tireless. Building
on the momentum from this Congress planning, Mr. Galantière
headed a group that worked out a program for the expansion
of American P.E.N.'s activities and for the financing of
this expansion. This program has been implemented by Mr.
Galantière's successors.[499]

Lewis may have thought back with bemused satisfaction to Independence
Day, 1955, when the French Consul General and other French and American dignitaries gathered on Bedloe's Island in New York Harbor to com-
memorate France's gift of the Statue of Liberty to the United States. Lewis

had been asked to speak on behalf of his countrymen, which he did by conveying the invented story of his youth:

> The first time I passed the Statue of Liberty on the way out of
> the land of my birth, I didn't even look at it, I was three
> months old and if I had been able to formulate a conscious
> desire, I suppose it would not have been for freedom but for
> security, or food. It thus happens that my first impression of
> this world-famous symbol was gained, not here but in Paris.
> There, as a little boy, I gazed upon the smaller replica of what
> I may call the patroness of this gathering. It stands at the
> base of a bridge, in the middle of the River Seine, to remind
> our French comrades-in-democracy—as this great monument reminds
> all Americans—that the French people are America's oldest ally—
> an ally in a war, not of conquest but of independence.[500]

The letters that Lewis sent and received from late 1973 took on the melancholy tones of summations and farewells.

To Henry Steele Commager, October 1, 1973:

> Dear Henry,
>
> ... For days, a young woman has been sorting out books for
> which I have no room—having retreated into a garret since
> my wife died, and really not knowing what books I can part
> with without excessive regret...Recall that you, unknown to
> yourself, first taught me American history in your Documents—
> when I had to find answers to my French schoolmates' taunts...
>
> Your affectionate debtor,
>
> Lewis[501]

June 1, 1974, from Mina Kirstein:

> Dear Lewis.
>
> I stood looking at that great long flower-box for several
> moments, mystified as to who could be sending me flowers in
> New York. They were the most Monet of flowers. He was always
> painting pink ones, just like the ones you sent...Your note
> was special balm, for it came on my anniversary—48 years[502]—
> and you are one of the two people in the world, except for my
> brothers, who remember Harry...I feel quite as you do about

the need for aloneness. At our age, the happiest encounters are perhaps the briefest. Nevertheless, I would risk a weekend if you would...I only need a day or two warning.

Bless you, too, dear Lewis.

Your loving, Mina[503]

July 10, 1974, from René Arnaud:

Dear old brother, we have well received your sweet letter dated December 26, and have been so happy to read all the details of your life, and all that interests you. I am envious of all the books you have as treasures, notably the first of Swann (edited from an author!) and the Montaigne of the 17th century...

I must go to London next month for three or four days to have a meeting about arbitration, which I am very much interested in. I have worked at it so much at the beginning of my career at the CCI [the Chamber of Commerce] and the system developed so greatly that I see with pleasure something I will leave behind me.

I am not talking about the present situation. The Arabs are nicely owning us: a direct consequence of the universal decolonization. If, as we say, to govern is to foresee, then we have not been governed.

Goodbye, old brother. Edith and I are sending you our best wishes for the year that is starting. Let's hope we will see each other!

René Arnaud[504]

August 12, 1974, from "Cela," her identity otherwise unknown:

Dearest Lewis,

I hated that so many things are bothersome for you—it never should be that the very best person should have to suffer and yet, inscrutable are the ways of the Lord, etc. No comfort at any time. Certainly, the business of aging is at its most tiresome through infirmities, otherwise I don't mind at all getting older myself because the years are after all just another number, and I never seem to register much that way. I see everyone as he was (or she) at our first meeting; so you are forever that dynamic man with a shiny dark hair and honest-to-God laugh and absolutely unending wisdom who said such lovely things to me in Tony's...

I wish I could do more for you than pray for you and love you.

Your loving Cela[505]

On August 30, 1974, Lewis was hospitalized with emphysema.[506]

From Lewis to Peter Colefax, June 27, 1975:

Dear Peter

Beautiful and gifted Elda,[507]

It's my eyes...nothing seems to sharpen and clarify...—

... My trouble is that I can't heat myself up: I get bored with my own thoughts or intents. In conversation, a companion can release from me a fair amount of talking. A printed text can—always has been able to—draw from me notes, comments, snorts or intellectual delights that may become thefts ("Wasn't it Lord Harvey who...")

... I will admit that I cannot end anything I start to write. As to beautiful women, I am ashamed to say that I had rather be persuaded that I have charmed them than that they are impatient for the proof that they have charmed me. That my weakness leaves me, this last year, no longer discontented with my mere gift for conversation, I only half accept...[508]

In a July 1975 letter to Martie Henze (wife of fellow Cold Warrior, Paul Henze)[509] Lewis lamented:

I am in my fourth year of no exit from our country: not even to Florida, Southern California, nor nowhere. Last year was quite dreary (I thought), this one murderous...

You...know how frankly crooked and quasi-criminal those who lead us at top and at bottom are; and of course I don't mean only in business, in unions, in professions, in government petty and large...

*Dear Marty, you couldn't get a duller letter, but the reason
is that I have long been a pretty tired fellow...*

God be with you both...And the scattered Henzes.

Lewis[510]

Sidney Offit came upon Lewis at lunch one day in 1975 and was invited
to sit. Lewis, wearing a napkin draped as a bib, was dining on oatmeal, his
dental condition denying him more ambitious fare. Lewis spoke "with his
characteristic French flourish" (Offit's words) of his adventures in 1920s
Paris, including some tales about Hemingway. A silence then settled on the
meal. Lewis glanced over at Offit and asked: "And who are you and why am
I telling you all this?"

Lewis to Peter Colefax, July 23, 1975:

> *I am tired. I've been from doctor to doctor: eyes, ears,
> lungs (no smoke, no climb, etc.). Can't see a street sign
> or door number; read without the unfitting glasses. I haven't
> left New York in three years now. This spring and summer most
> murderous stifling heat & stormy rain—*
>
> *Bless her, you lucky people, and him. I don't happen to know
> who else...*
>
> *Ever your grateful, Lewis*[511]

October 10, 1975, from Peter Colefax:

> *Dear Lewis,*
>
> *This is to bring you Elda's and my congratulations on joining
> Club 80 and to wish you easier days ahead. Happy birthday.
> We wish we could be with you and help you celebrate another
> milestone in a wonderful life—and one which has given so
> much warmth, stimulation and pleasure to so many...*
>
> *Meanwhile our love to you. Peter*[512]

Pierre Louis Duchartre to Lewis, December 12, 1975:

Very Dear Lewis,

We are sad because when you wrote your last letter you seem to be very sad, too sad...

The reaction of the entire family.[513]

Lewis was hospitalized at the De Witt Nursing Home from May to September 28, 1976. After that, he was cared for by Bethe Douglas who, at one time, had been a nightclub singer.[514] Lewis signed his will on November 10 and, in it, he bequeathed Bethe $100,000—the largest single specific bequest. He described Bethe as "My old friend, gallant in adversity."

The exertion now demanded of each breath, each morsel, each coherent thought told Lewis he was failing. Bethe's ministrations helped. Sometimes, she would stroke his forehead, and sometimes read aloud. As his vitality waned, the words of a poem Lewis had written—one he had never shared—brought him back to a time and place that had once been his and that, in those moments, in his mind, were his again:

Farewell to the trees of Paris and the silver-green band of silence, the Seine, winding under the sailing clouds in the wide Parisian sky; farewell to the ancient bridges,—the Pont Marie, the Pont Neuf, the Pont Royal,—and to the streamers of red and yellow light that lie on the surface of the water when night has fallen. Farewell to the sunlight of Paris that laves its ancient houses in the soft, vibrant air. Farewell to the little island of the blessed king Saint-Louis where the houses of the great and the tenements of the poor live in age-old comity; where Baudelaire lived in the incomparable Hotel de Lauzun; where the happiest years of my life were passed in love and reverie and high debate.[515]

On February 14, 1977, New Yorkers were driven indoors by a piercing Canadian freeze. The cold dry air infiltrated Lewis's apartment, stung his lungs, and brought on the terrifying sensation that he was suffocating. He was taken across town to Presbyterian Hospital, where sedation turned his desperate rasping gasps into gentle, insufficient inhalations, and eased his compulsion to strive. A day or two passed. He heard his sister Eda's voice. He saw her face. He felt her hand on his. On Tuesday, a wisp of warmth crept into the city from the south, portending the approach of spring.

The New York Times, February 22, 1977
Lewis Galantière, Translator of French Works, Dies

Lewis Galantière, writer, critic and authority on modern French literature, died Sunday evening at Presbyterian Hospital after a brief illness. He was 81 years old.

A past president of the P. E. N. American Center and an active figure in international cultural circles, Mr. Galantière was a friend of leading writers on both sides of the Atlantic for more than half-a century.

His own best-known work was as a translator, of Antoine de St.-Exupéry, Jean Cocteau, François Mauriac, Sacha Guitry and Jean Anouilh. His adaptation of Anouilh's "Antigone," first performed by Katharine Cornell in 1946, is still revived occasionally.

A well-known raconteur among men and women of letters, Mr. Galantière was reticent about his private life. According to friends, he was born in Chicago on October 10, 1895, of French parents, and was raised in France, but opted for American citizenship when he reached the age of 21.

Following World War I, he went to work for the International Chamber of Commerce in Paris. There he joined the teeming literary scene of the 1920's, meeting the young Ernest Hemingway, James Joyce and some of the French writers he would introduce later to American readers.

Worked for Federal Reserve

He returned to this country in 1928 and for the next 12 years worked for the Federal Reserve Bank of New York. Meanwhile, he and a co-author, John Houseman, wrote three light plays for the Broadway stage. Of the third, "And Be My Love," Brooks Atkinson wrote in 1934 that it was "a flawless comedy, but dull." Following the fall of France in June 1940, Mr. Galantière wrote a passionate denunciation of the new Vichy regime in New York Herald Tribune. It ended, "the world will witness the re-emergence of the French Phoenix from the ashes."

When the United States joined the war, he became director of French operations for the Office of War Information, serving in New York, then in London and finally in Paris. Afterward, he mingled two careers, one as a translator and critic of French literature, the other as a consultant on cultural relations.

As adviser to Radio Free Europe and the Free Europe Committee from 1952 to 1964, he was a participant in the cultural cold war of the epoch. He organized an American Round Table for the Advertising Council and many conferences under the Council on Foreign Relations. As president of the American branch, he presided over the International P.E.N. Congress in New York in 1966.

During this period he also translated and edited the much praised "Goncourt Journals 1851-70"; edited "America and the Mind of Europe," a collection of essays by leading Western intellectuals, and wrote numerous political and literary articles for magazines.

He was long a director of the American Civil Liberties Union, the Authors League of America and the American Translators Association, and was a familiar figure at the Century Association. Among his honors was the French Order of Arts and Letters.

Mr. Galantière's wife, the former Nancy N. Davis, died in 1969. They had no children.

EPILOGUE

In 1888 in Riga, Latvia, my grandfather, Aaron Lurie, attended the wedding of his eighteen-year-old sister, Cecile, to Joseph Galantiere, and, soon thereafter, the three sailed out of the Bay of Riga and to the frightening, exciting, unknown of the United States. A third Lurie sibling, Henry, had immigrated earlier.

Joseph, Cecile, and Aaron arrived in New York in early September, where my grandfather, then sixteen, apprenticed to learn the trade of a *tinsmith*, the term describing someone who made pots, gutters, and other items from sheet metal. Joseph and Cecile continued on to Chicago, where Cecile gave birth to three children: Lewis (the oldest), Eda, and Jacob. After the 1907 Bankers' Crisis, the Galantieres moved to Los Angeles.

Joseph Galantiere died in January 1919, two months after the World War I armistice, and Cecile and her two youngest children moved from Los Angeles to Denver to live with her brother Henry. At the time, Lewis was working for the War Department.

My grandfather, Aaron, relocated from New York to Hartford, Connecticut, where, over the first four decades of the twentieth century, he built a roofing and sheet metal business and became a Hartford City alderman. His wife gave birth to eleven children (nine of them girls), and Aaron purchased a family cemetery plot with room for more than a dozen graves. The plot is on the side of a hill, facing east, in the Emanuel Synagogue cemetery. A granite monolith about eight feet tall, bearing the LURIE name, marks the site. When Cecile died in 1930, she was interred in one of those graves. Her modest headstone reads "CECILE LURIE GALANTIERE 1863—1930," her date of birth mistaken by seven years. Down the hill and forty yards to the northeast is a simple gravestone, in a style like that of Cecile's. It reads "LEWIS GALANTIERE" "DIED FEB 20, 1977 AGE 81 YRS."

SELECTED BIBLIOGRAPHY

Alethea, David. *Lewis Galantière: The Last Amateur.* Monograph. University of Hawaii-West Oahu, 1992. Also published, expurgated, in Columbia University Library columns, Columbia University, 1992.

Allen, Debra J. *The Oder-Neisse Line: The United States, Poland, and Germany in the Cold War.* Westport, CT: Praeger, 2003

Anderson, Sherwood. *Memoirs.* New York: Harcourt, Brace, 1942.

———. *The Sherwood Anderson Diaries, 1936–1941.* Edited by Hilbert H. Campbell. Athens: University of Georgia Press, 1987.

Anouilh, Jean *Antigone.* Adapted by Louis Galantière. New York: Samuel French, Inc., 1973

Appel, Paul P., ed. *Homage to Sherwood Anderson, 1876—1941.* Mamaroneck, NY: Paul P. Appel, 1970.

Arestis, Philip, and Malcolm Sawyer. *A Biographical Dictionary of Dissenting Economists.* 2nd ed. Northampton, MA: Edward Elgar, 2001.

Baker, Carlos. *Ernest Hemingway: A Life Story.* New York: Charles Scribner's Sons, 1969.

Benson, Jackson J., ed. *New Critical Approaches to the Short Stories of Ernest Hemingway.* Durham, NC: Duke University Press, 1990.

Birmingham, Stephen. *Life at the Dakota.* Syracuse, NY: Syracuse University Press, 1996

Butler, Dorothy, and George H. Butler. *A Life in Armor: Extracts from the Notebooks and Letters of Alice Carter Butler*. Chicago: Pascal Covici, 1925.

Cate, Curtis. *Antoine de Saint-Exupéry: His Life and Times*. New York: Paragon House, 1990.

Chute, Marchette. *P.E.N. American Center: A History of the First Fifty Years*. New York City: PEN American Center, 1972.

Claridge, Laura. *The Lady with the Borzoi: Blanche Knopf, Literary Tastemaker Extraordinaire*. New York: Farrar, Straus and Giroux, 2016.

Cohn, Deborah. *The Latin American Literary Boom and U.S. Nationalism during the Cold War*. Nashville: Vanderbilt University Press, 2012

Colum, Padraic, and Margaret Freeman Cabell. *Between Friends: Letters of James Branch Cabell and Others*. Whitefish, MT: Literary Licensing, LLC, 2011.

Cook, Don. *Charles de Gaulle: A Biography*. New York: G. P. Putnam's Sons, 1983.

Einzig, Paul. *In the Centre of Things: the Autobiography of Paul Einzig*. London: Hutchinson, 1960.

Feinstein, Adam. *Pablo Neruda: A Passion for Life*. New York: Bloomsbury, 2004.

Fitch, Noel Riley. *Sylvia Beach and the Lost Generation: A History of Literary Paris in the Twenties and Thirties*. New York: W. W. Norton, 1985.

———. *Walks in Hemingway's Paris: A Guide to Paris For The Literary Traveler*. New York City: St. Martin's Griffin, 1992.

Galantière, Louis, ed. *America and the Minds of Europe*. London: Hamish Hamilton, 1951.

———, ed. *The Goncourt Journals, 1851–1870*. New York: Doubleday, Doran, 1937.

———. "Here Is Thy Sting." *New Republic*, July 2, 1930.

———. "The Most Unforgettable Character I've Met: Antoine de Saint-Exupéry." *Reader's Digest*, December 1957.

Gati, Charles. *Failed Illusions: Moscow, Washington, Budapest, and the 1956 Hungarian Revolt*. Stanford, CA: Stanford University Press, 2006.

Gregory, Horace, and Marya Zaturenska. *A History of American Poetry, 1900–1940*. New York: Harcourt, Brace, 1942.

Hansen, Arlen J. *Expatriate Paris: A Cultural and Literary Guide to Paris of the 1920s*. New York: Arcade, 2012.

Heil, Jr., Alan L. *Voice of America: A History*. New York: Columbia University Press, 2003.

Hemingway, Ernest. *Ernest Hemingway: Selected Letters, 1917–1961*. Edited by Carlos Baker. New York City: Charles Scribner's Sons, 1981.

———. *The Letters of Ernest Hemingway*. Vol. 1, *1907–1922*. Edited by Sandra Spanier and Robert W. Trogdon. Cambridge: Cambridge University Press, 2011.

———. *A Moveable Feast*. New York City: Scribners 1964.

Houseman, John. *Unfinished Business: Memoirs, 1902–1988*. New York: Applause Theatre Books, 1972.

Howe, Irving. *Sherwood Anderson*. Stanford, CA: Stanford University Press, 1951.

International Congress of the PEN Clubs. *The Writer as Independent Spirit: Proceedings of the XXXIV International P.E.N. Congress*. New York: PEN American Center, 1968.

Johnson, A. Ross. *Broadcasting Freedom—Radio Free Europe and Radio Liberty: The CIA Years and Beyond*. Washington, DC: Woodrow Wilson Center Press, 2010.

Kert, Bernice. *The Hemingway Women*. New York: W. W. Norton, 1983.

Freelon, Kiratiana. *Kiratiana's Travel Guide to Black Paris*. Chicago: Eunique Press, 2010.

Kutulas, Judy. *The American Civil Liberties Union and the Making of Modern Liberalism, 1930–1960*. Chapel Hill: University of North Carolina Press, 2006.

Labedz, Leopold, and Max Hayward, eds. *On Trial: The Case of Sinyavsky (Tertz) and Daniel (Arzhak)*. London: Collins and Harvill, 1967.

Levander, Caroline F., and Robert S. Levine, eds. *Hemispheric American Studies*. New Brunswick, NJ: Rutgers University Press, 2008.

Lucas, Scott. *Freedom's War: the US Crusade against the Soviet Union, 1945–56*. New York: New York University Press, 1999.

Lynn, Katalin Kádár. *The Inauguration of "Organized Political Warfare": Cold War Organizations*. Saint Helena, CA: Helena History Press, 2013.

MacMillan, Margaret. *Paris 1919: Six Months That Changed the World*. New York: Random House, 2001.

Mickelson, Sig. *America's Other Voice: The Story of Radio Free Europe and Radio Liberty*. Westport, CT: Praeger, 1983.

Moore, Honor. *The White Blackbird : A Life of the Painter Margarett Sargent by Her Granddaughter*. New York: W. W. Norton, 2009.

Nelson, Michael. *War of the Black Heavens: The Battles of Western Broadcasting in the Cold War*. Syracuse, NY: Syracuse University Press, 1997.

Neruda, Pablo. *Memoirs*. Translated by Hardie St. Martin. New York: Farrar, Straus and Giroux, 1977.

———. *Spain in Our Hearts*. Translated by Donald D. Walsh. New York: New Directions, 2005.

Nissenson, Marilyn. *The Lady Upstairs: Dorothy Schiff and the New York Post*. New York: St. Martin's, 2007.

De Poncins, Gontran, with Lewis Galantière. *Kabloona*. New York: Time-Life Books, 1941.

Puddington, Arch. *Broadcasting Freedom: The Cold War Triumph of Radio Free Europe and Radio Liberty*. Lexington: University Press of Kentucky, 2000.

Rascoe, Burton. *A Bookman's Daybook*. New York City: Horace Liveright, 1929.

———. *Before I Forget*. New York City: Doubleday, Doran, 1937.

Reynolds, Michael. *Hemingway: The Paris Years*. New York: W. W. Norton, 1989.

———. *The Young Hemingway*. New York: W. W. Norton, 1998.

De Saint-Exupéry, Antoine. *Flight to Arras*. Translated by Lewis Galantière. New York City: Harcourt, Brace, 1942.

———. *Pilote de guerre*. Paris: Gallimard, 1942.

———.*Wind, Sand and Stars*. Translated by Lewis Galantière. New York: Reynal and Hitchcock, 1939.

Saunders, Frances Stonor. *The Cultural Cold War: The CIA and the World of Arts and Letters*. New York, New Press, 2013. Originally published London: Granta Books, 1999.

Schiff, Stacy. *St. Exupéry: a Biography*. New York: Alfred A. Knopf, 1995.

Sitton, Robert. *Lady in the Dark: Iris Barry and the Art of Film*. New York: Columbia University Press, 2014.

Tommasini, Anthony. *Virgil Thomson, Composer on the Aisle*. New York: W. W. Norton, 1997.

Townsend, Kim. *Sherwood Anderson*. New York: Houghton Mifflin, 1987.

Tuccille, Jerome. *A Portrait of Hemingway as a Young Man*. Boston: Blue Mustang, 2010.

Van Vechten, Carl. *The Splendid Drunken Twenties: Selections from the Daybooks, 1922–30* (Urbana: University of Illinois Press, 2003).

Van Cassel, Elke. *A Cold War Magazine of Causes: A Critical History of the Reporter, 1949–1968*. Nijmegen, The Netherlands: Radboud University, 2007.

Warren, Robert Penn. *All the King's Men*. 2nd ed. New York: Harcourt, Brace, 1996.

Weber, Ronald. *The Midwestern Ascendancy in American Writing*. Bloomington: Indiana University Press, 1992.

Whitton, John Boardman, ed. *Propaganda and the Cold War: A Princeton University Symposium*. Washington, DC: Public Affairs Press, 1963.

Winkler, Allan M. *The Politics of Propaganda: The Office of War Information, 1942–1945*. New Haven, CT: Yale University Press, 1979.

ABBREVIATIONS IN NOTES

Baker EH Letters

Ernest Hemingway: Selected Letters, 1917–1961, edited by Carlos Baker (New York: Charles Scribner's Sons, 1981)

Bancroft Library

The Bancroft Library, University of California, Berkeley, CA, Helen Elizabeth Haines papers, 1849-1934

Butler Library

Butler Rare Books and Manuscripts Library, Columbia University

Firestone Library

Firestone Library, Princeton University.

Hoover

Hoover Institution Archives, Stanford University

Hoover-Puddington

Hoover Institution Archives, Stanford University, Arch Puddington Collection,

JFK Library

JFK Library, Boston, MA

Mudd Library

Princeton Mudd Library, Rascoe-Galantière Letters, 1918–1919; Hamilton Fish Armstrong Papers; PEN America Center Records

Newberry Library

Newberry Library, Chicago

Princeton University	Rare Books and Special Collections (RBSC) Library
Ransom Center	Ransom Center, University of Texas
Reynolds, PY	Michael Reynolds, *Hemingway: The Paris Years* (New York: W. W. Norton, 1989)
University at Buffalo	Libraries, State University of New York at Buffalo
UP Library	University of Pennsylvania, Rare Books and Manuscripts Library
UVA Library, Cab-Gal	University of Virginia Library, Special Collections, James Branch Cabell Collection, Letters from Lewis Galantière, Scrapbook 2, 1886–1919

NOTES

NOTES TO CHAPTER 1

1. Ernest Hemingway had been a celebrity when he returned to New York Harbor from the First World War's Italian front, the first American wounded in that war. A blizzard of shrapnel had sliced into his leg during an evening visit to a front-line foxhole. But the glow of his domestic celebrity was short lived and, back in Chicago, Ernest soon confronted the seemingly insurmountable challenge of becoming a paid fiction writer. He turned to another Chicagoan, Sherwood Anderson for advice. Sherwood's short-story collection Winesburg, Ohio, had recently received critical acclaim and become a popular success, and Hemingway figured that Sherwood was a guy who knew something about how to succeed in the writing business. He asked Sherwood whether he should pursue his writing career in Italy, the place of his most memorable life experiences, but Sherwood suggested that he instead go to Paris, where a community of American authors was doing wonderfully innovative stuff. Sherwood told him of Lewis Galantière, a Chicago friend with an encyclopedic knowledge of English, French, and German literature who, when he had lived in Chicago about three years earlier, had written book reviews for the Chicago newspapers. Sherwood's November 28 letter to Lewis had ensued.

2. Newberry Library, Sherwood Anderson Collection, Galantière 1919–1939, box 20, folder 993

3. Carlos Baker, *Ernest Hemingway Selected Letters 1917-1961* (New York: Charles Scribner's Sons, 1981), 59.

4. Kenneth Schuyler Lynn, *Hemingway* (New York: Fawcett Columbine, 1988), 150.

5. *The New Oxford Book of Literary Anecdotes*, ed. John Gross (Oxford: Oxford University Press, 2008), 279.

6. Lewis Galantière to Burton Rascoe. UP July 9, 1919. Burton Rascoe Collection, 1918–1919, folder 2.

7. Kirk Curnutt, *Coffee with Hemingway* (London: Duncan Baird, 2007), 101.

8. Michael Reynolds, *Hemingway: The Paris Years* (New York: W.W. Norton & Company,1989), 29.

9. Reynolds, PY.

10. Butler Library, Galantière Collection, box 9-001.

11. Butler Library, Galantière Collection, box 9-001.

12. In his October 21, 1923, *New York Tribune* column "A Bookman's Daybook," Burton reported that Lewis had sent him a copy of *Three Stories and Ten Poems* but that he had not yet gotten around to reading it.

13. Baker EH Letters.

14. The full title of the *New York Times Book Review* article was "Paris, the Literary Capital of the United States—French Atmosphere for American Writing." The following are additional excerpts from the December 23, 1923 article:

> *Take, for example, Babbitt, than which there is no more*
> *characteristic American novel. Sinclair Lewis wrote it*
> *abroad. The contrast of the foreign businessman inspired*
> *him, perhaps, to write a more biting satire on the*
> *American businessman than if he had chosen to write about*
> *Babbitt in the midst of Babbitts. . . .*
>
> *Gilbert Seldes recently returned to New York. He had*
> *left his duties as editor of The Dial to go to Paris last*
> *summer to join the little group of serious writers. In a*
> *tiny little court apartment on the Île Saint Louis, where*
> *not even the incessant honking of the Paris taxi horns*
> *could disturb, he completed his book on The Seven Modern*
> *Arts. He lived at the time with Louis Galantière, Paris*
> *literary correspondent of The New York Tribune.*

Side-by-side with the writers of the last generation who
have chosen to do their work in Paris, such as Alvan Sanborn,
Ezra Pound and F. Berkeley Smith, all of whom have married
into French families and are completely Francophile, we have
such strange mushrooms in the literary field as Gertrude
Stein.

15.   The *Chicago Tribune European Edition* began life in July 1917 as the *Chicago Tribune Army Edition*: a four-page tabloid intended for the soldiers of the American Expeditionary Force who then numbered fewer than 20,000. By May 1918, those military ranks had grown to over a million and the newspaper had expanded to a full-coverage publication with a Sunday magazine supplement. Despite its formal name, by 1924 most people referred to it as the "Paris Edition." Its roll of contributors would, over time, include Henry Miller, Ezra Pound, George Seldes, William L. Shirer, Harold Stearns, Gertrude Stein, James Thurber, and Lewis Galantière appearing as Louis Gay.

16.   Butler Library, Galantière Collection, box 8-001.

17.   *The American Mercury*, May 1, 1924.

18.   Hemingway pulled his punch, a little, by identifying Lewis in this ar-

ticle only as "Lewis Gay," a name that would not have been familiar to most American readers of *The Transatlantic Review*.

19. *Transatlantic Review*, April 1924.

20. Baker EH Letters, 114.

21. Pavley and Oukrainsky would later form America's first major touring ballet company.

22. *Shamokin Dispatch*, December 24, 1927.

23. *Hemingwaysparis.blogspot.com* 10508

24. Dorothy and Lewis became engaged in the fall of 1923. Lewis sent an announcement to Burton Rascoe (another Chicago pal who, at the time, was literary editor of the *New York Tribune*) and asked him to publish the news:

    > September 9, 1923
    >
    > Dear Burton,
    >
    > . . . you will see from the attached note—which is for your paper's Society Editor—that I am engaged to be married to Dorothy Butler, a Glencoe girl who has been living here with her mother for the past year & a half. I am very happy about it. If you ever see G. Seldes, he will tell you about Dorothy. We jump off in the Spring— probably in June. Could you come over?
    >
    > Love to you & Hazel, Lewis
    >
    > **UP Library, Burton Rascoe Collection, Burton-Galantière, 1923–1926, folder 4**

    Lewis also wrote to Sherwood Anderson with the news:

    > I'll tell you first of all that I am to be married—yes! You old slob! Married myself in June, to an American girl whose name is Dorothy Butler and who has everything I

*want. We became engaged in November and we are awaiting
the arrival of her two brothers before jumping off . . .*

*I am—we are, I must learn to say now—we are planning to
live permanently in Paris. I have a decent job here—oh!
Nothing wonderful—with enough time off to do a little
journalism on the side, and it may be that when I am
married and settled in a home, with a heap of petty
material worries out of the way, I shall be able to try
my hand at writing something more than 1500 words long -
something that will stand up on its own feet.*

**Newberry Library, Sherwood Anderson Collection,
Galantière 1919–1939, box 20, folder 993**

25. The following is the full text of Dorothy's letter to Hadley:

May 23, 1924

Dear Hadley,

*I am about to explode in righteous indignation.—The
worm has turned—Lewis has put me in the position of the
boobish kid who stays to face the music while the rest
run away. Once too often—I think he needs a lesson in
having the courage to stick to his convictions, or else
to give them up openly,—change his mind, and take a
different tack.*

*You and Ernest have said so many times, plaintively to
Mama [Dorothy's mother], that Lewis was "so different"
since he has been in love with me,—the inference being
that I was the cause of the break in the friendship—
Perhaps I am handing myself an orchid, and if you
have any reason to dispute me, do so by all means, but
it seems to me I've been the only person who's been
perfectly square and open and above board.*

*In the first place, Lewis told me last winter (Great
Scott—a year ago last winter) that you were no friend of
mine—He said "Hadley tried to talk about you to me when
you were away. Said you were selfish and I don't know
what else she would have said if I hadn't shut her up."
Naturally that made me furious—I wanted to have things*

out with you and not keep on piling up resentment, but Lewis persuaded me not to, and that perhaps it wouldn't work—

Besides I've always been decent about your friendship with Mama. I didn't want to mess that up—I've never told her about our quarrel with you specifically, and she's always regretting our split—To return to the fray—when the baby was coming I wanted sincerely to be nice to you, and was. Before we announced our engagement and after the baby came, I said to Lewis "I'm going to write Hadley." He said "Oh, I wouldn't." and more to that effect.

Then when you came back, after being in correspondence with Mama, you didn't even let her know your address, which hurt her very much—He ran into you by accident at Sylvia Beach's—Lewis says nothing was said to him about your address, and I know nothing came to my ears except that you lived over or under or in a sawmill.

Last Saturday after Mama had been to see your sweet baby, she again tried the little peace-maker—said "Why don't you two go around?" I looked at Lewis who burst out "Not on your life—we won't go near them—fine friends they've been to us!"

Now I guess we're up to date, except that Lewis went up there without me, which made me furious enough to write this—it puts me in such a false position to be the only one not under the shadow of the olive branch—

I assure you Hadley. I have never been selfish about Lewis's friendships, and I'm always sincere in my own.

I'm awfully sorry for the whole coil. (["Coil"] What have I been reading?!) But Lewis has been cowardly, as I think most people are, about saying one thing behind your back, and acting another—to say nothing of you and Ernest—and I just wanted to tell you that I have been consistent, and that, in spite of appearances, I have nothing to do with snatching Lewis's friendship away from you.

He would sign this too if he were here—I told him I was going to write it.

Sincerely,

Dorothy

I must in justice say that Lewis Galantière ("The Critic," as Ernest calls him) is such a sincere admirer of Ernest's work that he welcomed an opportunity to hearing more of it.

JFK Library, Hemingway Collection.

26. Possibly a psychiatrist.

27. Newberry Library, Malcolm Cowley Papers, box 31 folder 643.

28. Butler Library, Galantière Collection, box 5.

29. *Chicago Tribune European Edition*, "The Social World," June 15, 1924, 6:

> *An American wedding of interest was solemnized in the private salons of the Hotel Ritz yesterday afternoon, when Miss Dorothy Butler, daughter of Mrs. Alice Carter Butler of Chicago, became the bride of Mr. Lewis Galantière, of Paris.*
>
> *The service, which was a very impressive one, was conducted by Mr. Horace J. Bridget, leader of the Chicago Ethical Society, who came from London to officiate. The bride wore a becoming robe de style of white faille trimmed with white camellias, and carried a shower bouquet of the same flower. She was attended by Miss Eileen Delaney, who came from Holyoke, Massachusetts specially for the wedding. Mrs. Butler was dressed in pale gray and carried a bouquet of orchids. Mr. George H. Butler, brother of the bride, who arrived from America last week, acted as best man.*
>
> *A reception and dance followed which was attended by, among others, Mr. Eugene K. Butler, younger brother of the bride, M. René Arnaud, Mr. and Mrs. William Aspenwall Bradley, M. Jean Cocteau, M. and Mme. Pierre Duchartre, Miss Alice Hall, Mrs. Lorna Lindley, Mr. and Mrs. Gerald Murphy, Miss Jean Murray, M. and Mme. Jean Priox, Miss Barbara Parrolt, Mr. Stephan Parrolt, Mr. J. Kinglsey*

Rooker, Mr. Gilbert Seldes, Mr. Donald Ogden Stewart, M. and Mme. Pierre Vasseur and Mr. and Mrs. Victor Llona.

The civil service took place on Thursday at the mairie [town hall] of the seventeenth arrondissement and was witnessed by Miss Alice Hall and Mr. Gilbert Seldes. The young couple are leaving last night on a wedding trip and will be at home upon their return at 24 Quai d'Orleans.

30. Dorothy Butler and George H. Butler. *A Life in Armor: Extracts from the Notebooks and Letters of Alice Carter Butler* (Chicago: Pascal Covici, 1925).

31. Ibid.

32. Reynolds, PY, 249.

33. Baker EH Letters, 137. "Boid" was one of several nicknames that Hemingway gave Bill Smith.

34. Stacy Schiff, *A Biography of St. Exupéry* (New York: Alfred A. Knopf, 1995), 122.

35. A.E. Hotchner, *Hemingway in Love: His Own Story* (New York: St. Martin's Press, 2015) 70.

36. Ibid. 86.

37. Ibid. 86.

38. A. E. Hotchner, *Daily Mail*, October 22, 2015.

39. Ernest Hemingway, *A Moveable Feast* (New York: Hemingway Copyright Owners, 2009) various.

40. An excerpt from Arthur Rimbaud's poem, *Chanson de la plus haute tour* that translates roughly as "By being too sensitive I have wasted my life."

41. *The New York Times Book Review*, May 10, 1964, Section 7, page 1.

42. Butler Library, Galantière Collection, box 2.

NOTES TO CHAPTER 2

43. Over the next twenty years, Joseph and Cecilia occupied successive tenements on Halsted Street, then on Forquer Street, and then on South Sangamon Street.

44. The Galantière surname, although of French origin, identified Prussian Jews in the leather crafts, including bookbinding. Book binding entailed stitching and gluing paper pages within leather-bound cardboard covers and embossing the covers and spines with text and filigrees in gold leaf.

45. *Los Angeles Herald*, May 2, 1910.

46. In special cases, the dean of the law school, Frank Monroe Porter, had the authority to admit as a "special student" an applicant who had not met the required educational qualifications, provided they were met by the start of the student's junior year.

47. *The Music Student 2*, February 1916.

48. Other exam questions included the following:

    Who wrote the following? Select fifteen and characterize as play, poem, novel, etc.

Laocoön	Tristram Shandy
Bible in Spain	Stones of Venice
Playboy of the Western World	The Princess
Imitation of Christ	Water Babies
Spirit of Youth and the City Streets	Ode to a Grecian Urn [sic]

The Sunken Bell	*Your United States*
Childe Harold	*Peer Gynt*
Rise of the Dutch Republic	*Joseph Vance*
Consuelo	*Making of an American*
Essays of Elia	*Winning of the West*
Marius the Epicurean	*Cloister and the Hearth*
The Decameron	*War and Peace*

Discuss one of the following subjects. Write two pages or more.

The Italian Renaissance

The Protestant Reformation in England

The Holy Roman Empire

49. In the first decade of the 1900s, the University of Chicago's Laboratory School (a primary and secondary school) incorporated a year's attendance at the university and, if Lewis had attended the laboratory school, it could have included that university experience. Weighing in favor of that possibility was that the laboratory school offered courses in French. Weighing against that possibility was that Lewis would have attended the university courses when younger than fourteen, his age in the year that the family had moved to Los Angeles.

50. Helen Haines served on the editorial staffs of *The Library Journal, Publishers Weekly,* and *The American Catalogue* but by 1908 had resigned due to poor health. At the same time, Haines resigned as a vice president of the American Library Association and moved with two of her sisters to Pasadena. There, by 1914, Helen's health had improved sufficiently to allow her to teach at the library school.

51.　In his biography, *Before I Forget*, Burton described the allure of Kroch's:

> ...This was the small bookshop operated on the south side
> of Monroe Street between Wabash and Michigan avenues by
> A. Kroch... In those days, in 1912 and until sometime
> after the war, Kroch's bookshop was an intimate little
> store specializing in the importation of foreign art
> prints and books in foreign languages...

> "Papa" Kroch, as all his intimates were later to call
> him, had and has excellent taste in literature...He was
> the despair of book salesmen from the Eastern publishing
> houses who could not understand why a man in the retail
> book business would not handle novels which were in large
> and persistent demand, and, moreover, who chose to order
> books out of their samples which they had had little luck
> with elsewhere. The answer is that "Papa" Kroch has grown
> rich and influential and has had a marked influence upon
> the taste of his time, whereas many of the publishing
> houses which then battened briefly upon best sellers have
> long since gone out of business and the books of some of
> their best sellers have been entirely forgotten.

52.　In the same biography, Rascoe spoke of his friendship with Lewis:

> In Kroch's bookshop were three salesmen, Lewis
> Galantière, Benjamin Silbermann and A. van Ameyden Van
> Duym, all linguists, all keenly interested in the best
> literature of the day...Kroch and his salesmen were not
> mere salesmen: they read the books they sold and could
> talk intelligently about them; each regarded himself
> as an implement in the inculcating of cultivated taste
> among the book buyers of America, and the taste among
> the book buyers at the time, as attested by the lists
> of best sellers, was limited and provincial. Kroch and
> his salesmen were instrumental, in Chicago, at least, in
> arousing curiosity over general ideas, the development
> of literature and art in England, Ireland and on the
> European continent, and in the translations from the
> literature of contemporary Europe which the publishers,

> *Huebsch, Knopf and the young firm of Boni & Liveright, were trying to introduce to the American public.*
>
> *My closest friend in the shop was Lewis Galantière. He and I lunched together two or three times a week at the nearby Tip-Top Inn on the top floor of the Pullman Building. Our luncheons together were singular in that often neither one of us said anything throughout the meal: we each sat with some European book or magazine, perhaps the Mercure de France, the Revue de Deux Mondes, or the Nouvelle Revue Française (with which a group of new and talented Frenchmen were doing such exciting things). We were in agreement over so many things that we rarely had any arguments: our conversation was, when it took place, rather to give each other items of intellectual information or to call one another's attention to stimulating things to read.*

53. Here is a sample of that sparring, excerpted from an April 18, 1916, letter from Burton to Lewis:

> *Dear Lewis,*
>
> *Damn you! You've got my dander up and am going to play an Apollo to your Marsyas. sMore about Stevenson, which I must work into the article: ...*
>
> *Cabell, I tell you, is his equal in prose style and superior to him in intelligence and creative ability...*
> *Yours, Burton*

UP Library, Burton Rascoe - Galantière letters, undated

54. Sherwood Anderson, *Memoirs* (New York: Harcourt, Brace, 1942).

55. Padraic Colum, Editor; Margaret Freeman Cabell, Editor, *Between Friends: Letters of James Branch Cabell and others* (New York: Literary Licensing, LLC, 2011), 14.

56. The following are excerpts from the Galantière-Rascoe-Cabell correspondence:

Burton Rascoe sent Cabell a copy of his appraisal of the author's works with this cover letter:

December 31, 1917

My dear Mr. Cabell:

I am enclosing herewith a review which very feebly records my reactions to your wholly delightful books...

The impression [your books]...have produced upon me constrains me to salute you as the highest creative genius (or talents, if you will) and the most keenly discerning intelligence now producing American literature.

UP Library, Cab-Ras

Lewis sent this note with a copy of the same review:

January 6, 1918

My dear Mr. Cabell,

... I enclose also a more significant notice of your work. This was written by my very good friend, Burton Rascoe. He is, I verily believe, the greatest and, I might almost say, the most intelligent admirer you have...Since I had the pleasure of first quoting to him from The Cream of the Jest, I feel quite proud to have brought you, in spirit, together...

If you will write him a note thanking him for the review, I am sure that he will be immensely pleased.

UVA Library, Cab-Gal.

Lewis to Cabell, February 3, 1918

My dear Mr. Cabell,

... Truly, I am astonished at the ill-success in the past of your books. Doubtless in distinct contradiction to what has gone before, my experience with your books has regenerated my faith in American readers...So the good work progresses. One request: that you make no mention of thanks in any letter to me. Without any idea *of Chauvinism, I am trying to do 'my bit' for American letters.*

UVA Library, Cab-Gal.

Here, Cabell's dedication in *The Lineage of Lichfield*

The Epistle Dedicatory

To Lewis Galantière

You have herewith the book which you once desired me to make, in just the utterly unreadable form which you suggested. Indeed, I can now see that in no less devastating manner could I well dispose of the questions you then asked, a bit sceptically, as to "the connecting theme" of my books in gross...

... it was your suggestion, some while ago, that I compile and put in order such a selection as would make plain the family connection...

... the quite obvious connection is the fact that they constitute a largish family tree, which I herewith present for your confusion.

Lineage of Litchfield (New York: Robert M. McBride, 1922).

Lewis's letter to Cabell, May 9, 1922

I have to thank you for giving me, in too-generous measure as judged by my dessert, exactly what I asked of you. The book is a very personal one, as touches yourself, and thus it is one which occupies a very special place in my affection.

UVA Library, Cab-Gal.

57. Lewis's December 15 piece in the *Chicago Examiner* appeared under the banner headline "H'M!—LET'S SEE!—SAYS LEWIS Galantière":

Reviewing is a perilous business and ruins man's native humility. Reviewers are, if you approach their raison d'etre in a spirit more serious than it deserves, a race of upstarts. Reviews are pernicious, and any man who takes his cue from a review without having first himself

examined the book under discussion is a heedless donkey
and an incompetent book-buyer.

Look at it squarely. By what right do I or does any
other scribbler of ephemera tell you, an intelligent
reader of excellent literature, what you ought or ought
not to read? Knowledge? Experience? Judgment? Ability
to estimate? Oh, I say! Did you ever know a reviewer,
or talk to one? And did you ever meet a cheekier, more
cocksure, irritating and shallow dispenser of platitudes
in your life than a professional reviewer, or than I am,
if you happen to know me? The one line of value in all
that I write is here: Never read a review for information
or instruction. Read it as literature—of a sort—and if
the writer doesn't amuse you, if his style, apart from
its substance, cannot hold you, read instead the book he
warns you against. Voilà.

58. *Publishers Weekly* 93, part 1, March 2, 1918.

59. Lewis framed the denouement as favorably as he could in a March 9,
     1918, letter to Burton Rascoe:

> *Dear Burton:*
>
> *... Burton, I've got something else on my mind that I*
> *wanted to tell you before you left for the East but I*
> *didn't know how it would affect you on your trip. I*
> *wanted very much too, to wait until you got back before*
> *I left, but I couldn't afford the money it cost me to*
> *live in Chicago. Sort of to ease myself, I told Roy Goble*
> *and Sherwood of this, and it hurt me that I wasn't able*
> *to tell it to you. You may hear of it some time and I'd*
> *rather you hear it from me than another.*
>
> *It's about my affair with Kroch. You know, I have been*
> *wanting to leave him for some time, and there was at the*
> *bottom of it a prime cause which neither he nor anyone*
> *else knew of. When we moved out of Michigan Avenue and*
> *put in a totally different stock of books somebody had*
> *to know fairly accurately what was in those books. It*
> *devolved upon me to read them or to skim through, at*

*least, most everything that was sold in the Shop. I used
to take the books to luncheon and look them through, and
I took a great many of them home to read on the train
and of an evening. A certain percentage of those books,
though from their very nature not a great percentage,
were very interesting to me, and I found, commencing last
Autumn, that it was a very simple matter to leave a book
at home that I had taken out, figuratively, for review.
By the last month they had run into a matter of nearly
a hundred dollars, and I was becoming concerned for my
kleptomania.*

*If Kroch had been a different kind of man I should've
been able to quit but it gave me a malicious satisfaction
to take his property; a satisfaction I could not curb...
[But when] we had a row again, I quit. Well, it bothered
me that I could neither return these books nor make
restitution, so I wrote Kroch a letter—damned fool that I
was!—Telling him exactly what I had done, and enclosing a
list of such books as I had taken...I don't know how far
Kroch will go, particularly since he has that foolish,
foolish letter from me...If he ever mentions the case to
you tell him to show you the letter or else don't listen
to him. It's simple enough for any man to say that he had
a letter of confession, and at the same time, though we
have a letter, have one of totally different nature.*

*Well, that thing's clumsily unloaded. Sherwood and Roy
were great about it. Sherwood laughed...They both cheered
me up a lot...My love to Hazel and to the children, and
believe me altogether the same, Lewis.*

**UP Library, Burton Rascoe Collection, Burton-Galantière,
1923-1926, folder 4 0**

60. Lewis Galantière to Burton Rascoe, March 9, 1918, UP Library, Burton Rascoe Collection, Rascoe-Galantière, 1918–1919, folder 2.

61. A presumption of eugenics was that members of the Anglo-Saxon race possessed "good blood," meaning superior genes to those of other races. Advertisements of the time adopted the theme.

Chicago Tribune, Paris Edition, April 20, 1924

62. Lewis Galantière to Burton Roscoe, July 15, 1918, UP Library, Burton Rascoe Collection, Galantière Box "Undated & Incomplete."

63. Ibid.

64. In the 1900 census, Joseph reported that he was born in 1868 and Cecilia in 1869. In the 1910 census, he changed the years to 1871 and 1872.

65. Lewis Galantière to Burton Rascoe, January 9, 1919. UP Library, Burton Rascoe Collection, Rascoe-Galantière, 1918–1919, folder 2.

66. Excerpts from letters to Burton Rascoe:

    March 1, 1919

    ... The Saturday paper contained your screed about Sonnica la cortesana. I was very much interested, for I had not known of the translation and just finished the

original after coming back to camp from the north. I
found the book among my father's fiction.

UP Library, Burton Rascoe Collection, Rascoe-Galantière
1918-1919, folder 2

March 28, 1919

I am reading a quasi-college course: Aristotle and
Spenser, Homer and Milton, Worrying through Theocritus in
a little Gk-Latin edition that was my father's.

Ibid.

April 7, 1919

...Saturday, I found ...an edition of Longinus in Greek
& Latin, and a Callimachus in Greek. With the aid of
lexicons and English translations, and marginal notes in
my father's hand, I am reading Sophocles in Greek, and
taking a shy at the Iliad in a little Chiswick (2 vol)
edition my father had....

Ibid.

The largest single cache of Lewis's papers are maintained in Columbia University's Butler Rare Books and Manuscripts Library. Among the thousands of pages of documents, the photographs, and the several books in that repository, and among the books that Lewis gave to New York's Century Association of which he was a member, there is not a letter, card, photograph or other remembrance of Lewis's parents, his brother, or his sister. Nor are there the books, purportedly annotated by Joseph Galantière, to which Lewis had alluded. According to surviving family members and persons familiar with the donation of the papers to the university, the absence of these things was not due to their having been removed prior to donation, but because they had not existed.

NOTES TO CHAPTER 3

67. A presidential commission placed the management of the country's thirty-two military camp libraries in the hands of the American Library Association's "War Service," and the War Service enlisted public libraries nationwide to manage and fund the camp libraries. The Library Association's general director, Herbert Putnam, also served as the Librarian of Congress.

68. Lewis again lamented his lack of a career in a September 27, 1919, letter to Burton Rascoe:

> The Army has chosen an individual named L L Dickerson to direct library war work in peace time, and I have heard from two excellent sources that I am to be offered something or other, I have no idea what, when the personnel is decided upon...
>
> ... My library war work has been unimportant, though commended by a host of library people, and I don't doubt I could get a decent library job in civil life: but I prize only, of my Service experience, the re-making of the man...
>
> ... People rejoice when they are able to trip me up on the subject of Syrian troglodytism or mathematics: so much do they think I know. In Los Angeles, [architect] Harold Chambers's stenographer announces (from hearsay) "your learned friend is outside." And what does it amount to. Vanity and curiosity in equal measure prompted me to delve into a thousand mysteries and to be master of none. I don't know English literature as I should, nor yet French, or Spanish, or Russian, or Italian. Ficke knows more of Japanese than I do: Pound more of Chinese.
>
> **UP Library, Rascoe Collection, Rascoe-Galantière, 1923–1926, folder 4.**

69. UP Library, Rascoe Collection, Rascoe-Galantière, folder 2.

70. Newberry Library, Sherwood Anderson Papers, Galantière correspondence 1919–1939, box 20, folder 993.

71. For example, in June 1919, H. L. Mencken described Anderson's *Winesburg, Ohio* as groundbreaking:

> Here [is] a new order of short story...It is so vivid,
> so full of insight, so shiningly life-like and glowing,
> that the book is lifted into a category all its own.—"The
> Smart Set," August 1919

72. Excerpt from a December 17, 1919, letter from Lewis to Burton Rascoe:

> I ran into [Harold] Stearns [a contributing editor to
> "The Dial"] the other day...He is to come here to dinner
> tonight. I intend to get some information about the
> Dial from him...It seems to me I ought to be able to
> run a foreign department, say, worthy of two or three
> pages that would be interesting. I should like to
> treat of literature, of course, but not of that alone:
> of illustration and illustrated books; of bookmakers,
> binders, publishers, periodicals, and most things
> culture-literary from abroad. Mencken believes this day
> is one for success in translations because of the general
> paucity of English & American stuff. I think so too,
> and I should like to do something with it. The "London
> Letter" and the "Paris Letter" type of thing seems too
> superficial, too desultory and too thin for any worth. A
> column more meaty, such as I am dreaming of, ought to
> have a good response in many directions.
>
> **Galantière to Rascoe, June 23, 1919, UP Library, Rascoe
> Collection, Rascoe-Galantière, 1918–1919, folder 2.**

73. Lewis wrote this in a January 3, 1920, letter to Burton:

> Our America [Waldo Frank's assessment of the postwar
> American writers and artists and their works] annoyed
> me with its excessive Jewishness, and its cracked
> interpretation of American history. I hold that a great

> *body of men wrote our Constitution, not a collection of*
> *second-rate economists, and that they were animated by*
> *high purpose. With the flaws of the Constitution I have*
> *no concern, but I don't believe the spirit of these men*
> *has ever been equaled in history; not by the Barons*
> *at Runnymede or anywhere else. These birds, Stearns*
> *& Frank & Mencken, have set me to reading serious*
> *American history. I am now on volume 3 of Rhodes.* [James
> Ford Rhodes wrote about the American Civil War and
> Reconstruction.]

74. Among the guest lecturers were Dean Wigmore of Northwestern University and John Erskine of Columbia University.

75. The ICC initially consisted of the five allied nations: the United States, Great Britain, France, Italy, and Belgium.

76. Harry Sinclair Lewis and Harrison Smith, eds., *From Main Street to Stockholm: Letters of Sinclair Lewis, 1919–1930* (New York: Harcourt, Brace, 1952), item 48, p. 57.

77. Galantière to Rascoe, December 26, 1920, UP Library, Burton Rascoe Collection, Galantière Box "Undated & Incomplete."

78. There are references to a Ms. Helene Edel in Lewis's letters, but they are ambiguous as to the relationship.

79. Germany had capitulated while still largely undamaged by war. France and the low countries were in need of extensive reconstruction, which, it was thought, would be paid for from reparations promised by Germany under the terms of the Treaty of Versailles, and from the forfeiture to France of important German patents and natural resources.

80. Lewis described some of his ICC assignments in a letter to Burton Rascoe:

> *October 20, 1921*
>
> *The other day I was delivered of 8000 words on commercial*
> *arbitration which are now signed by Owen Young of the*
> *Gen. Electric Company and I am now working up several*
> *3500–4000 word tracts on the Wiesbaden Agreement*
> [the agreement set out some of Germany's World War I
> reparations obligations to France, and that some Allied
> countries saw as giving France unfair preferences], *Upper*
> *Silesia, and International Bills of Lading.*
>
> **UP Library, Burton Rascoe Collection, Rascoe-Galantière**
> **1920–1922, folder 3.**

81. A *Normalien* is a student or former student of the highly selective teacher training college the Normal School of Technical Education in Paris.

82. From "France after the First World War," Lewis's contribution to *Appreciations of Frederick Paul Keppel*. New York: Columbia University Press, 1951.

83. This was from the account given to the author by the eighty-five-year-old Michel Arnaud during their August 15, 2015, lunch in Paris.

84. From a February 3, 1921, letter from Lewis to Sherwood Anderson:

> *Madame Gay is a small, homely person with short legs, a*
> *big nose, a lisping, fluent and earnest speech, who is, I*
> *should say, in her 30s. But if knowledge of literature*
> *and critical feeling for it count; if you want of*
> *your translator whole-sound appreciation, accurate,*
> *instinctive insight into your meaning and honest, deep*
> *enthusiasm for your work, you have these in Madame Gay.*
> *I was greatly impressed with her intelligent conception*
> *of your stories, with her scrupulous desire to turn*
> *out only a first-rate rendering and with her courageous*
> *appreciation of the difficulty she has to surmount.*
>
> **Newberry Library, Sherwood Anderson Collection,**
> **Galantière 1919–1939, box 20, folder 993**

85. Lewis wrote to Burton about Sherwood's visit:

> Sherwood is here, with Tennessee & Paul Rosenfeld. He
> is very happy and touched & bewildered by the beauty
> of Paris. "T" has been suffering from a bad cold these
> couple of days past; I hope to take them into the country
> for the weekend. Rosenfeld, a moon faced, Jewish type,
> very cultivated, rather dainty of manner, a charming
> fellow, strikes me very favorably...Last night we took in
> (T staying in bed) La Nuit des Rois at Copeau's theatre
> and then had a drink with Copeau.

> **UP Library, Burton Rascoe Collection, Rascoe-Galantière
> 1920-1922, folder 3.**

86. Kim Townsend, *Sherwood Anderson* (New York: Houghton Mifflin, 1987), 178.

87. Gertrude Stein later wrote about Anderson's visit, referring to herself in the third-person voice of *The Autobiography of Alice B. Toklas*:

> Gertrude Stein was moved and pleased as she has very
> rarely been. Gertrude Stein was in those days a little
> bitter, all her unpublished manuscripts, and no hope of
> publication or serious recognition. Sherwood Anderson
> came and quite simply and directly as is his way told her
> what he thought of her work and what it had meant to him
> in his development...Gertrude Stein and Sherwood Anderson
> have always been the best of friends, but I do not
> believe even he realizes how much his visit meant to her.

> **Gertrude Stein, *The Autobiography of Alice B. Toklas*
> (reprint, New York: Vintage, 1990).**

88. UP Library, Burton Rascoe Collection, Rascoe-Galantière 1920–1922, folder 3.

89. Ibid. Épaté is French for "impress."

90. Firestone Library, Sylvia Beach letters, box 19, folder 38.

91. Lewis and Sinclair Lewis met in Washington, DC, during the fall of

1920, when Sinclair's book *Main Street* first attained best-seller status. Sinclair wrote to his publisher, Alfred Harcourt, that Lewis had insisted that the book be translated into French, and Sinclair had asked Lewis's help to make that happen. Here is the relevant excerpt from Sinclair Lewis's November 26, 1920, letter to Harcourt:

> Lewis Galantière, an intelligent chap I know here in Washington, friend to Sherwood Anderson, Guy Holt, Burton Rascoe, et. al., is going to France, to be stationed there on a business mission. He insists that Main Street must be translated into French. He seems to know something of French publishers and of the proper approach. He is a fine lad and I have given him a card to Spingarn so that he may talk over this with him. [Joel Elias Spingarn, a literary critic and professor of comparative literature at Columbia University]
>
> Corking, 17,609 [copies of his book sold] already. We'll get that 109,009.
>
> Thaznuff
>
> SL
>
> **Lewis and Smith, From Main Street to Stockholm: Letters Of Sinclair Lewis, 1919-1930. Online courtesy of the Sinclair Lewis Estate.**

92. UP Library, Burton Rascoe Collection, Rascoe-Galantière 1920–1922, folder 3.

93. The first publication of *Ulysses* was to have been a run of 750 copies on Joyce's birthday, February 2, 1922. But due to problems with the cover, the printer, Darantiere, released only two copies. One went to Joyce's wife and the other to Lewis. Joyce did not inscribe later copies until February 13. Of those the first went to Harriet Weaver, the second to Sylvia Beach, and the third to Margaret Anderson.

94. Letter from Lewis to Burton Rascoe:

March 25, 1926

Dear Burton:

*... Joyce won't stand for the idea of a book of
conversations. Says he has nothing to say; can't talk
anyway; doesn't know why people ask him out to dinner,
since he is so poor a conversationalist; etc, etc.
Offered, however, to give me all the help I might need
in writing either an article or a hook about Ulysses.
Suggested that I work up a series of lectures on Ulysses,
with his collaboration. I don't know about the lecture
idea. Strikes me I wouldn't be much of a lecturer—also,
there wouldn't be much in it. Also, how attractive would
another book about a book—even if the book is Ulysses—
be to the reading public. I just had another look at
Gorman's book. It is pretty superficial and abominably
written, but good enough for people who need help in
reading Joyce...Sylvia Beach wants me to write a sort of
guide to Ulysses, or "How to read U." I don't. Anyway,
I have been re-reading Ulysses, and find it rich enough
to do any amount of writing about it. Joyce sang me a
parody of John MacCormack's "Man dear, did ye never hear
o pretty Molly Brannigan."...He also told me of a dream
he had about Molly, Bloom, and a crowd of people on
the edge of a field in a mountainside in Ireland...Joyce
works every day from nine in the morning to seven in the
evening, but his eyes are so bad that he works at a very
low rate of speed. He promised that when he had finished
the section of the new book he was now writing, he would
phone me to come up and hear it read. He tells me that
hundreds of legends are in circulation about him: he is
dead, he is in a madhouse, he goes into the Seine with
his seven children for a swim every morning that god
sends into the world, rain or shine, warm or cold, etc.
etc. We might some day try to collect all these.*

**UP Library, Burton Rascoe Collection, Rascoe-Galantière
1923–1926, folder 4.**

A month later, Joyce wrote to Harriet Weaver, suggesting that the
idea still seemed possible:

> *I am to read [from Finnegans Wake]...to a small group, this time including a young American—Galantière—who is preparing a course of lectures of Ulysses.*
>
> **James Joyce Letters, ed. Richard Ellman (New York: Viking, 1966), 3:140.**

95. UP Library, Burton Rascoe Collection, Rascoe-Galantière 1920–1922, folder 3.

96. Here is the reference to Madam Lecompte's *Au Rendez-vous des Mariniers* that appears in *The Sun Also Rises:*

> We ate dinner at Madame Lecomte's restaurant on the far side of the island. It was crowded with Americans and we had to stand up and wait for a place. Some one had put it in the American Women's Club list as a quaint restaurant on the Paris quais as yet untouched by Americans, so we had to wait forty-five minutes for a table. Bill had eaten at the restaurant in 1918, right after the armistice, and Madame Lecomte made a great fuss over seeing him.
>
> **Ernest Hemingway, *The Sun Also Rises* (New York: Simon & Schuster, 2014) 62.**

Few signs of the restaurant remain, but one element still visible is the sill under the second floor window.

97. UP Library, Burton Rascoe Collection, Rascoe-Galantière 1920–1922, folder 3.

98. Newberry Library, Sherwood Anderson Collection, Galantière 1919–1939, box 20, folder 993

99. For Lewis, Paris was a place to live and work. For Harold Stearns and Sinclair Lewis, it was a place to act-out with abandon. Here is how Stearns described it:

> I rang up Lewis Galantière, and asked him to come to my aid and help me pilot Sinclair [Lewis] around—which he graciously did. It was as hectic a five days and nights as I have ever put in; Sinclair was full of vitality. He wanted to go everywhere at once, to see everything, to visit every bar, explore the "Quarter"—and we cut quite a dash in Montparnasse those few nights, too.
>
> And thus, what had begun as a simple weekend jaunt from London over to Paris and France ended in fact in my staying on in Paris over 250 weekends, that is to say, for five years.
>
> **Harold Stearns, *The Street I Know: The Autobiography of the Last of the Bohemians* (Lanham, MD: Rowman & Littlefield, 2014), 206.**

Lewis gave his perspective of that week, in an August 17, 1921, letter to Burton Rascoe:

> I have just got rid of Harold Stearns after seven days of continued eating drinking and running about. He went down to Sinclair Lewis's house in Kent for a cup of tea. The two decided suddenly to come to Paris, and wired me to meet them last Thursday (this is Wednesday). Sinclair went home Sunday. I have been, as I say, on a continued bat, and the liquor I've drunk has curdled in my gut and corroded the lining of my stomach. Harold is nothing but a rubber hose. He drank twice what I did—three times as much!—But it had no effect on him whatever. Every night he was awake until three, when he wasn't spending the

*night in the arms of a broad. Red Lewis was funny as
hell, most so when he was tight. One evening he thought
a nice girl, a friend of mine, had insulted him—and you
should have seen the dignified air Main Street can assume.
He was beastly to the poor girl; talked about himself as
"personage" who had "condescended" to speak to a stranger,
etc., etc...Very, very funny, except that the girl was
a friend of mine. And when I butted in he said in a tone
half menace, half solemnity "Lewis, please don't make
me lose an old friend, as I have just lost a new one!" I
howled with glee, and he got sore as hell. Harold kept
muttering under his breath (while Sinclair continued to
insult the poor woman) "The God damn fool! Jesus! Why
doesn't he shut up. Hey waiter ("Monsieur," he called
him), another Grand Marnier. Christ! Lewis (to me): Let's
get out & go where he ain't.".. .Well. The damned thing
turned day into night & night into day. I spent 1000
francs on booze, taxis & women (also food. Good food)
and let my office go to thunder. Autrement dit, I play
the American all over. Sinclair has gone back to England,
firmly convinced that he knows France, Paris, the French,
the Parisians, the language, the American in Paris...
God! He's full of theories—the theories of a Rotary club
member. But he's a damn nice guy, a little nervous with
wonder at the success of his book, and probably worried
as to how best to save & spend at the same time the
money he's made. Harold is silent & slovenly as usual but
he's a white man. He has, intellectually, an enviable
foundation, I think, but his mind moves so damned slowly,
it exasperates me. He wants to sit & drink, never to sit
& drink & talk, and I have no affection for a drinking
sphinx. However, I got a few words out of him one evening
& really enjoyed. He thinks of living here this winter,
and if I find an apartment I shall take him in. He's
silent, and that's a virtue. Besides, I like him.*

**UP Library, Burton Rascoe Collection, Rascoe-Galantière
1920–1922, folder 3.**

Lewis let Stearns stay with him in his apartment, and gave him money when the money that Sinclair Lewis had "loaned" him ran out. Stearns acknowledged as much:

> ...Sinclair's money helped the first few weeks; Lewis Galantière was very nice, too; the newspaper boys, especially Sam Dashiel and dear old Roscoe Ashworth, were always buying me a meal, and, as they would say almost with embarrassment, "slipping" me a few francs now and then.

Harold Stearns, *The Street I Know: The Autobiography of the Last of the Bohemians* (Lanham, MD: Rowman & Littlefield, 2014), 207.

But Lewis soon ran out of patience:

> He is really an impossibly careless, sloppy, and unpresentable person with a character so feeble that he takes the money I give him for food & buys booze & ladies,—and then tells me childish lies which I pretend to believe. Damn him! I shall, because of him, be losing my conviction that human frailty is an amusing and not a serious spectacle.

Lewis Galantière to Burton Rascoe, October 20, 1921, UP Library, Burton Rascoe Collection, Rascoe-Galantière 1920–1922, folder 3.

> ...he has succeeded in disgusting me completely. He is a man quite without character and thought. I don't mind losing the money I have loaned him, (Heaven knows I have never considered it a loan.) I don't like my friends to be as completely without moral fibre as he is. The other day I gave him a job, only so that he might have the three hundred francs which it would bring him. He promised to write the stuff I wanted in five days; it is now nearly three weeks, and he has turned half of it in to me and as a result of his procrastination, I have been catching hell from the boss. The boss quotes to me this brutal advice of a business man: "Never have anything to do with an unlucky man."

> Lewis Galantière to Sherwood Anderson, November 11,
> 1921, Newberry Library, Sherwood Anderson Collection,
> Galantière 1919–1939, box 20, folder 993.

And two weeks later:

> *If I have not said so before, I should say now that I*
> *am completely hep to Mr. Stearns. I suffer the supplice*
> *about once a week of buying him lunch and for the sake of*
> *appearances, but I assure you that I had rather give him*
> *the 20 francs and be without his depressing company.*
>
> Lewis Galantière to Sherwood Anderson, November 11, 1921,
> UP Library, Burton Rascoe Collection, Rascoe-Galantière
> 1920–1922, folder 3.

100. Pierre Mac Orlan was a novelist and songwriter. The brothers Tharaud (Jean and Jérôme Tharaud), Jean Giraudoux, Remy de Gourmont, and René Maran were all writers. Lewis's gratuitous bigotry was de rigueur among "sophisticates" during most of his life.

101. In his first effort, Lewis critiqued a recent work by Comte de Gobineau, *L'Abbaye de Typhaines* that started out dry, academic, and sober, but it was the setup for his satire of Germans, whose admiration of Gobineau was, in Lewis's opinion, pretentious.

102. Ernest Boyd was a literary critic, writer, and translator.

103. UP Library, Burton Rascoe Collection, Rascoe-Galantière 1920–1922, folder 3.

104. Ibid.

105. Ibid.

106. Ibid.

107. The following are excerpts from Lewis's columns published in the *New York Tribune* and the *Chicago Tribune Paris Edition*:

December 10, 1922

THE DEATH OF PROUST

MARCEL PROUST is dead. The news spread quickly through Paris and produced a curious astonishment. It was as if every one were astonished at his own surprise, for we all knew of his fragile health, and if we had thought twice about it we should have reflected that he would soon disappear. But when a man lives as Proust lived, a pale, enigmatic mystery to the public, seen rarely in a fashionable club or the supper rooms of a great hotel, one becomes habituated to the thought of the living man. I doubt if the death of older men like Anatole France, for example, will occasion less surprise, so little do we remember its inevitability.

Through an intimate friend of Proust I was enabled to meet him once.

EZRA POUND IN SELF-EXILE

It is likely that if you went into the courtyard of 70 Rue Notre Dame des Champs you would be startled by strange wailings and squeakings. You would knock and a voice would call, "Come in!" Opening the door you would see Ezra Pound sitting on a low stool, his head tilted back and his lips to the mouth piece of a bassoon that stands six feet high. His cheeks are puffed, he blows with all his strength and he has progressed so far as to be able to blow a high or a low note at will. If you ask what it is all about Pound will tell you calmly that he has written an opera, libretto and music, that he is now orchestrating it and that to do this he is getting intimately acquainted with a variety of instruments.

RANDOM NOTES

The first of five concerts of modern music, directed by Jean Wiener, was devoted to the compositions of Darius Milhaud...one was never under the impression of assisting at the flowering of a great musical genius. The audience were generous in appreciation but without fervor. There were few hisses and there was no fighting.

March 4, 1923

> *PARIS.—Le bon vieux temps—that feeling phrase—is again in order. France has come back to herself, despite her little private war in the Ruhr, and Paris is the peace-time Paris again. Late in the year we shall have the fun of hearing campaign speeches for the General Election of 1924, and the crowds at the Batignolles, or in the Bastille quarter, will cry once more, "A bas la calotte" at the Catholic candidates, to be answered by the "A bas la commune" of their opponents...*

* * *

> *I attended recently another of the Jean Wiener concerts of modern music. As usual, it proved highly diverting. A quartet by Webern, played almost throughout with muted strings, had the air of a successful endeavor to reproduce the sensations of a patient emerging from the influence of ether. Cloudy harmonies and vague, muffled noises of a world dawning on a nascent consciousness struggled to impress themselves upon a bewildered audience. When, precisely, this came to an end, only the players knew. The audience hesitated, looked at one another for encouragement, decided finally to plump for the music and applauded with ostentation.*

Excerpts from Lewis Gay's March 2, 1924, column on Carl Van Vechten show that his pen could be venomous:

> *EVERYBODY knows the story of the Quaker who slipped on the tiled floor of a hotel and hurt himself damnably. A bell boy rushed forward to help him up. Once on his feet, the Quaker said: "Boy, doest thee swear." And the boy, taking his cue from the gentleman's garb, answered earnestly, "Oh! no sir, no sir." The Quaker sighed. "Hm." said he. "That is a great pity. I should have paid thee handsomely hadst thou sworn for me."*

> *Gentle reader, forgive me. I am that Quaker. I have slipped on Mr. Carl Van Vechten's The Blind Bow-boy and I pray you to swear for me, for this is the most vulgar and pretentious writing that the lot of the reviewer has ever forced him to read. I do not know anything more irritating*

than the cheap snobbery, the flabby verbosity, the vapid, hideous emptiness of this book. Mr. Van Vechten's mind seems to be a pasteboard box rattling with the names of perfumes, tissues, restaurants, hotels, resorts, books, writers, painters, composers, and international imbeciles. It is sound without fury, words without sense, noise without rhythm; it is a fiction composed of the smartaleckry, the false elegance, the italicized French words, the stockings, underwear, and breath-perfumers of the advertising pages of Vanity Fair. It is simply and putridly too amazingly nil for expression...

When he is not writing like E. P. Roe or cataloging a Greenwich Village bookshop or a Fifth Avenue lingerie shop, Mr. Van Vechten is sprinkling through his pages the deft subtlety of "not unbecoming," "not unimportant," "not without attraction," "not devoid of interest," and other out-worn stylistic small change.

108. "Paris News Letter," *New York Herald*, November 18, 1923.

NOTES TO CHAPTER 4

109. For a couple of years after the merger, the surviving paper was called the *New York Herald–New York Tribune*.

110. With the appearance of his last regular column on May 11, 1924, Lewis thanked Burton for the opportunity he had been given:

> Dear Burton,
>
> ... You have certainly been a peach to run my Paris Letters so regularly. I haven't sent you a word of gratitude, but it's evident from everything I hear that being in your paper has "made" me (so far as my own stuff could contribute to it) as nothing else could have done, and if I don't send you thanks often it isn't because I don't feel them...
>
> Your ever affectionate
>
> Lewis

And, again, in July:

> Dear Burton,
>
> ... Except for that job [The Paris Newsletter]—for which no one else would conceivably have engaged me—I should be utterly unknown in New York today. It brought me kudos and friends and a few other jobs, and I don't need to tell you how much indebted to you I feel. Of course, there is our ten year old affection, now as spontaneous as in 1916, but it doesn't alter the fact that except for you I should be a nonentity in literary journalism instead of the possessor of a slight reputation.
>
> **Both UP Library, Burton Rascoe Collection, Burton-Galantière 1923–1926, folder 4.**

111. Baker, EH Letters, 232.

112. Ibid.

113. Lewis sent Burton a note of thanks and of his disconcertion about his financial prospects.

> May 4, 1925
>
> Burton:
>
> I have wanted to send you a line ever since I came down...to tell you how happy I have been ever since the night you gave us the party, and since seeing how wonderfully Hazel & you took Dorothy to your hearts, and how she responded, and—all the rest that can't go on paper because it's too fine and wonderful...
>
> ... I had a sort of collapse last night after unpacking my trunk, at about six o'clock, and I am still dead with weariness, for no known reason—unless it is the coming of spring, and the sultry Washington weather. The work here will go well enough, I think, so I am not worried about that at all. My only worries are about cursed money. I should like to find some way to get hold of a couple of thousand dollars—but that's another story...
>
> ... When I get back to Paris I shall have no home for a couple of weeks, shall then be forced to go to Brussels till the end of June.
>
> **UP Library, Burton Rascoe Collection, Burton-Galantière 1923-1926, folder 4.**

114. March 11, 1925, letter to Sherwood Anderson:

> Sherwood,
>
> ... have you seen Hemingway's stuff, and don't you believe (as I do) that the boy has a real right to be writing. I think In Our Time was magnificent. Liveright [the publisher] is doing a book for him that ought to be a knockout.
>
> **Newberry Library, Sherwood Anderson Collection, Galantière 1919-1939, box 20, folder 993.**

Lewis said the same to Burton Rascoe in an October 15, 1925, letter:

Hemingway's own book [In Our Time] is out and I have it.
He brought it round the other day. I haven't reread what
I already knew, nor read the new things, but I have a
lot of faith in him. He has his eye on his object better
than any young ster [sic] I know, and he has moments
of penetration and delicacy that are astounding. It is
these latter that give him worth beyond the quality of a
reporter...

UP Library, Burton Rascoe Collection, Burton-Galantière
1923-1926, folder 4.

115. Ibid.

116. Butler Library, Galantière Collection, box 23.

117. Ibid.

118. UP Library, Burton Rascoe Collection, Burton-Galantière 1923–1926, folder 4.

119. Newberry Library, Sherwood Anderson Collection, box 20.

120. At the time, Europe had twenty-six tariff and travel barriers. That problem was exacerbated by the fractioning of the Austro-Hungarian Empire into eight parts after World War I, the short duration of bilateral trade agreements, and the instability and volatility of currency exchanges and exchange rates, respectively. Lewis's article summarized the forces at work and, with prescience, spoke of the need "to break down barriers of race prejudice." It appeared in the August 29, 1926 issue of the *New York Times* and was titled "Trade Barriers Hold Back World's Business."

121. Condé Montrose Nast (March 26, 1873–September 19, 1942) was the founder of Condé Nast Publications, publisher of magazines that eventually included *Vanity Fair, Vogue,* and the *New Yorker.*

122. Qtd. in Carlos Drake, *Mr. Aladdin* (New York: G. P. Putnam's Sons, 1947), 91.

123. In 1927, Joyce obtained an injunction to stop Roth's publication of *Ulysses*, and Sylvia Beach organized an international protest, including protests by 167 authors. In a January 26, 1927, letter to Sylvia Beach, Lewis offered his advice:

> I am interested to hear that Ben Connor [Joyce's attorney] is concerning himself with the Roth affair. I hope that you will ask them, if he has not already done so, and if Hays is not his New York correspondent, to call off Arthur Hays, for if these two lawyers work independently, it will cross each other's track and mess up affairs without any good results to Joyce. The whole trouble with this affair in the past has been one of too many cooks,—Jane Heap, Lloyd Morris, Herbert Gorman, stray newspaper people, myself, Hays, etc., etc. is the old story of everybody's business and nobody's business.
>
> I am very happy about the protest being signed by writers of international renown. It should be circulated (1) to the press Bureaux (associated, United, international, and consolidated, for America); (2) to the correspondence of leading American newspapers in Paris, with the recommendation that they send long mail stories about the matter (the agencies will surely handle the telegraphic week). Ask Harold Callander of the NYTimes (rue de la Paix) to write a Sunday magazine story about the piracy. Dosch-Fleurot of the World will help, of course, as will Guy Hickok of the Brooklyn Eagle. But Hemingway or Bill Bird should be called into consultation about this. (3) the American literary journals and literary supplements of newspapers should be sent the protest.
>
> **University at Buffalo, James Joyce Collection.**

124. Firestone Library, Sylvia Beach Papers, Series 1: Correspondence, C0108, box 19.

125. Adrienne Monnier, Sylvia's intimate companion, ran a French language bookstore, La Maison des Amis des Livres.

126. University at Buffalo, James Joyce Collection.

127. Ransom Center, William A. Bradley Literary Agency, 1923–1982, Galantière correspondence, 27.10

128. Kennedy Library, Hemingway Collection, Box IC43, January 6, 1927, (EHPP-IC43-022-001)

129. Donald Ogden Stewart, "An Interview," *Hemingway/Fitzgerald Annual*, 1973: 83–85, 85.

130. *Torrents of Spring* was eleven days in the making and was ninety pages long. Hemingway had two purposes in writing the book. The first, as noted, was to diminish and distance Anderson's work from his own. The second was to sever his publishing contract with Boni & Liveright so that he could move to Scribners. Hemingway's Boni & Liveright contract gave him a right of termination if they rejected any of his submissions. Boni & Liveright also represented Anderson. They rejected *Torrents* for its demeaning satire of their esteemed client, as Hemingway expected they would, and he terminated their contract.

In 1969, Sherwood Anderson's wife, Eleanor, published *Homage to Sherwood Anderson*. It contained remembrances that had been donated by Sherwood's friends and by some estimable acquaintances, including Paul Rosenfeld, Waldo Frank, Thomas Wolfe, Henry Miller, William Soroyan, Ben Hecht, and Gertrude Stein. That year—1969—was long after Hemingway had become an icon of Western literature, and eight years after he had died. Lewis's contribution resolved the Anderson-Hemingway contest in Anderson's favor:

> Sherwood came to Paris in the company of Tennessee Mitchell and Paul Rosenfeld. It may have been the

*spring of 1921. It must have been, because it was not
many months after he left that he sent me a letter to
introduce a free-lance newspaper man and amateur boxer
called Hemingway, and Hemingway, I know, arrived in
the winter of '21-22. Hemingway was a very complex and
interesting fellow. I knew him intimately for about
six months, after which we drifted apart. He was very
interesting, and I often wonder what has become of him.
Sherwood had a lot of faith in him and liked him very
much. I read a book he wrote called "The Torrents of
Spring" and told him he was letting himself be influenced
too much by Sherwood. Perhaps what I said annoyed
him. The book has long been forgotten, but anyone who
remembers it will know exactly what I mean.*

**Paul P. Appel, *Homage to Sherwood Anderson,
1876-1941*(Mamaroneck, N.Y.:Paul.P.Appel Publisher, 1970),
102.**

131. JFK Library, Hemingway Collection, box IC43 Vanity Fair, 7 Mar. 1927, NY, (EHPP-IC43-022-002).

132. Bancroft Library, Helen Haines letters.

133. UP Library, Burton Rascoe Collection, Burton-Galantière 1923–1926, folder 4.

134. Butler Library, Galantière Collection, box 1.

135. Iris had acquired her knowledge of movies circuitously and harshly. She passed the entrance exam at Oxford University and was about to enter when World War I intervened. She spent 1915 writing poetry, some of which was published in the British journal *Poetry and Drama*. Ezra Pound, who was then in London, read her poems and wrote:

April 2, 1916:

Dear Madam,

*Have you any poems unpublished? It is one of my functions
to gather up verses for an American publication called*

Poetry. They have even been known to print and decently to pay for what I select and send in to them, although they are not always prompt in this matter. At any rate I should be glad to see some of your stuff I think some of it might be 'available.'

Very truly yours,

Ezra Pound

University at Buffalo, Ezra Pound papers

Iris sent Pound her poems and Pound gave Iris his suggestions, including the rule about prose that he thought the most crucial—the one he would later emphasize to Hemingway. Here it is:

July 27, 1916

... The whole art is divided into:

      a. concision, or style, or saying what you mean in the fewest and clearest words.

      b. the actual necessity for creating or constructing something; of presenting an image, or enough images of concrete things arranged to stir the reader.

Beyond these concrete objects named, one can make simple emotional statements of fact, such as 'I am tired,' or simple credos like 'After death there comes no other calamity.'

I think there must be more, predominately more, objects than statements...Also one must have emotion or one's cadence and rhythms will be vapid and without any interest.

It is as simple as the sculptor's direction: "Take a chisel and cut away all the stone you don't want." ...

Ezra Pound, *The Selected Letters of Ezra Pound* **(New York: New Directions Publishing, 1950), 91.**

Pound arranged for two of Iris's poems to be published in the July 1916 edition of *Poetry* magazine and, that year, she moved to London and hung around with Pound and his fellow writers Ford Madox Ford, T. S. Eliot, Edith Sitwell, William Butler Yeats, and, most consequentially and passionately, the writer-painter Wyndham Lewis. Iris had two children with Wyndham Lewis: a boy, Robin Lewis Barry, born in 1919, and a girl, Maisie Wyndham Lewis, born the following year. Iris placed her son in the care of her mother and placed her daughter with a financially well off but childless couple, the Spencers. Iris lived with Wyndham Lewis in the lower level of a house near Notting Hill Gate and served as his muse and his submissive. When Lewis wanted the house to himself or himself and another woman, he sent Iris to the cinema. When she returned, he required her to describe, in detail, the movie she had seen. Lewis had a Svengali hold over Iris, as she wrote:

> I would have followed him anywhere. The others—Pound, Eliot, Ford—had shown they thought he was the best. Of course I followed him. Four years followed. I was very happy but suffered a lot. I was a prisoner...I was tolerated...My function was to be quiet all day and droll in the evening, to flatter, to listen and to stimulate.
>
> **Qtd. in Robert Stilton, *Lady in the Dark: Iris Barry and the Art of Film* (New York: Columbia University Press, 2014), 73.**

In 1923 a weekly conservative magazine, *The Spectator*, hired Iris to be both a secretary and columnist on the subject of household furnishings. She married the magazine's assistant literary editor, Alan Porter. He was twenty-four, she twenty-eight. The marriage was her act of self-liberation from Wyndham Lewis:

> one sunny day in June, I suddenly felt free...The charm no doubt from both sides was broken. Anyway I myself went away.
>
> **Ibid.**

Seeing that America was monopolizing moviemaking, the British government moved to promote its own film industry, after which *The Spectator* created a new editorial position—film critic. The publisher's son, Alan Strachey, interviewed Iris for the position; she wrote:

> I was now interviewed, I think by the fils Strachey, for I seem to recall a sofa in his office with a surprising number of very bright cushions piled on it.
>
> **Ibid, 84.**

She got the job.

136. Butler Library, Galantière Collection, box 7-001.

137. Ibid.

138. Ibid.

139. Ibid.

140. Ibid.

141. Butler Library, Galantière Collection, box 17.

142. *The New Republic*, July 2, 1030.

143. Qtd. in Robert Stilton, *Lady in the Dark: Iris Barry and the Art of Film.* (New York: Columbia University Press, 2014), 74.

144. Iris's second marriage ended in 1950. Her association with filmmaker Luis Buñuel made her a target of the U.S. anti-communist movement, and she left the United States for Europe, rarely to return. In her later years she lived in the south of France with Pierre Kerroux, a younger man she met at the 1947 Cannes Film Festival. The two gardened, renovated houses, and operated an antique shop. Iris died of cancer in Marseilles in 1969 at the age of seventy-five.

145. Ford Madox Ford, Sondra J. Stang and Karen Cochran, *The Correspondence of Ford Madox Ford and Stella Bowen* (Bloomington, University of Indiana Press, 1993), 335.

146. *Shamokin (PA) News-Dispatch*, December 24, 1927, 8.

NOTES TO CHAPTER 5

147. At the ICC, Lewis had analyzed and reported upon the maneuvering of countries and banks for advantages in reparations, loan repayments, and reconstruction and industrialization contracts. And he had prepared a weekly bulletin of economic information for the domestic U.S. Chamber of Commerce that had proven valuable to the country's leading businessmen (as they were then all men). To do these things, he had traveled throughout Europe and met with leading financial and political power brokers. Witness this letter to Burton Rascoe:

> July 4, 1922
>
> ... I flew over to Prague the other day, and back this morning, after a two-days' conference in Czechoslovakia; bully trip both ways, landing only at Strasbourg—a regular stop—coming and going. We had a good talk with Beneš, who has a splendid personality.
>
> **UP Library, Burton Rascoe Collection, Burton-Galantière 1923–1926, folder 4.**

But there was also time for play, as seen in Lewis's July 27, 1922, letter to Burton Rascoe:

> July 27, 1922
>
> ... I've been enjoying a nice rest here [Bushey Grange, New Watford, England, about 15 miles northwest of downtown London]. I read & write mornings, play tennis or golf afternoons & talk or dance after dinner. Occasionally, we go up to London (40 min. away) to the theater, or on necessary errands. I saw Galsworthy's Loyalties & enjoyed it enormously; also Gladys Cooper (a beauty with talent) in The Second Mrs. Tangueray, which plays better than it reads.

(Gladys Cooper was thirty-four years old when Lewis rendered this opinion. Forty years later, she would appear in a *Twilight Zone* episode, "Nothing in the Dark," in which, as an old woman, she refuses to admit anyone to her basement apartment, out of fear that the person might be Death coming to claim her. The actor who played Death, costumed as a policeman, was a young Robert Redford.)

> I'm going back to Paris on the first. Then I may go to Italy for a fortnight, or I may hold over until September & go down to Vienna for a series of conferences & lectures I've been hearing about: Bertrand Russell, Gilbert Murray & great people from other countries are to speak during the fortnight 7–21 September.
>
> **UP Library, Burton Rascoe Collection, Burton-Galantière 1920–1923, folder 3,**

148. For date of hire: Minutes of the Board of Governors of the Federal Reserve Bank of New York, February 2, 1928.

149. Yale University, Gilmore Music Library, Virgil Thomson Collection.

150. *St. Louis Post-Dispatch*, July 8, 1928, 3.

151. Federal Reserve Bank of St. Louis Memoranda, memorandum, https://fraser.stlouisfed.org/files/docs/historical/frbny/strong/strong_1000_9_european_trip_1928.pdf.

152. *New York Times*, June 25, 1928, 1.

    The Federal Reserve Archival System for Economic Research "FRASER,"

    https://fraser.stlouisfed.org/files/docs/meltzer/craint89.pdf.

153. *Palm Beach Post*, January 17, 1929.

154. Max Saunders, *Ford Madox Ford: A Dual Life*, vol. 2, *The After-War World* (Oxford: Oxford University Press, 1966).

155. At about this time—1944—Dorothy started losing touch with reality. She visited Jenny Bradley in Paris during the summer of 1946 and, the following spring, sent Jenny a rambling letter. Here is an excerpt:

> ... First and foremost, coming to Europe was my liberation, not for me alone, but for any value I have as a factor in the struggle for sanity—what I have always been stuck with—an artist, a creator, with a social conscience that cannot by-pass contemporary responsibility—(I hope you can read this scrawl—I am writing it in the midst of things thrown about in my passionate rebellion at which I can still laugh as an example of my ineptitude at adjusting myself to what is called realism: it isn't now and never has been...).

Ransom Center, William A. Bradley Literary Agency, 1923–1982, Dorothy Galantière correspondence.

Two subsequent letters from Dorothy to Malcom Cowley, a liberal columnist, dealt with Ezra Pound's imprisonment in the United States—as a traitor and then for insanity. Here are extracts; the bold font has been added:

> October 1949
>
> Dear Mr. Cowley—
>
> ... I know Ezra Pound; and his behavior in Paris to me held him up to scorn in Paris and New York—A New York newspaper called him "the middle-aged Adonis of the Rive Gauche"—He is a despicable and unbalanced person—(This was when I was a student years ago, with my family in Paris) when his early work revealed him as he is—

Newberry Library, Malcolm Cowley papers, box 31, folder 643.

> January 1951:
>
> Dear Malcolm Cowley:—

NOTES • 291

> *I recall vividly the one conversation I had with you at the Mosses' table in Paris—Lewis Galantière—"The Middle-Aged Adonis of the Rive Gauche" had just appeared in Burton Rascoe's column—*
>
> **Ibid.**

156. Lincoln founded Hound & Horn in 1927, when an article he had submitted to Harvard's literary magazine—the Harvard Advocate—was rejected. Over the next seven years, he built Hound & Horn into a journal that was well respected in the art world.

157. The other founders were John Walker and Edward W. W. Warburg. Edward Warburg founded the Museum of Modern Art and served on its board of trustees from 1932 to 1958. He remained active in the art world and, throughout his life, contributed his time and money to relief organizations and Jewish philanthropies.

    Lincoln, Edward Warburg, George Balanchine and Vladimir Dimitriev founded the American Ballet Company in 1939, which became the New York City Ballet. Lincoln served as its General Director until 1989. He helped to create Lincoln Center in New York and the American Shakespeare Festival in Stratford, Connecticut. During World War II, Lincoln served with the Army's Monuments, Fine Arts, and Archives program, reclaiming and protecting works of art that had been looted by the Germans. The unit became known as the "Monuments Men."

158. Margarett was a fourth cousin of John Singer Sargent.

159. Other art critics praised Margarett's work. In 1929, *Art News* declared, "Miss Margarett Sargent...has mounted a more fiery Pegasus who has taken her for a somewhat breathless ride among the colorful phenomena of modern art." Forbes Watson wrote "Her subjects seem ready to step from their frames and become really alive."

Both quoted by Moore, Honor in *The White Blackbird : A Life of the Painter Margarett Sargent by Her Granddaughter* (New York: W. W. Norton, 2009), 176.

Helen Appleton Read said that her emphasis on line was her "outstanding contribution as an artist."

Ibid, 155.

160. Ibid. 203.

161. Butler Library, Galantière Collection, box 2-001 undated.

162. Ibid.

163. Ibid.

164. Throughout the times mentioned, Joseph Galantière had been selling tobacco in Chicago and Los Angeles.

165. Butler Library, Galantière Collection, box 2-001, July 25, 1919.

166. Ibid., July 27, 1919.

167. Ibid., July 29, 1919.

168. Ibid.

169. Ibid., box 5.

170. Ibid., box 1.

171. Here are some of Lewis's other ruminations about or letters to Margarett. They are in chronological order, to the extent known. All are from the Butler Library, Galantière Collection, box 2-001.

Undated

A little while ago I sat alone at lunch,...I thought of the gravity in your eyes and your voice when sometimes you look at me and say you can't understand why I love

you. I thought of the first time I saw you in a red
smock. I thought of you standing in the dark room when I
had shut the door behind us and did not yet put on the
light...while I held you, standing, in my arms, and heard
you whisper "I love this room, I love this room. No, not
because it's yours, just because of itself." And then
heard you laugh a little at your denial that you loved it
because it was mine...

And most of all I thought how grateful I was for your
love...And the things you believed of me, though they
might not be native to me, I saw coming true to myself,
growing into existence in the generating sunlight of your
faith. What I say now is not conceit, darling: it is what
happens when I am with you, even when I am merely writing
to you: your power is so great that your faith could move
mountains, does move them; since it takes me, and in
those moments when we are together makes an unreal fine
being of me.

May 21, 1929

Do you remember that two nights ago we seemed to have
reached the edge of possibility; and that last night
we picked up its frontiers and flung them light-years
forward? As I write it, that which was not called upon
rises up, and they tremble in the power of its intensity.
What a hand is yours! What a mouth! What heaven you
bear...

Beloved, one thing worries me, and that is that you're
ill. My hand can't always be there to give you heat: You
must have that attended to, and soon. Don't wait: these
recurrent pains hurt and worry me. I long to kiss the
little scar that we shall live with when it has been
done.

Undated

there are times when I feel I'd welcome a storm, but
until we see clearly into the future we should be careful

not to ruffle its waters. You have so much at stake
that I shiver sometimes with fright of what I should be
depriving you of if the storm broke and you were blown
away from your cruel, but still for certain reasons
welcome, mooring. I resent your ties, I want them broken,
that I won't want you to bleed when they break. I want
you to be freed by the rotting of the rope around your
wrists, not by the knife which might go too deep, and cut
you in the process of freeing you.

Undated

If your head aches I will bathe it tenderly; if you
are lonesome, I will come to you cheer you; if you are
incomprehensibly depressed I will soothe you and my
heart will talk to you and pour out upon you all the
comfort that it holds...But I will not listen to suicidal
idiocies, and I will insist that you exercise as much
fortitude in your spiritual torments as you do in your
physical and material misadventures.

June 16, 1929

the world is still dark. If I could but let the future
take care of itself! But I am always tinkering with it,
trying to adjust it to my desire. It is that passion I
have for feeling myself in command of my life, rather
than feeling myself its servant, the servant of the
years...

... I have always told myself that whatever happened to
me, for good or ill, was the product of my own strength
or weakness, the result of something within me and not of
forces outside me...Thus...I pick up a book and try to
change the direction of my thoughts when I feel I'm about
to give way to depression, about to indulge myself in
self-pity or the general pleasure of feeling myself the
victim of circumstance...

... I was kind, certainly; and she grew to hate, to
loathe my kindness, because it made her feel culpable

*towards a man she was already through with. I taught her—
she says—all she knows of sexual pleasure; but having
experienced it, she doubtless wearied of it...*

*... I do not know what I did not give her, except the
satisfaction of her desire for a master...*

*... She took our love with feverish intensity, she
was throughout a smoldering volcano. Still, I was—she
said "grim" but that is generous—I was as solemn as a
Unitarian preacher, full of precepts and holy words and
nauseating repetition of "soul" and "happiness" and
"bliss" and "gravity" and "serenity" and God only knows
what other dark-great colors. Ugh! And all that without
one smile at myself! Still, dammit, I was moved; I meant
what I wrote; I loved her in a way I didn't believe human
beings could love. I was absolutely hers (unfortunately
for me, as it now turns out)...*

*"You're a fool, you're a fool, you're a fool!...Do you
forget her fright, perhaps it was her horror, when
you suggested—you poor innocent imbecile-in-love, that
someday she might be your wife? Do you forget that what
she most craved is freedom? And that perhaps she broke
with you in part because she felt your love was too
deep, too possessive, at bottom too serious to fit into
her plans for herself, her passion for freedom?"... My
son, you are a fool to think she wants to be changed, or
that she would allow anyone to change her. One thing she
resented about you was that she could see in your eye the
stupid passion of the missionary, come to change her...
Remember always that her dissatisfaction with self is
accompanied by a gazelle's flight from intrusion upon the
sacredness of self.*

172. Mina Kirstein Curtiss, then an English professor at Smith College, lived twenty miles north of the college, in Ashfield, Massachusetts, in the geographic middle of the state. Mina, like Lewis, was fluent in French and, during her career, translated or edited works by Marcel Proust, Alexis Leger (also known as Saint-John Perse), Edgar Degas, and Philip Halevy. Mina had married Henry Tomlinson Curtiss in

1926. He died a year later but time did not diminish her love. On July 7, 1929, Lewis wrote of Mina,

> She has most things one could want: two houses she loves, a busy outdoor life (farms, dogs, horses, garden, etc.) that she lives with intense happiness. She likes teaching at Smith. She has friends who are fond of her. She has no material—I mean money—worries. But something is lacking. Well, as she spoke, I knew that something must be Harry Curtiss, who died suddenly, at 38, about a year and a half ago.

Butler Library, Galantière Collection, box 1-002.

In 1935, Mina joined Orson Welles and John Houseman, as a researcher and scriptwriter for the *Mercury Theatre of the Air*. She was with them on Halloween 1938, when Welles scared the Eastern Seaboard with his *War of the Worlds* broadcast. In 1942, Houseman enlisted Mina and Lewis to serve in the Office of War Information. Their friendships endured over the following decades.

173. Butler Library, Galantière Collection, box 1-002.

174. Ernest Hemingway, *Ernest Hemingway: Selected Letters, 1917–1961*. Edited by Carlos Baker. (New York City: Charles Scribner's Sons, 1981), 326.

175. *Hound and Horn*, Volume 3, No. 2, Jan-March 1930, 259-262.

176. The play featured Clark Gable, in his Broadway debut.

177. *New York Times*, August 12, 1930.

178. John Houseman, *Unfinished Business: Memoirs, 1902–1988* (New York: Applause Theatre Book Publishers, 1989).2

179. *New York Times*, December 3, 1933, 159.

180. Of his Jewish identity, Houseman said this:

> ...for so many years, [a psychological insulation] had
> enabled me to "pass," whenever it suited me, among
> Jews and gentiles alike, without the faintest feeling
> of betrayal or guilt. From the repeated chameleon's
> maneuvers which I found myself forced to perform
> throughout my childhood, I had developed a mechanism
> of adjustment so automatic and so complete that I was
> honestly unaware of the denials and deceptions that these
> transformations required of me. On a simple semantic
> level, phrases like "to Jew down," "don't be a Jew!," "a
> fat Jew," even "dirty Jew" formed part of the standard
> vocabulary of my schoolmates to whose customs I was so
> scrupulously trying to adhere. Yet I would have been
> horrified and hurt if I had ever heard them applied to my
> father while he lived, or to those cousins, uncles and
> aunts whose elegant Parisian apartments I visited during
> the holidays. Unable or unwilling to make the distasteful
> connection, I remained blithely unaware of the problem.
> (Years later, on a belated pilgrimage to the family vault
> in the Cimetière Montparnasse, I noticed three plaques
> next to my father's grave. They were those of two aunts
> and one cousin—MORT 1944 A AUSCHWITZ, ASSASSINÉS PAR LES
> ALLEMANDS.)

Houseman, *Unfinished Business*.

181. Butler Library, Galantière Collection, box 2-001.

182. Sometimes termed the "Mid-Atlantic accent" (referring to the longitude and not latitude), its hallmark is the nonrhotic "R." Franklin Roosevelt had a similar accent. Lewis, whose formative Chicago years had embossed no dialect, adopted Houseman's "Mid-Atlantic accent" as his own.

183. Anthony Tommasini, *Virgil Thomson: Composer on the Aisle* (New York: W. W. Norton, 1997).

184. Houseman, *Unfinished Business*.

185. Ibid.

186. This was how Virgil Thomson appraised John:

> Jack was never first-class as a director. He always had somebody around with quicker ideas, and he would use them as assistants. But what he could do with his smooth English manners was arrange compromises and rob one till and put it in another and make the money last when he didn't have enough, and find out who could get what for free and who were the very best people to bring together. He was a marvelous, creative producer. He didn't have original ideas as a director. And he knew it. But he didn't like it rubbed in.

> **Tommasini, *Virgil Thomson*.**

187. The name of the play was changed to *And Be My Love* prior to its opening in Montreal. It was the story of a man who preys on spinsters and widows, and then he falls in love with the niece of one of his victims, who rejects him. The *Montreal Gazette* interviewed Lewis before that production, and quoted him as having done "most of the writing of the dialogue," with Houseman having been the critic, reviser, and "dramatic formalist." The interviewer ascribed to Lewis participation in the Algonquin Round Table: "He belongs to the famous Bohemian circle presided over by the celebrated Dorothy Parker. Robert Benchley, noted drama critic of New York is one of his intimate friends." While Lewis knew the Round Table members, he had not sought membership in their klatch.

188. Gerald Bordman, *American Theatre: A Chronicle of Comedy and Drama, 1930-1969* (Oxford: Oxford University Press 1996), 93.

189. John Houseman, *Run-Through, A Memoir* (New York, Simon and Schuster, 1972) 171.

190. Butler Library, Galantière Collection, box 4.

NOTES TO CHAPTER 6

191. UP Library, Burton Rascoe Collection, Burton-Galantière 1923–1926, folder 4

192. Balogh would serve as Wilson's advisor throughout his four terms in office, 1964 to 1970 and 1974 to 1976.

193. Selected letters between Balogh and Galantière

> *November 14, 1930*
>
> *Princes House*
>
> *95 Gresham Street*
>
> *London, ec2*
>
> *Dear Lewis,*
>
> ... [I attended] *the League of Nations Gold Conference at Geneva...*[and] *am directed to ask you privately about the impression of the first preliminary* [Gold Memorandum] *report as made in America, especially among our friends in the Reserve System...*
>
> *Yours affectionately,*
>
> *Thomas Balogh*
>
> Butler Library, Galantière Collection, box 1-002.

> *November 22, 1930*
>
> *My dear Balogh,*
>
> *All that I dare tell you of the sentiment here regarding the Gold Memorandum is that its publication was considered most unfortunate. If, however, you are interested in my private views, as well as I can summon them at the moment, here they are:*
>
> > ... *The whole question of central banking in its international aspect is in the air. The central bankers*

*themselves have only now begun to think about it... and
they can hardly be expected to do their thinking in
public... The Memorandum must seem to them an example of
misguided "open diplomacy." ...*

*... While you are studying the question of a so-called
gold shortage, you might also suggest remedies for a
surplus of gold. This has been our problem in recent
years and it is likely to be the French problem for some
time to come. Certainly, for the immediate future it
seems a more acute problem than that of a shortage of
gold.*

*You may make what use you can of this commentary in your
studies: but I beg you not to cite them as Federal Reserve
Judgments upon the report or to communicate them in toto
as representing the American view...These are [my] private
reflections which, of course, have already been made known on
the 10th floor...*

Yours ever, Lewis Galantière

Ibid.

December 8, 1930

My dear Galantière,

*... I do agree that the computation of gold requirements
is wholly nonsensical...Your French problem of surplus
of gold is no problem...In general, I do think that the
question was treated much too simply and that there is
very much more to do especially as regards the position
of the different countries...*

*Do write very soon and repudiate my objection to your
criticism.*

Yours ever most affectionately,

Thomas Balogh

Ibid.

December 22, 1930

My dear Balogh,

I did not say that the central bankers were disinclined to think about the problems. I said they disliked thinking in public...I...repeat that the problem is at present rather one of surplus gold than of a gold shortage. To put the same thing differently, gold shortage is hypothetical but gold maldistribution is actual. Our business is to get gold out of this country; the business of the French is to get gold out of theirs. Ultimately, this can only be done by persuading Frenchmen and Americans to lend abroad...

Best holiday wishes and affectionate greetings.

Ibid.

January 1, 1931

Dear Galantière,

I have perused with great attention your admirable criticism of the slightly important Gold Calf which fills my dreams. It seems to me that you are right in most of the points but I still maintain that something ought to be done...

I see with great joy that you have turned playwright. I think that is a much better venture than writing about gold, anyhow; more useful for the world and more profitable for yourself. A pity that I did not discover the poetical vein in myself.

With best wishes for a better New Year,

I remain,

Your most affectionate, Balogh

Ibid.

194. Ibid.

195. Balogh to Lewis, June 12, 1936, ibid.

196. L. G. (Leslie Galfreid) Melville, assistant governor of the Common-wealth Bank of Australia, to Lewis Galantière, December 28, 1937. Butler Library, Galantière Collection, box 3. In 1944, Melville would lead the Australian delegation to the 1944 Bretton Woods conference.

197. Butler Library, Galantière Collection, box 1.

198. H. Sudermann's *Excursion to Tilsit* (1930) from the German and the following from French: Joseph Delteil's *Napoleon* (1930), François Mauriac's The Family (1930), Pierre Louys' Aphrodite (1933), Sacha Guitry's *If Memory Serves* (1935), and the Goncourt brothers' *The Goncourt Journals, 1851–1870* (1937). Lewis also wrote an essay introducing a volume of François Villon's poems in 1932. Butler Library, Galantière Collection, box 3.

199. All of the citations alluded to were of René's 150-page history (mostly illustrated) of the Second French Empire (1852 to 1870), initially published as *Le Coup d'etat du deux décembre* and then, by Hachette in 1928, as simply *Le 2 décembre*.

200. Butler Library, Galantière Collection, box 1-100.

201. Antoine Jean-Baptiste Marie Roger de Saint-Exupéry was born at the turn of the century into a Parisian noble family with its origins in the Crusades. His musings on man, machines, and nature were engaging and lyrical, encompassing saga, parable, philosophy, poetry, and polemic. His gentle but heartbreaking novella *The Little Prince*, is the most widely read book in the French language.

Powered flight came to France the year Saint-Exupéry turned eight, when Wilbur Wright circled the Hunaudières racetrack. At twelve, Saint-Exupéry talked his way into the back seat of a Ber-thaud-Wroblewski monoplane for his first flight. At eighteen, living in Paris, he watched from his apartment's rooftop as Zeppelins spilled their bombs on the city by night and Big Bertha shelled it by day. He was still eighteen when the armistice was signed. The following year, he joined the Second Fighter Group and was posted to Le Bourget in Paris in October 1922. After the military released him from active duty the following year, he accepted a bookkeeping job. Its tedium became an indelible memory. In October 1924, he worked as a traveling truck salesman, the negligible demands of which gave him time and solitude, which he used to write. His first published story, "The Aviator," appeared in *Le Navire d'Argent* on April 1, 1926.

Flying was a novelty in the summer of 1926 and, for a fee, Saint-Exupéry took tourists aloft on their "baptismal" flights out of Le Bourget field. In October, an air mail company—Latécoère—hired him as a mechanic, but he was soon piloting an open-cockpit Breguet 14 biplane on runs from Toulouse, France, to Alicante, Spain, flying between the capricious cloud bases of the Pyrenees, and the treetops that streamed below. Navigation was by visual landmarks, fog permitting, and by dead-reckoning when not. This was the kind of adventure that stirred Saint-Exupéry:

> the hostile gods drag you down and the altimeter plummets
> "9,000...7,000...5,000 ...4,500...3,000" as [they] do
> you along with it; you're forced to turn around because
> the mountain is now higher than you are and the gods are
> laughing. And you try to escape through a valley, with
> the confidence of an omelet in a frying pan, because the
> hostile gods are playing tennis, and you are the ball.
> [This from a letter to Renée de Saussine, in whom Saint-
> Exupéry was romantically interested.]

By early 1927, his routes extended to Casablanca and then to Dakar, the latter being especially dangerous because Moors had recently killed two Latécoère pilots there.

On February 7, 1927, Saint-Exupéry's Breguet blew a tie-rod and crashed in the Sahara, leaving him and his copilot, René

Riguelle, stranded for three days. The experience would later re-emerge, sometimes as allegory, in his books *Southern Mail*, *Wind, Sand and Stars*, and *The Little Prince*.

Flying the mail demanded self-discipline, a commitment to task, and courage. That experience and the laconic camaraderie of his fellow pilots (men he admired and whose collegiality he aspired to merit) aroused in Saint-Exupéry a sense of self-worth that he had not previously known:

> For the first time since I was born it seemed to me that my life was my own and that I was responsible for it.
>
> **Stacy Schiff,. St. Exupéry: A Biography (New York: Alfred A. Knopf, 1995), 150.**

In July 1929, Gallimard published *Southern Mail* to good reviews. In late September, Saint-Exupéry sailed to Buenos Aires where, for the next fifteen months, he both flew the mail and managed operations. On June 13, 1930, one of Latécoère's pilots, Henri Guillaumet, set out from Santiago, Chile, for Buenos Aires in a two-seat open-cockpit biplane. Caught by weather, he exhausted his fuel and crash-landed on a frozen lakebed in the Andes, at an altitude of 10,500 feet. Seven days later, having been given up for dead, Guillaumet emerged at San Carlos. Saint-Exupéry flew to retrieve him. For Saint-Exupéry, Guillaumet epitomized the ideal of the aviator brotherhood.

Saint-Exupéry returned to France in February 1931 and completed his book *Night Flight*, most of which had been written in South America.

202. Newberry Library, Sherwood Anderson Collection, Galantière 1919–1939, box 20, folder 993.

203. Ibid.

204. *Atlantic Monthly*, April 1, 1947.

205. Lewis quoting Saint-Exupéry, ibid.

206. In her comprehensive biography of St. Exupéry, Stacy Schiff spoke of Lewis's influence:

> Anyone doubting the long reach of Galantière's editorial arm has only to consult his papers at the Rare Book and Manuscript Library (Butler), Columbia University, New York, or to compare the American and French editions of the text, all of which have greatly informed this discussion of the two volumes. Saint-Exupéry writes repeatedly in his correspondence with Becker of the changes and additions requested by Hitchcock and, especially, by Galantière. He harped on the idea that he wanted the book to amount to more than simply a collection of memories and can be heard saying as much on the Festival recording, "Leur Oeuvre et Leur Voix," on which he prefaces his reading from the French-language preface.

Schiff, *St. Exupéry*, 301n.

207. Newberry Library, Sherwood Anderson Collection, Galantière 1938–1939, box 7, folder 262.

208. Hilbert H. Campbell, ed., *The Sherwood Anderson Diaries, 1936–1941* (Athens: University of Georgia Press, 1987).

209. National Archives, Military Personnel Records Center, St. Louis, MO.

210. Sherwood Anderson recorded their visit in his diary:

> July 1, 1939: First full day at Ripshin. We put up hay. I caught up correspondence...Lewis and Nancy Galantière settled—they came at 9:20 Marion and I met them.
>
> July 3, 1939:...Ella Ketchin, of Washington, a government official, and Nancy lying out in the yard. Conversations with Lewis. He is unsure of himself. Nice man but

> *oversells himself as sophisticate.* [And yet, in his memoir, Anderson described Lewis as "that perfect gentleman and the only real sophisticate I have known." That memoir was for public consumption.]
>
> *July 8, 1939: We got a fine big piece of luggage, all arranged for picnics from Lewis and Nancy. Nancy had been ill but got downstairs.*
>
> *July 14, 1939: We all drove to Marion and Lewis and Nancy Galantière left for California.*
>
> **Campbell, The Sherwood Anderson Diaries.**

211. *Foreign Affairs*, October 1949.

212. As noted, Norris was descended from a heralded family. Norris's great-grandfather, Isaac Davis, had been an officer in the Massachusetts militia during the American Revolution, in command of minutemen at the Battle of Concord. Norris's grandfather, John Davis, had been a Massachusetts governor and U.S. Senator and Congressman. His father, Horace Davis, had sailed around Cape Horn to San Francisco in 1852, too late for the gold rush but in time to make a fortune in the flour business. Horace served as a U.S. Congressman from 1877 to 1881, as president of the University of California from 1888 to 1890 and as president of the board of trustees of Stanford University from 1885 to 1916.

Norris was born in San Francisco on June 26, 1876, and graduated from the Harvard School of Engineering in 1898. He fought in the Spanish-American War and then in World War I, attaining the rank of lieutenant colonel. Back in San Francisco, he married Margaret Therese Morgan, and the couple had two children, daughters Margery and Nancy. When Margery was married in a Unitarian Church on August 24, 1935, the society page of the Los Angeles Times effervessed "Channel City Deb Married in Splendor":

The ceremony was performed at high noon August 24 at Casa Paz del Mar, the home of the bride's mother...Into the huge drawing room of the casa, its wall hung with priceless paintings of Italian masters, the wedding party approached an improvised altar through an aisle marked with satin ribbons and standards of white larkspur. Banks of the same flowers were behind the altar, and for further background was an old Chinese screen flanked with Woodwardia ferns.

Los Angeles Times, August 24, 1935.

213. The colonel divorced Therese in 1933. The vitriol in the family during the seven years of the divorce proceeding had been intense. It culminated on July 3, 1933, as reported in the *Los Angeles Times* the following day:

WRIT ENDS LONG FIGHT ON DIVORCE

Mrs. Therese Davis Wins Decree From Californian After Seven Year's Suits

Therese Morgan Davis, San Francisco and Santa Barbara society matron, was divorced on grounds of desertion here today from Col. Norris K. Davis of San Francisco. Granting of the decree ended seven years of litigation in the courts of California and Nevada.

Mrs. Davis obtained the divorce on her cross-complaint, filed after the State Supreme Court had reversed a judgment obtained here in 1930 by her husband, who previously had sought a California decree.

A contest had been indicated with both parties demanding a jury trial, but Col. Davis today made no attempt to resist granting of the divorce to Ms. Davis.

The Davises separated in 1920, shortly after his return from service overseas.

During the 1930s, Norris owned several companies, including a winery in Napa Valley. He married once again, to a woman twenty-four years younger than he.

214. Newberry Library, Sherwood Anderson Collection, Galantière 1938–1939, box 20, folder 993.

215. Ibid., box 34, folder 1821.

216. Pella Bay is about 150 miles from the magnetic north pole and fifteen hundred miles north of Duluth, Minnesota.

217. Eskimo culture was forever altered by the construction of Canadian military installations during World War II.

218. Gontran de Poncins and Lewis Galantière, *Kabloona* (New York: Reynal and Company; reprint, Chicago: Time-Life Books, 1941).

219. Newberry Library, Sherwood Anderson Collection, Galantière 1919–1939, box 20, folder 993.

NOTES TO CHAPTER 7

220. The treaty ostensibly dealt with war reparations, initially set at about $32 billion (the equivalent of $450 billion in 2015), under a payment schedule that was restructured by the 1923 Dawes Plan, under which U.S. banks lent Germany the money to pay reparations to the European Allies so that those Allies could then pay their U.S. war debts—initially $10 billion. German reparations obligations were again restructured in 1928 under the Young Plan.

221. On January 24, 1936, Lewis attended a white-tie dinner hosted at the German Consul General's luxurious East 77th Street residence, to honor Mr. Emil Puhl, a director of the Reichsbank and Dr. Hans Hartenstein, who headed the Reich's Office for Foreign Exchange Controls. Lewis had been obliged to attend as a representative of the Federal Reserve Bank, although he would certainly have attended anyway, out of curiosity about Hitler's intentions and about the caliber of these men—Puhl and Hartenstein. The record does not reveal whether Lewis could have then thought Puhl capable of stashing Nazi looted gold—some pried from human teeth—in safe houses. Puhl was later convicted of war crimes. But Hartenstein was a known factor. In 1933, he had negotiated the exodus of Jews from Nazi Germany to Israel and, when offered a promotion on the condition that he join the Nazi Party, turned it down and resigned from the German civil service.

222. In his September 1937 "Four-Year Plan Memorandum," Hitler chose to arm for war rather than invest in the manufacturing of consumer goods (which would improve Germany's balance of payments and standard of living). Here are excerpts from Hitler's "Memorandum":

*Since the outbreak of the French Revolution, the world
has been moving with ever increasing speed toward a new
conflict, the most extreme solution of which is called
Bolshevism, whose essence and aim, however, are solely
the elimination of those strata of mankind which have
hitherto provided the leadership and their replacement
by worldwide Jewry. No state will be able to withdraw or
even remain at a distance from this historical conflict...*

*It is...Germany's duty to secure her own existence
by every means in face of this catastrophe, and to
protect herself against it...the extent of the military
development of our resources cannot be too large, nor its
pace too swift...*

*However well balanced the general pattern of a nation's
life ought to be, there must at particular times be
certain disturbances of the balance at the expense of
other less vital tasks. If we do not succeed in bringing
the German army as rapidly as possible to the rank of
premier army in the world...then Germany will be lost!*

223. Extract from Dr. Einzig's letter to Lewis, July 26, 1938

Dear Mr. Galantière,

*First of all let me congratulate you upon your excellent
translation of "Le Journal des Goncourts." It must be a
relief to be able to get away at times from the eternal
subject of finance.*

*I have not forgotten the very valuable help you gave
me in connection with my book "The Theory of Forward
Exchange." May I once more take advantage of your good
nature by asking you for information and assistance
regarding a subject which at present constitutes my
main interest in life? This subject is German economic
penetration into the Danube basin and the Balkans, and
the possibility of resistance to that penetration. I am
sure that in your position you have followed closely
the developments in South-Eastern Europe, and that you
realise the danger of German political control of a
number of countries as a result of economic penetration.*

[Dr. Einzig then asked whether the United States would intercede to discourage Germany's ambitions.]

Butler Library, Galantière Collection, box 1.

224. Lewis replied after speaking with a colleague, the economist Emilio Gabriel Collado. The following is an excerpt from Lewis's letter:

August 5, 1938

Dear Dr. Einzig,

I am answering your letter of the 26th of July on the eve of leaving for my holiday and after weeks of work in sweltering heat, so that what I now hastily write must be briefly and may be confusingly said.

You ask, in substance, what my personal views are of the possibility of official American action to prevent or offset German political-economic penetration in Southeastern Europe. It is doubtless as obvious to you as to me that public opinion in this country, strongly anti-authoritarian though it be, is highly unlikely to permit the Administration to embark deliberately upon the sort of policy discussed in your letter. A nation which seems to have made up its mind not to "entangle" itself with even the great democracies of Western Europe is not going to allow its governors to take a stand about Southeastern Europe, whatever the ideological basis of that stand. It seems clear enough that the only line of action the United States Government can take would be that bounded by its trade agreements policy. A trade agreement has been concluded with Czechoslovakia, negotiations with Turkey are in process, and I believe there have been tentative conversations with representatives of Yugoslavia. With these last two, I should think negotiation would be difficult because of their exchange controls and quota discriminations, on the one hand, and our rigid "purity" in these matters, on the other...

These are of course my personal views, and I dare say that other Americans might readily express quite different ones...

Yours sincerely,

Lewis Galantière

Ibid.

225. The following is an extract from René Arnaud's September 26, 1937, letter to Lewis:

15 Bis Orlean St, Neuilly sur Seine [René's home, in a northwest outskirt of central Paris]

Dear Pal

... Newspapers must have told you that there was an explosion in the wing of offices opposite my own. No important rooms were destroyed; it was a stupid and incomprehensible act. They want us to believe that it was the work of Franco anarchists, to discredit them in France. But that would be too subtle a purpose...

Hitler and Mussolini are hugging each other, protesting that they want peace. Hum! Luckily, I have seen, during a short military stint, how well we are prepared—It's great! I understand hélas!...that you prefer staying outside the mélée. Sadly, if it starts, it would be more difficult for you to stay outside than it was the last time...

Yours, René Arnaud

Ibid.

226. René Arnoud, *Tragédie Bouffe: A Frenchman in the First World War* (London: Sidgwick and Jackson, 1964). René inscribed this in Lewis's copy:

To Lewis Galantière and his charming wife

In memory, Lewis, of the 20s and of these long talks at the "Rendez-vous des Mariniers" where our friendship was born.

A sincere homage, René Arnaud

227. The 1919 Treaty of Saint-Germain had allotted part of the Austro-Hungarian Empire, whose residents were predominantly ethnic
Germans, to Czechoslovakia. It was to have been a buffer for Czechoslovakia against future German aggression. The Germans referred to
this area as the Sudetenland.

228. Newberry Library, Sherwood Anderson Collection, Galantière 1919–
1939, box 20, folder 993.

229. Had annexation of the Sudetenland to Germany been put to a vote
by the Sudeten people, its majority German population would have
likely voted for annexation. Honoring that vote would have been consistent with the principle—advanced by Woodrow Wilson and advocated by the Allies during the Versailles peace negotiations—of the
right of peoples to self-determination.

230. Following the Munich Pact, Czech president Edvard Beneš, whom
Lewis had met in 1922, resigned. Fearing assassination by the Nazis, he fled to England in October 1938. He was succeeded in office
the following month by Dr. Emil Hácha. On March 13, 1939, Hitler
met with the leader of the Slovak region of Czechoslovakia, Roman
Catholic monsignor Jozef Tiso. At that meeting, Hitler persuaded
Tiso to proclaim the independence of Slovakia. Tiso did so, on his
own authority but under the threat of Hungarian annexation of Slovakia (with Hungary backed by the German military). The following day, President Hácha, facing the German invasion of his country
and threatened by Hitler with the punitive bombing of half of Prague
into rubble, surrendered the rest of Czechoslovakia. On March 16,
1939, Tiso yielded up the Slovakian region and Hitler announced,
from Prague, that Czechoslovakia had "showed its inherent inability
to survive and has therefore now fallen victim to actual dissolution."
During the Nazi occupation, Tiso would hold positions of power and

be instrumental in the deportation of Jews to death camps. After the war, he was tried and sentenced to death for treason and collaboration with the Nazis. He appealed the sentence to Evard Beneš, who was once again president of Czechoslovakia. There would be no reprieve and Tiso was hanged on April 18, 1947.

231. Butler Library, Galantière Collection, box 9-001.

232. Ibid., box 7.

233. Ibid., box 1.

234. Ibid.

235. Here, Lewis's prediction of how the war would unfold:

> [Hitler's] error was to believe Poland could be obtained without bringing England and France into "active" war. Hitler now knows that he must gamble everything on succeeding in a Blitzkrieg against England during the next four months or lose the war. [The Battle of Britain was in fact fought over a four-month interval: from the end of June until the end of October 1940.]
>
> His reserves of materials are only sufficient for one sustained offensive effort and once expended cannot be replaced. Nor can the "helots" be effectively absorbed under present war conditions. Therefore, Hitler must and will play every card he possesses between now and August. But he will fail to win his Blitzkrieg and it is the Allies who will win the war decisively by the spring or early summer of 1941.
>
> After the activity of the next four months, her gasoline situation will be acute and irreparable and the seizure of Norway has aggravated the gasoline problem in that American supplies are now largely cut off. Already in industry the quality of her steel production is showing the effect of her lack of manganese. Fabricators are closing down their works due to the poor quality of

German steel supplies. Her reserves of war metals at the start of the war were not large, judged in the light of the consumption to be expected in a "big" war.

Russia is too weak to play any part in the war. She will, however, be a strong nation of over 200,000,000 people to be reckoned with twenty-five to thirty years from now.

The Maginot line is practically impregnable and now stretches from the Channel to the Italian frontier. The British Navy commands the seas. Hence the Blitzkrieg will be directed at England itself.

Hitler has had a long run of overruling his military heads and being proved right in the event—the most recent example the occupation of Denmark and the Norwegian ports in a day and a half. He may be expected to continue attempting the apparently impossible.

The Allies will suffer reverse after reverse—largely due to their being behind in preparedness owing to the late date at which they woke up to the Hitler threat. Enormous destruction and suffering will be endured...The Allied reverses this summer will be such that emotions will be so stirred in the United States that that country will enter the war in 1940—possibly before election day. In that event, her role will be to furnish credits, become a partner in the blockade, and possibly loan some part of her Navy. The U.S.A.'s joining the blockade will mean that no goods can reach Germany either via Italy or via Russia from North, Central or South America. Within two months of the U.S.A. coming in, the war will be over.

Even if the U.S.A. does not enter the war, the Allies will win early in 1941 because Germany will have used up so much of her reserves by the end of August, 1940 that thereafter she will only be able to carry on a "small" scale war.

Butler Library, Galantière Collection, box 17.

236. Ibid., box 7.

237. Ibid., box 1.

238. After the initial German successes, Maxime Weygand was placed in charge of the French military. His tactics were too late and too meager to halt the invasion, and he soon joined with Pétain in seeking an armistice.

239. Butler Library, Galantière Collection, box 1.

240. *To the New York Herald Tribune:*

> A singularly insincere and pusillanimous regime has now been erected in France in the guise of "reforms proposed by Marshal Pétain," as Laval put it on July 9. Three hundred and ninety-five Deputies and 225 Senators of the Third Republic have rushed to Vichy in the hope of sharing in the spoils that will result from the carving up of the carcass of France by the sinister Laval—a man who has been false to every political group of his nation; by the ludicrous and ineffectual dentist, Marquet, the Beau Brummell of Bordeaux, by the intriguing banker, Baudoin and by the simple-minded Catholic soldier, Weygand, who, with his elder, the French Hindenburg, has lent a great name to a group of spoliators in the absurd expectancy that this shameless gang will bring forth a Christian and an orderly France.

> For the glorious device, the very sound of which lifted men's hearts throughout a century and a half of human advancement—Liberté, Egalité, Fraternité—these men have substituted the hollow insipidity of a borrowed cacophony—Travail, Famille, Patrie. It is not that Work and Family and Fatherland are not great words—they are. But what man other than a serf would wish to work without liberty, to raise a family where there was no equality before the state and the law, to have a fatherland in which there was no fraternity?

> This criticism of the new device is fundamental: but objections may be raised which are more immediate. Work for whom? If MM. Laval et Compagnie (excluding the soldiers) stood for something new and revolutionary, were

*not the archetype of corrupt Third Republic politicians,
one would grant that the Frenchman might henceforth work
in the common interest, for the common good. But we know
very well that what Laval and his clique stand for is a
concentration of wealth that will make the "200 families"
look like Little Brothers of St. Francis...*

*Family? But there can be no family in the Fascist state.
The Catholics as such, who are nearly as stupid as the
possessing classes as such, seem to have learned nothing
from the history of the last decade. The heart of the
family principle is—who will rear the children? In the
Fascist state youth belongs to the entire nation. Parents
and teachers are, as the Nazis have it, Treuhaender—
trustees. For all practical purposes they are less than
this, they are mere boarding-house keepers.*

*In 1935 the Nazi government gave German parents the
option of sending their children either to governmental
or to parochial schools—but with the warning that those
who opted for the parochial school would be deemed to
have taken sides against the party. In the same year it
was decreed that every German member of the teaching
profession must join the party through the Nazi Teachers'
Association (Nationalsozialistischer Lehrerbund). Exactly
thus will Laval seek to betray Pétain and Weygand.
Fatherland? Nobody expects France to possess independence
in Nazi Europe—it is to be doubted that she will possess
even dominion status. Go outside the German orbit and ask
the black in the Transvaal for whose fatherland he works
and brings up a family: this will be the status of the
French family under Hitler's hireling. Laval.*

*But to talk about Patrie at all in these German terms
of blood and soil is to misapprehend and misrepresent
totally what it means to be a Frenchman. France is
not mere soil. France is not a symbol of fealty and
fraternity of blood. France is a way of life, a view
of the world, a civilization. The essence of France is
not something exclusive but inclusive; it is something
spiritual and universal, not something material and
national.*

Anybody can be a Frenchman. Anybody who can read and savor Montaigne and Rabelais, Descartes and Pascal, Voltaire and Diderot, Molière and Flaubert, Fenelon and Renan, Turgot and de Tocqueville, can become part of the Patrie called France—and up to yesterday, at any rate, every born Frenchman would have welcomed him into the great family of the French spirit.

It was precisely because France and America, each in its own way, were inclusive and not exclusive, that they were sister nations. It was because of this that their peoples were drawn to each other, were animated by deep sympathy for each other even when they were ignorant of each other's languages, histories, institutions.

Here is a Patrie that cannot be sacked, gutted, despoiled by such unFrench Frenchmen as Laval, even though the nation remain for a time stunned and its spirit numbed. It will not be changed in essence, it will not be regimented; and it will react. The French are not a patient people. They are not a timorous people. They are—very significantly—not like the Germans, a people who need to be whipped up and organized by self-appointed or hereditary leaders in order to spring into action.

It is not a Laval, nor a dandy of the stripe of Marquet that will be able to alter the course of the stream of French civilization. And when the erstwhile hungry Germans have grown fat again, and have sunk into that state of sentimentality to which they are brought by magnums of the sickly-sweet champagne they love, the lightning of the French spirit will blast Laval's Gestapo and the world will witness the re-emergence of the French Phoenix from its ashes.

"France's Spirit Only Numbed, Lewis Galantiére Predicts That Its Revival Will Destroy Oppressors," *New York Tribune*, July 12, 1940.

241. Butler Library, Galantière Collection, box 17.

242.   *Old Jewry*

London, e.c.2.

metropolitan 8001

My dearest Louis,

... You ask me about my ideas on the European situation?...I think you are aware that I was terribly apprehensive about a possible German-Italian cooperation. Economically speaking it would be obvious. Politically speaking, both Italy and Germany belong to that party which is bent on revising the Peace Treaties and which is therefore not in a defensive but in an offensive position. Both are suffering from over-population...
In both countries a regime has been established whose continued prestige rests on foreign rather than internal successes. Here we have people who are suffering from an inferiority complex and do not regard their position in the absolute as Anglo-Saxons would do and ask themselves whether they feel better themselves this year than they did last, but whose measure of comparison is the "other fellow" and especially the impression which that power makes on the "other fellow."

I do not want to bore you with mass psycho-analytical remarks, but I have little doubt in my mind that the Germans are essentially masochistic; that ever since the Revolution they were hard pressed by a big Oedipus complex, trying to remedy their sin of killing the Papa by putting themselves back into the infantile position of the child who is chastised but cared for by the old fellow and whose life flows in the repressed certainty of the nursery. Voila! the basis of Nazi-ism. Add to it, s'il vous plait, a high pressure propaganda and extreme economic suffering, a love of phrases, an absolute lack of information on the part of the people, and you will understand that Hitler's popularity within has not developed in the same way as abroad.

Thomas Balogh to Lewis Galantière, September 6, 1934, Butler Library, Galantière Collection, box 1-001.

243. Here are the hypotheses that Lewis set out in his grant request. The words in quotation marks are from his application form:

> Germans were "hypnotized" by the memory of Germany's mediaeval ascendancy over western Christendom and were enthralled with a "mirage of world dominion."

> Whereas the humanist ideas of the Dutch, French, and English had created an affluent middle class that cherished political liberty, the Lutheran Reformation had degraded the German peasantry, had debilitated the burgher (i.e., middle) class, and had established a God-blessed and absolutist nobility.

> The "mirage of world dominion" and the absolutist rule of the nobility had imbued Germans with an "irrational, intuitional and universalistic" romantic philosophy—that they were a chosen people and that non-Germans were "limited, incomplete and inferior."

> The Prussian aristocracy had adopted this "metaphysical idiosyncrasy" as a state theology that distracted the people from their miserable living conditions.

> And with this metaphysical theology, when wedded to a totalitarian economic system (as distinct from Western European free economies), the German people had chosen Nazism over the liberal and democratic Weimar Republic.

Butler Library, Galantière Collection, box 2.

244. Professor Guérard's recommendations of Maurice Chevalier, "not the vaudeville artist, but the author of *The Ironic Temper*," had been to no avail. Butler Library, Galantière Collection, box 1-001.

245. Butler Library, Galantière Collection, box 7-001.

246. Butler Library, Galantière Collection, box 1

247. Excerpt from Lewis's article, "Irresponsible Germany," in the May
1940 issue of *Forum and Century*:

> Two of the fundamental characteristics of the German
> are...the incapacity for prompt decision and the instinct
> to take shelter behind collective consultation before a
> line of action is adopted...

> [No] *forces, external or internal, could have defeated
> German republicanism had the Germans desired to be
> republicans. None of them could have destroyed the German
> Republic had that republic been the product of the
> deliberate will of the German people...*

> How does one go about dissociating any people from
> its government for purposes of war? The two—people and
> government—are the same, are indissolubly fused, and
> cannot be separated. The government will evolve from age
> to age, perhaps from generation to: it will change in
> form, in external aim, in internal policy; but it will
> change only as the people themselves first change...

> ... [It is wrong to argue] *that Hitler has forced on all
> the Germans, against their will, the adventure on which
> they have since 1933...*

> Of course many Germans are shocked by excessive anti-
> Semitism, just as many Americans are not in the least
> shocked by a light touch of anti-Semitism. Of course many
> German villages had, in Sam Blythe's phrase, their "pet
> Jew." But to assume that the German who is shocked by
> a pogrom is also made miserable by the Greater Germany
> drive of the Nazi regime is to ignore a thousand years of
> German history and indoctrination...

> ... while many Germans may have had no taste for this ugly
> business [the invasions of Czechoslovakia on March 15,
> 1939, and of Poland on September 1, 1939], they certainly
> felt that they stood to gain by it; ...[they] saw in
> the two campaigns, as in the absorption of Austria, a
> glorious augmentation of the splendor and power of the
> German Folk.

... Whence arises this insistence that not once but twice in twenty years—and each time in respect of a different form of government and a different social category of leadership—the world must hasten to dissociate the Germans from their governors?

Whether they fight for Hitlerism or fall into Stalinism or elect a third way out, the responsibility is still theirs. And this people will not face this responsibility in the future any more than in the past, so long as the whole of the democratic world, from the British Ministry for Propaganda to Miss Nora Wain, continues to assure it that it is a dear, sweet people, truly better than its governors, and absolved from all responsibility for what is done in the name of the German Folk.

Those people are doing a puzzled and harassed world no good who encourage the German people to believe that they are the irresponsible victims of their governors, that they are unanswerable to the world for what their governors do, and that it is somehow reserved for them alone to share in the fruits of civilization without the assumption of any duty or the fulfillment of any trust towards Western society as a whole.

248. Hoover, Albert Léon Guérard Papers, 1942-1948

NOTES TO CHAPTER 8

249. *Atlantic Monthly*, April 1947, 133.

250. Ibid, 136.

251. From Saint-Exupéry's, *Flight to Arras*, as translated by Lewis Galantière.

252. Ibid.

253. Butler Library, Galantière Collection, box 1.

254. *Harrisburg (PA) Telegraph*, July 19, 1943, 6.

NOTES TO CHAPTER 9

255. Butler Library, Galantière Collection, box 17.

256. The following are more excerpts from Pétain's proclamation:

> As for collaboration—offered in the month of October, 1940, by the Chancellor of the Reich under conditions that made me appreciate their deference—it was a long-term labor and has not yet been able to bear all its fruits...That is the goal toward which we are heading; but it is an immense labor, which requires on our part as much will as it does patience. Other tasks absorb the German Government, gigantic tasks in developments to the east in defense of a civilization and which can change the map of the world.

> I would also recall to the great American republic the reasons why it has no cause to fear a decline of French ideals. Certainly our parliamentary democracy is dead, but it never had more than a few traits in common with the democracy of the United States. As for the instinct of liberty, it still lives within us, proud and strong...

> Authority no longer emanates from below. The only authority is that which I entrust or delegate...This is what I have decided: Activity of political parties and groups of political origin is suspended until further notice...

> I will double the means of police action, whose discipline and loyalty should guarantee public order...

> A group of Commissars of Public Power is created...These high officials will be charged with studying the spirit in which the laws, decrees, orders and instructions of the central power will be carried out. They will have the mission of ferreting out and destroying obstacles which abuse of the rules of administrative routine or activity of secret societies can oppose to the work of National Revolution.

> *Powers of regional prefects...over all heads of local*
> *services is direct and complete.*
>
> *... all Ministers and high officials must swear an oath of*
> *fealty to me and engage themselves to carry out duties in*
> *their charge for the well-being of the State according to*
> *the rules of honor and propriety.*

257. Butler Library, Galantière Collection, box 1.

258. Ibid.

259. Robert Sherwood, a decorated World War I veteran, movie critic, and playwright, headed the Office of War Information, or OWI, of which the Foreign Information Service was part. The OWI had started out as the Office of the Coordinator of Information, which President Roosevelt created in July 1941 and was bifurcated after the United States entered the war. One part dealt with military intelligence and covert operations (the Office of Strategic Services, or OSS, under William J. Donovan) and the other with propaganda (again, the OWI under Robert Sherwood).

260. National Archives, Military Personnel Records Center, St. Louis, MO.

261. National Archives, Military Personnel Records Center, St. Louis, MO.

262. National Archives, Military Personnel Records Center, St. Louis, MO, January 11, 1942 Memo from Nelson P. Poynter to Robert E. Sherwood, with a copy to Colonel Donovan.

263. National Archives, Military Personnel Records Center, St. Louis, MO.

264. Houseman, *Unfinished Business,* 244.

265. Website maintained by Chris Kern, Washington DC, http://www.chriskern.net/essay/voaFirstBroadcast.html.

266. Butler Library, Galantière Collection, box 17.

267. Bancroft Library, Helen Haines letters.

268. *Atlantic Monthly*, April 1, 1947.

269. Ibid.

270. Roosevelt and Churchill were less sanguine about the French Navy. In its June 23, 1940, armistice agreement with the French, Germany had "solemnly and firmly declared that it had no intention of making demands regarding the French fleet." But Winston Churchill had little regard for German promises and gave French Admiral François Darlan two choices for disposition of the fleet: fight the Germans or sail the vessels with reduced crews to either a British port or a French port inaccessible to the Germans. "If you refuse these fair offers, I must with profound regret, require you to sink your ships within 6 hours." Darlan chose a third course: he promised Churchill that he would scuttle his ships at the first warning that they might be seized. Ten days after the armistice was signed, the British shelled the French ships at port in Mers-el-Kébir, Algeria. About thirteen hundred French servicemen were killed and the Vichy government severed diplomatic relations with England. Darlan was incensed; de Gaulle was not. Speaking of the action in a July 8, 1940 broadcast, de Gaulle said,

> By virtue of an agreement contrary to all honor [the armistice], the government then established in Bordeaux agreed to place our ships at the mercy of the enemy. There cannot be the slightest doubt that, on principle and of necessity, the enemy would have used them either against Britain or against our own Empire. I therefore have no hesitation in saying that they are better destroyed.

271. In preparation for the North African landings, the American consul in Algiers, Robert Daniel Murphy, was instructed to determine whether the French military stationed there would cooperate or would resist

an Allied invasion. He said they would support the Allies, and so Allied soldiers were instructed to withhold fire unless fired upon. When the Allied forces approached, French coastal batteries and naval vessels opened fire at Casablanca and Oran, costing lives on both sides during the first two days of the invasion. A third landing site, Algiers, capitulated readily, due in part to the preparatory work of the French resistance, which, in the early hours of November 8, 1942, sent four hundred members to seize the telephone system, radio station, and other key sites there. It was at that time and place that American Consul Robert Daniel Murphy asked Admiral Darlan to join the Allies. Darlan was then commander of the French Vichy forces and, by coincidence, had picked the day of the invasion to visit his hospitalized son in Algiers. During the height of his power in the Vichy Regime, Darlan had been its minister of foreign affairs, minister of the interior, and minister of national defense and had been named Pétain's eventual successor. That ended in April 1942, when the Germans backed the restoration of Laval, whom they trusted to be more compliant.

With General Giraud cooling his heels on Gibraltar, Darlan appeared to be the only French official whom the French North African troops would obey if ordered to stand down. On November 10, at the instruction of Roosevelt and Churchill, Eisenhower named Admiral Darlan the "High Commissioner." Darlan gave the order to cease fire and the French North African troops obeyed. Upon learning of Darlan's betrayal, Hitler ordered the German occupation of all of Vichy France.

The United States now had a partner in François Darlan. De Gaulle, who had not been told of Operation Torch in advance, was incensed that Roosevelt and Churchill had sidelined him and that Darlan, whom de Gaulle considered a Nazi collaborator, was leading a Vichy-derived government. Many of the Algerian French population and many Americans and British who identified with de Gaulle's Free France felt the same way. De Gaulle's representatives in the United States urged that he, and not Darlan, be recognized as the legitimate French provisional authority. On November 29, 1942, Saint-Exupéry, writing in the *New York Times*, stirred the pot by saying that the choice of a provisional government should be left to Britain and the United States. Saint-Exupéry's intent had been to quell French factionalism, but his words were taken by many to be anti–de Gaulle and anti-Free French. De Gaulle was incensed when he learned of Saint-Exupéry's suggestion that the Americans and British should choose the interim leader. In his mind, by rights, the prize was his.

High Commissioner Darlan's ascendancy became moot when, on December 24, a twenty-year-old monarchist, anti-Vichyite, and member of the Resistance, Bonnier de La Chappelle—placed one bullet in Darlan's chest and a second in his skull. Darlan was replaced—by the Allies—with General Giraud who, like Darlan, retained the North African administrative holdovers from the Vichy regime. Giraud also retained many of the regime's policies, including that of withholding French citizenship from Algerian Jews.

272. On June 13, 1942, President Roosevelt folded General Donovan's foreign intelligence and covert operations into the Office of Strategic Services (later the CIA) and placed Robert Sherwood's propaganda functions, including VOA, in a separate agency: the Office of War Information (later, the U.S. Information Agency).

273. National Archives, Military Personnel Records Center, St. Louis, MO.

274. *Wilkes-Barre (PA) Record*, October 5, 1942, 1.

275. Rales is an abnormal crackling or rattling chest sound caused by congestion of the lungs.

276. Butler Library, Galantière Collection, box 05, folder 3. 10329

277. Ibid.

278. *The Decline and Fall of the Roman Empire* is a six-volume treatise by Edward Gibbon. First published in the 1780s, it ran about 5,000 pages.

279. Butler Library, Galantière Collection, box 05, folder 3. 10330

280. Ibid. 10322

281. *New York Times*, April 5, 1943, page 8, column 2.

282. Butler Library, Galantière Collection, box 17.

283. National Archives, Military Personnel Records Center, St. Louis, MO.

284. Lewis's February 1, 1944 OWI Position Description

> Regional Specialist for the French-language operations of the Overseas Operations Branch is responsible for the coordination and execution of the French output of the Overseas Operations Branch of the OWI in the departments of...recorded radio shows distributed to Outposts on platters to all French-speaking regions of the world... cable-wireless and syndicated news...booklets, leaflets, posters and other printed material...and execution of the psychological warfare policy of the Overseas Operations Branch.
>
> He works under the direct supervision of John Houseman, Chief of the Radio Program Bureau of the Overseas Operations Branch. At the same time, he is in direct touch with the Chief of Region II (Washington Office) for the purpose of examination and execution of all matters of long-range policy relating to the French-language world as well as with the chiefs of the Overseas Publications Bureau, the Motion Pictures Bureau and

> *the Cable-Wireless Bureau concerning French-language*
> *production by the staffs of those bureaus.*
>
> *Among* [the French-language] *regions, may be mentioned*
> *Northern Italy, Spain, the Balkans, the Eastern*
> *Mediterranean, Turkey, and Egypt. His duty, in its*
> *broadest aspect, is to place his specialized knowledge*
> *at the service of all the departments of the Overseas*
> *Operations Branch concerned with the French-language*
> *areas and his general responsibility is for the*
> *coordination and execution of policy in the several media*
> *and for the quality of the French-language output of the*
> *Overseas Operations Branch...*
>
> *The present incumbent of the position is Lewis*
> *Galantière...Educated chiefly in France. In OWI...he*
> *organized the French Radio Section which now broadcasts*
> *over eighty 15-minute programs every 24 hours. Writer on*
> *economic and literary subjects and translator of many*
> *prominent French authors.*

Ibid.

285. During his recuperation, Lewis continued to supervise a staff of OWI writers, editors, translators, and broadcasters. One of his subordinates, Mr. Jean Longuet, was incompetent, inattentive, and insubordinate and, on June 16, 1943, Lewis fired him. (Butler Library, Galantière Collection, box 17.) Two weeks later, a banner headline appeared on page 6 of the *New York Post*: "Longuet Blames Vichyites for OWI Ouster."

Longuet accused Lewis of both being a secret admirer of Pétain and of having "engineered" his (Longuet's) discharge from the OWI because he was a member of the French Socialist Party. On the day that the *Post* ran the article, the de Gaulle delegation sent a telegram to the *Post* saying that Longuet's statement was "wholly inaccurate and untrue." The delegation also sent a letter to Lewis expressing its hope

> *that this attack upon you shall be withdrawn in its*
> *entirety and that the damage to your reputation and your*

> *integrity brought about by this publication be erased in*
> *a subsequent article.*

On August 7, 1943, the *Post* published a retraction of suitable length, substance and contrition. Its headline, "OWI Denies Lewis Galantière Is Pro-Vichy or Fascist," was the same size and font as that of the original article, and its closing statement was unqualified:

> *On the basis of the information now furnished for the*
> *first time by OWI officials and Mr. Galantière, the Post*
> *regrets and withdraws any reflections on Mr. Galantière or*
> *his loyalty, arising from its story of July 2.*

286. Bancroft Library, Helen Haines letters.

287. Bernice Kert, *The Hemingway Women* (New York: W. W. Norton, 1999), 392:

> *in London...old friends turned up—Freddie Spiegel,*
> *Lewis Galantière, as did Ernest's brother Leicester*
> *(attached to a documentary film unit in London) and Life*
> *photographer Robert Capa.*

288. *Collier's Weekly* magazine staffed only a single reporter to cover the European Theater. Hemingway offered his reportage services to Collier's, certain that it would hire him and discharge its current reporter, Martha Gellhorn. Martha was then Ernest's wife, but their marriage was near its end. Hemingway resented Martha's long absences on reporting assignments and her lapsed adoration, and she had tired of his cruelty and self-absorption. Gellhorn stowed away on a hospital ship off the coast of Normandy, where she lent a hand with the wounded and then went ashore to do the same for the troops on the beaches.

289. In the judgment of Winston Churchill and, especially, Franklin Roosevelt, Charles de Gaulle was petty, intransigent, self-aggrandizing and unrealistic: the self-proclaimed leader of a government that did not exist. In Charles de Gaulle's view, Churchill and Roosevelt were untrustworthy Vichy collaborators. The perceptions of all were accurate.

From 1940 to 1944, President Roosevelt and Secretary Hull had done their best to sideline de Gaulle in favor of an alliance with the Vichy regime. (Relations with the Vichy regime were maintained because, ostensibly, it was the validly chosen French government. But also, through that channel of communications, the United States hoped to have a voice in military and political matters.) Thus Churchill and Roosevelt had dealt with Pétain, then Darlan, and then Giraud, but not with de Gaulle.

Roosevelt and Churchill's transactions with de Gaulle had been a chronicle of repeated betrayals, apologies, obduracy, suspicions, slights, and resentments on both sides. Examples abounded.

The Levant

Under the League of Nations mandate, France had been given dominion over Syria and Lebanon. In 1941, Vichy gave Germany the use of a Syrian airbase that was then manned with German and thirty thousand Vichy French troops. A joint British and Free French advance on Syria and Lebanon had Free French soldiers battling Vichy soldiers, at a cost of thousands of French lives (plus the eye of one fighter of the Palestinian Brigade, Moshe Dayan). The Allies prevailed, and de Gaulle and his British counterparts who were on the scene agreed to terms of armistice: (1) de Gaulle would participate in the surrender negotiations and (2) the Free French would thereafter have authority over Syria and Lebanon. The London Foreign Office ignored the agreement and directed that negotiations be between the British and Vichy commanders. There was to be no continuing Free French presence; Vichy soldiers were to be returned to France; and—the final insult—the Free French were to have no direct contact, let alone a recruitment opportunity, with any of them. An infuriated de Gaulle responded by letter:

> *Free France, that is to say France, is no longer willing*
> *to entrust to the British military command the duty*
> *of exercising command over French troops in the Middle*
> *East. General de Gaulle and the French Empire Defense*
> *Council [the name of de Gaulle's government-in-exile]*
> *are resuming full and entire disposal of all Free French*
> *forces of the Levant as from July 24, 1941, at midday.*

Reading de Gaulle's letter, the British saw they had gone too far and modified the armistice arrangements. But the sense of shared purpose that had existed between de Gaulle and the British was broken. In an interview with the *Chicago Daily News*, de Gaulle gave his assessment of Britain's co-dependency with Vichy:

> *England is afraid of the French Fleet. What in effect*
> *England is carrying on is a wartime deal with Hitler in*
> *which Vichy serves as a go-between. Vichy serves Hitler*
> *in keeping the French people in subjection, and selling*
> *the French Empire piecemeal to Germany. But do not forget*
> *that Vichy also serves England by keeping the French fleet*
> *from Hitler's hands. Britain is exploiting Vichy the same*
> *way as Germany, the only difference is in purpose. What*
> *happens is, in effect, an exchange of advantages between*
> *hostile powers which keeps the Vichy government alive*
> *as long as both Britain and Germany are agreed that it*
> *should exist.*

When Churchill read de Gaulle's Chicago Daily News rebuke, he instructed his cabinet ministers to deny the general access to 10 Downing Street:

> *in view of General de Gaulle's disturbing behavior in*
> *recent weeks, departments should for the time being adopt*
> *a cautious and dilatory attitude towards all requests by*
> *the Free French.*

De Gaulle and Churchill later reconciled, as they did repeatedly after even more ferocious falling-outs.

Saint-Pierre and Miquelon

The small islands of Saint-Pierre and Miquelon lay just off the southern coast of Newfoundland, about a hundred miles south of Botwood Harbor. During prohibition, the Canadian islands' economies had boomed but, with the repeal of prohibition in 1933, their inhabitants had returned to fishing. In 1939, the islands' residents were pro–Free French but were governed, loosely, by pro-Vichy admiral Georges Robert, who was then living on the Caribbean island of Martinique, two thousand miles away. Secretary of State Cordell Hull negotiated an agreement with Admiral Robert under which the admiral immobilized his naval vessels (except for small patrol boats) at Saint-Pierre and Miquelon, and the United States refrained from challenging the pro-Vichy governance of the islands.

When the Battle of the Atlantic intensified, radio transmitters on the islands broadcast weather information that helped German submariners anticipate Allied ship movements. To stop those broadcasts, the State Department arranged for a Canadian military team to silence the transmitters without interfering with the islands' Vichy administrators, thus preserving the core of the Secretary Hull–Admiral Robert agreement. Unaware of those plans, de Gaulle told Churchill that he hoped to conduct a naval operation to claim the islands for the Free French. Churchill told de Gaulle not to do it but withheld information about the American-Canadian plan. De Gaulle agreed to forbear, but then learned of the proposed Canadian action. Fuming, he ordered Free French admiral Emile Muselier to invade the islands, which the admiral did on Christmas Day 1941, placing the pro-Vichy administrator under arrest. De Gaulle did not give Washington or London advance notice of the operation. The effect upon Roosevelt and Hull was profound. They would not thereafter tell de Gaulle of their military plans, including those of the invasion of North Africa—Operation Torch—or Normandy, Operation Overlord.

Elsewhere

From May 27 to June 11, 1942, Free French troops under General Pierre Koenig fought valiantly at Bir-Hakeim in the Libyan desert, allowing British troops to retreat and regroup after an onslaught by Erwin Rommel and his 88-millimeter guns. Headlines in France, Britain, and the United States cast the Free French and de Gaulle in heroic terms and gave credibility to de Gaulle's standing as leader of the French nation. Following Operation Torch, consultations between Giraud and de Gaulle resulted in the two men sharing power, but de Gaulle, being the more knowledgeable and skillful politician, soon outmaneuvered Giraud and, in November 1943, became the sole political head of the Free French.

During the run-up to D-day, Dwight Eisenhower, as Supreme Commander of the Allied Forces, prepared a declaration that he proposed to read to the people of France. In essence, it proclaimed that he and not the Free French would control the civil administration of France and that de Gaulle would be consulted only if he deemed it necessary. What follows is a part of Eisenhower's proclamation. The underlining has been added:

> Prompt and willing obedience to the orders _that I shall_
> _issue_ is essential. Effective civil administration
> of France must be provided by Frenchmen. All persons
> must continue in their present duties unless otherwise
> instructed. Those who have common cause with the enemy
> and so betrayed their country will be removed. As France
> is liberated from her oppressors, you yourselves will
> choose your representatives and the government under
> which you wish to live.

John Eisenhower, *General Ike: A Personal Reminiscence* (New York: Simon and Schuster, 2004), 161.

Don Cook, *Charles de Gaulle, A Biography* (New York, G.P. Putnam's Sons, 1983), 213

Eisenhower asked de Gaulle to address the French people immediately following his broadcast knowing that, in doing so, de Gaulle would appear to agree that the American Supreme Commander controlled France's civil government. De Gaulle did not play along. He insisted that an hour elapse between the speeches, so that their individual pronouncements would seem disassociated. The broadcasts went out over the BBC. Here is what de Gaulle said; again the underlining has been added:

> The decisive battle has begun...For the sons of France, whoever they may be, wherever they may be, the simple and sacred duty is to fight the enemy with all available means. The <u>directives issued</u> by the French Government and by the <u>French leaders who have been delegated to issue them</u> must be followed to the letter.

Don Cook, *Charles de Gaulle, A Biography* (New York, G.P. Putnam's Sons, 1983), 217

290. Ibid.

291. In 1939, his wife, Dorothy Schiff, the daughter of one of the founders of Kuhn, Loeb & Co., had bought the *New York Post* and appointed Backer its editor. It was a job he bollixed until March 28, 1942, when Dorothy instructed him to resign for reasons of "ill health." According to Ms. Schiff's biographer, Jeffrey Potter, she and President Roosevelt had had a romantic if not sexual liaison from 1936 to 1943, about which Backer knew and in which he took some satisfaction. As explained by his wife,

> George was overwhelmed by the president, and it was he who really sold me on him. George saw it all in a sort of droit du seigneur way, his wife being tapped by the

> *lord of the manor. He was proud of it, and it gave him*
> *tremendous prestige with his friends.*
>
> **Marilyn Nissenson, *The Lady Upstairs: Dorothy Schiff and***
> ***the New York Post* (New York: St. Martin's Press, 2007), 32.**

292. Butler Library, Galantière Collection, box 24.

293. Ibid.

294. Ibid.

295. Philip H. Cohen was OWI director of the American radio station for Europe. In September 1944, he sent a memorandum to OWI director Hamblet, recommending that OWI's Dutch Radio Section broadcast into Holland. Lewis sent Hamblet a contrary recommendation. Hamblet sided with Lewis, who then sent a memorandum to Mr. Cohen alone, explaining the several ways in which he—Cohen—had exhibited incompetence:

> *September 8, 1944*
>
> *The recommendation [to Hamblet] results from my recent inspection of the product of the Dutch Radio Section (oral and written) and my discussions with the staff. I have given the staff and its product a good deal of time recently...Mr. Coster-Smit gave evidence that he considered my attempts to improve the Section's output a personal attack against him. Mr. Schadee...has refused to broadcast "under" Coster-Smit. Schadee demands, in effect, that he be made Chief of the Radio Section. I refused to recommend this because I do not consider him qualified either to select news or to write it, and he has not given evidence of that quality of journalistic inventiveness (or showmanship) essential to a proper radio chief. His wife does distinctly possess this gift; she is exercising it with remarkable energy, devotion and success in her newsreel work; but I conceive that I cannot recommend a man for a job merely because his wife is an energetic and capable woman.*

*All of the foregoing took place before I read your
memorandum to Mr. Hamblet. Since you retain a copy of
that memo in your files, I cannot but ask you to place in
them this refutation of it.*

*I did not say to Mr. Hamblet what I now say to you (and
said on Thursday night on the telephone to Saudak)—that
if I intervened in the Dutch Radio situation it was
because our Dutch broadcasts were no credit to OWI and
you were doing nothing to improve them.*

*Nobody in the Dutch Radio Section had ever written a
line of copy or stood before a microphone before coming
to ABSIE. You knew that; yet you made no effort to train
them, to go over their work with them, to ask for reports
from producers, from listeners or from me concerning
them. So far as I know, you are unaware to this day what
goes into their broadcasts, what is the quality of their
reporting, their writing, their voices, the reading of
their lines. You do not know if their scripts are always
ready on time or always late. And until you know these
things, what you say about the Dutch Section clearly
cannot carry much weight.*

*Your memorandum—necessarily personal since you know
only the personalities and not the product involved—is
erroneous even in its discussion of persons.*

*Houbolt was not merely a man unable to speak or write
Dutch: he was unable to make up his mind concerning what
he wanted in his broadcasts, and constantly altered his
texts after they were censored (without resubmission to
the censor). Worse than that: he constantly expressed
the greatest contempt for the Dutch people, refused to
put anything of direct interest to the Dutch into his
broadcasts...I do not believe that any chief of ABSIE
who knew Houbolt's professional demerits and knew the
contents of his broadcast would hasten to his defense...*

*If my intrusion into your domain—which I freely confess—
has the result of stirring you into taking the Dutch
Section in hand, I cannot but be pleased, since it means*

that I shall be free hereafter to do my own work, and not part of yours.

Butler Library, Galantière Collection, box 24.

296. Lewis Galantière to Peter and Sonia Colefax, August 18, 1944, Franklin D. Roosevelt Library, Alexander Sachs Papers, box 27, Galantière folder. Peter Colefax was Chairman of American Potash, and a Director of Kerr-McGee and other corporations.

297. The laconic Guillaumet, whom Saint-Exupéry admired over all other pilots, had been shot down over the Mediterranean three years earlier.

298. In 2008, a German fighter pilot, Horst Rippert, announced that he had shot down Saint-Exupéry's P-38. Said Rippert,

> *If I had known it was Saint-Exupéry I would never have shot him down. He knew admirably how to describe the sky, the thoughts and feelings of pilots. His work inspired many of us to take up our vocation.*

The Telegraph, March 16, 2008, World News, page 1.

299. Saint-Exupéry's Lightning was found, in a hundred pieces, in 2004. It was less than two miles off shore, between Marseille and Cassis.

300. "Firsthand Recollections of trip to France, August 1944," typed memorandum, Butler Library, Galantière Collection, box 24.

301. Franklin D. Roosevelt Library, Alexander Sachs Papers, box 27, Galantière folder.

302. Don Cook, *Charles de Gaulle, A Biography* (New York, G.P. Putnam's Sons, 1983), 225.

303. Dietrich von Choltitz surrendered the city without detonating explosives that he had strategically placed throughout its infrastructure. Upon surrendering, Choltitz was transported to Trent Park, in Northern London, where his conversations with other senior German

officers were secretly recorded. In one, Choltitz admitted that, while stationed in Russia, he had ordered the liquidation of the Jews.

304. Ibid., *Charles de Gaulle, A Biography*, 225.

305. Lewis had obtained this information from Captain André Manuel, chief of Free French Intelligence Service, and from Robert Moulié, London director of the French *Information* Agency.

306. Butler Library, Galantière Collection, box 24.

307. Ibid.

308. Franklin Roosevelt to his son, Elliott Roosevelt, January 1943.

309. Butler Library, Galantière Collection, box 23.

310. Ibid., box 1.

311. Ibid., box 23.

312. Ibid.

313. Ibid.

314. Ibid.

315. Ibid., box 26.

316. In the 1920s, *La Guerre 1914–1918: Tragédie Bouffe* was reviewed by only a single literary critic, Jean de Pierrefeu of the *Journal des Débats*. He thought it extraordinary:

> I regret that a manuscript which moved me profoundly by its accent of savage sincerity could not be considered [for the Balzac Prize]. It is the notebook of a combatant at Verdun, written minute by minute with an awful lucidity. The soul of the soldier is presented naked stripped of all convention, in the moments when it is that of a frightened beast, and in those of its

heroic impulse. The author has not deigned to invent the slightest romantic incident in his desire to paint the truth. It was impossible to class this manuscript as a novel. But what an admirable document on battle! What a contribution to the psychology of the combatant! I hope that a publisher will give to the public this pitiless fragment of truth.

Butler Library, Galantière Collection, box 8.

317. The reference is to Edmond Dantes in Alexander Dumas's *The Count of Monte Cristo*. Butler Library, Galantière Collection, box 30.

318. As noted, *Au Rendez-vous des Mariniers* was Madame Lecomte's working-class restaurant at 33 Quai d'Anjou, where Lewis and René and Ernest Hemingway dined.

319. J.J. Wilhelm, *Ezra Pound: The Tragic Years, 1925-1972* (Pennsylvania State University Press, 2010), 308.

320. Houghton Library, Harvard University, E.E. Cummings collection

NOTES TO CHAPTER 10

321. Bancroft Library, Helen Haines letters.

322. *Dunkirk (NY) Evening Observer*, February 20, 1946.

323. Butler Library, Galantière Collection, box 2-001.

324. J. P. Wearing, *The London Stage 1940–1949: A Calendar of Productions, Performers and Personnel*, Lanham, MD: Rowman and Littlefield, 2014.

325. Bancroft Library, Helen Haines letters.

326. The play debuted on February 10, 1949. Jean Anouilh, *Antigone*, translated by Barbara Bray (London: Bloomsbury, 2000), 50; *Post-Gazette*, December 1, 1948, 10.

327. Lewis's *Antigone and the Tyrant* was an adaptation of Jean Anouilh's adaptation of Sophocles' *Antigone*. All three employed the same plot and characters:

Oedipus had two daughters and two sons. After the death of their father, the sons were to share power by ruling Thebes in alternate years. Instead, they engaged in civil war and killed each other. Their uncle, Creon, assumed the throne and, to set a civic example, ordered that one of his nephews be honored as a symbol of virtue and the other, Polynices, left unburied as a symbol of corruption—to be preyed upon as carrion. Antigone, one of the two sisters, buried Polynices because she believed it was the moral and decent thing to do but knowing that, for that act, Creon would condemn her to death. This Creon did, even though his son, Haemon, and Antigone were engaged to be married. Creon would not relent; he believed that, when a ruler gave a command, it had to be obeyed, even by him, or chaos would ensue.

Creon's sentence upon Antigone led to the suicide of three people: his son, Haemon, who couldn't bear the loss of Antigone; Creon's wife, Eurydice, upon learning of her husband's actions and her son's death; and Antigone, who hanged herself rather than suffer the sentence of being entombed alive.

In Sophocles's version, Creon's tragic error was that that he offended the gods by denying funeral rights to a dead man. Ultimately, Creon realized the error of his arrogance, but too late to avoid the consequences. The character of Antigone, although the instrument through whom Creon demonstrates his hubris, was not of equal weight to the story.

Jean Anouilh wrote his adaptation of *Antigone* for a German and French audience in occupied France. His Creon was a stand-in for Pétain and Laval, who were attempting to govern a country divided between collaborationists and resistance. To satisfy his German censors, Anouilh's Creon placed civic order above all. Creon (Pétain and Laval) selflessly governed a faction-riven Thebes (France) as best he could, while his Antigone (the callow, adolescent French people) disobeyed Creon for no valid reason other than that she, like her father Oedipus (possibly de Gaulle) was impulsive, imprudent, and self-destructive. When, having learned of her crime, Creon turned solicitous of Antigone and gave her the chance to save herself without compromising her morals, Antigone threw her life away by repeating the criminal act. In Anouilh's version, she does this not for the sake of protesting an unjust law but to escape what she anticipated would be the insufferable burdens of her oncoming adulthood. Anouilh compounds Antigone's frivolousness when, facing death, she confesses to herself and her guard that disobeying Creon had been a mistake. These character flaws in Antigone were sufficient reason for the German audience to overlook the rest of the story—that of rebellion against oppressive and unfair rule. Why the French, especially members of the French resistance, were uncritical is less clear. As a stand-in for the people of France, Antigone was an unprincipled or, at best, irrational gamine. It may be that the French were satisfied with that thin gruel because they had no other. The French and German audiences of occupied France each construed Anouilh's ambiguities as favoring their respective points of view. The play ran for five hundred performances.

When Lewis returned to the United States from France, he had probably already rewritten Anouilh's *Antigone* in his mind if not on paper. Given the changes that he made (discussed below), he obviously disdained the moral ambiguities in which Anouilh had indulged. In Lewis's mind, Pétain and Laval had been German quislings, hubristically bent on evil, against whose rule Antigone (many French citizens) had resisted at the cost of their lives. Lewis did not explicitly condemn Anouilh for his shading of the characters but offered his version of the play to set the record straight. Here is how Lewis described his effort on the eve of its Broadway opening:

> The reader will have to take my word for it that only a citizen of a German-occupied country (or, by analogy, a Southerner of 1863) would be able to come away from M. Anouilh's play with the feeling that Antigone's case was stronger than Creon's. For I should be less than frank if I did not say that the play in which Miss Cornell and Sir Cedric Hardwicke will open at the Cort Theatre tomorrow night is not in every respect the play which M. Anouilh gave to Occupied France in 1943.

This was understatement. From the play's opening lines, Lewis's Greek chorus accentuates Creon's tyranny and removes Antigone's selfish motives and vacillations.

Anouilh's version (translation from the French to the English by Barbara Bray), the chorus speaking:

> *The people gathered here are about to act the story of Antigone...She's thinking that soon she's going to be Antigone. That she'll suddenly stop being the thin dark girl whose family didn't take her seriously, and rise up alone against everyone. Against Creon, her uncle...the king. She's thinking she's going to die...though she's still young, and like everyone else would have preferred to live. But there's nothing to be done...she has felt herself hurtling further and further away...from all the rest of us, who are just here to watch, and haven't got to die in a few hours' time.*

Lewis's version:

> *These people that you see here are about to act out for you the story of Antigone...Antigone is young. She would much rather live than die. But there is no help for it. When you are on the side of the gods against the tyrant, of Man against the State, of purity against corruption— when, in short, your name is Antigone, there is only one part you can play; and she will have to play hers through to the end...from the moment the curtain went up, she began to feel that inhuman forces were whirling her out of this world, snatching her away...making her an instrument of the gods in a way she cannot fathom but that she will faithfully pursue. You have never seen inhuman forces at work? You will, tonight.*

At the end of Anouilh's play, Antigone proclaims that Creon was right and that she no longer knows why she chose death over life. In Lewis's version, death is the penalty inflicted upon her for refusing to countenance a collaborator.

Anouilh's version; the scene is Antigone dictating a letter to her guard, for delivery to Haemon:

> *My darling. I've chosen to die. And perhaps you'll stop loving me... And Creon was right: it's awful, but here, with this man [the Guard] beside me, I don't know any more what I'm dying for... I'm afraid... Oh, Haemon! It's only now I realise how easy it was to live... I don't*

> *know any more what I'm dying for... I'm afraid...* [To the
> Guard] *No, cross all that out! It's better no one should
> ever know. It'd be as if they were to see me naked, touch
> me, after I was dead. Just put, "I'm sorry." I'm sorry,
> my darling. It would have been nice and peaceful for you
> all without me. I love you...*

Lewis's version:

> *My darling. I had to die, and perhaps you will not love
> me any more...Perhaps you think it would have been
> simple to accept life... But it was not for myself. And
> now, it's all—so dreadful here alone. I am afraid...
> And those shadows...* [To the guard] *No. Scratch that out.
> Nobody must know that. They have no right to know. It's
> as if they saw me naked and touched me, after I am dead.
> Scratch that out. Just write: "Forgive me."*

And, finally, in Anouilh's *Antigone*, the author offers Creon's justification for collaboration. Anouilh's version, Creon speaking to his page after his son's suicide:

> *I'm going to tell you something the others don't know.
> There you are, face to face with what's to be done. You
> can't just fold your arms and do nothing. They say it's
> dirty work. But if you don't do it, who will?*

Lewis does not let Creon off the hook. Instead, the chorus speaks its indictment:

> Creon: *The task is there to be done. They say it's
>   dirty work. But if I didn't do it, who would?*
>
> Chorus: *Why must dirty work be done?...And there we
>   are...All dead: useless, rotting. Creon was the
>   most rational, the most persuasive of tyrants.
>   But like all tyrants, he refused to distinguish
>   between the things that are Caesar's and the
>   things that are God's. Now and again—in the
>   three thousand years since the first Antigone—
>   other Antigones have arisen like a clarion call
>   to remind men of this distinction. Their cause
>   is always the same—a passionate belief that*

> *moral law exists, and a passionate regard for the sanctity of human dignity.*

328. Butler Library, Galantière Collection, box 7-001.

329. Butler Library, Galantière Collection, box 26.

330. Butler Library, Galantière Collection, box 25.

NOTES TO CHAPTER 11

331. The World Bank and the International Monetary Fund were created at the 1944 Bretton Woods Conference to rebuild the war-shattered economies of Europe. When, in 1946, Stalin declined to participate in either, the U.S. Treasury Department asked George Kennan, then the U.S. ambassador to Moscow, why. Kennan's telegram of February 22, 1946, explained that the Soviets did not seek coexistence with the capitalist world but, rather, its subservience: that Stalin would intervene at every opportunity to undermine the West and impose his brand of communism. Kennan advised the State Department to counter the Soviets at every turn by assisting nations with vulnerable economies, and to counter Communist propaganda by publicizing the virtues of freedom over compulsory collectivization. This was the ideological essence of the Cold War.

The Cold War was "cold" in the sense that the chief combatants—the United States and the USSR—invested heavily in armaments research, development, and deployment and in the sense that the armed conflict was conducted between proxy governments, except during the major confrontations of the Korean Conflict and Vietnam War, and during the U.S. military interventions in the Congo and Santo Domingo. The facsimile of a declaration of war was spoken by Winston Churchill on March 5, 1946, at Westminster College in Fulton Missouri:

> It is my duty...to place before you certain facts about the present position in Europe. From Stettin in the Baltic to Trieste in the Adriatic an iron curtain has descended across the Continent. Behind that line lie all the capitols of the ancient states of Central and Eastern Europe...all are subject, in one form or another, not only to Soviet influence but to a very high and in some

> *cases increasing measure of control from Moscow...I do not believe that Soviet Russia desires war. What they desire is the fruits of war and the indefinite expansion of their power and doctrines.*

Toeing to Moscow's line, the Soviet Bloc countries criminalized the expression of political ideas—written and spoken, read and listened to—that were not approved by the state. Phone lines were bugged; homes were bugged; bathrooms, workrooms, bus stations, churches... no person could hazard confiding in another or being confided in by another. Neighbors were compelled to report neighbors (or did so out of malice) and school children were encouraged to report the conversations of their playmates' parents. Fear—of arbitrary arrest for casual remarks—saturated every moment of consciousness. George Orwell described the tyranny in *1984*:

> *Always, at every moment, there will be the thrill of victory, the sensation of trampling on an enemy who is helpless. If you want a picture of the future, imagine a boot stamping on a human face—forever.*

332. Bancroft Library, Helen Haines letters.

333. Elke Van Cassel, Elke, *A Cold War Magazine of Causes: A Critical History of the Reporter, 1949–1968* (Nijmegen (The Netherlands): Radboud University, 2007).

334. Qtd. in ibid.

335. Lewis Galantière to Helen Haines, March 14, 1949, Bancroft Library, Helen Haines letters.

336. Lewis Galantière to Helen Haines, July 27, 1949, Bancroft Library, Helen Haines letters.

337. In 1951, Lewis would become a member of the Council on Foreign Relations.

338. Bancroft Library, Helen Haines letters.

339. Galantière, "America Today, a Freehand Sketch," *Foreign Affairs*, July 1, 1950.

340. Lewis titled a sequel article, for the Radio Free Europe Press, "The New Capitalism." Here are excerpts:

> In the democratic polity the primary function of the apparatus of the State is to ensure diffusion of power for the purpose of preventing any individual or group from coercing other individuals or groups. This optimum aim is not attained in every community; but diffusion of power is, unquestionably, broadly characteristic of Democratic national life, and the daily chronicles of Western society report defeat after defeat of those who, in local communities, attempt to thwart it.
>
> In Western democracies, power being decentralized, it follows that decision-making also is decentralized. Decentralization of decision-making, in turn, encourages the development of millions of citizens who are willing and able to exercise initiative, people for whom the characteristically Anglo-American adjective, "self-reliant," was long ago found...
>
> American experience suggests that where many men exercise initiative, economic advance is rapid...In the free society, the citizen being genuinely permitted to serve his own interest, he really takes the initiative without which the interests of society cannot be advanced...
>
> There are those who believe that...ethical goods can be provided only by a kind of lay priesthood made up of servants of an all-powerful state, in whom the incentives to deal wisely, justly, unselfishly with those they rule over will be of a moral nature exclusively. This Platonic notion...[that] loyalty was the greatest of virtues, is not shared by many Americans. It is an idealistic inheritance which descended to Karl Marx, perhaps also to some men still in the Kremlin, certainly to the social

democrats, but which the least skeptical people in the world—the American people are historically conditioned to view with skepticism.

... It is true also that nowadays the small business man is handicapped by government demand for records and statistics which, proportionately, cost him much more than they cost the large company, and by a tax schedule which makes growth more difficult for him...[W] e get, in the aggregate, more initiative, boldness, and inventiveness out of the small business man than out of the prudent quasi-bureaucratic corporation official...

[The] owner-manager would not found a business if there were no promise of profit;... the salaried manager could not continue in employment if his efforts did not produce profits for ownership. [E]very economic enterprise, public or private, is obliged to budget for a profit...Without profits there can be no investment funds to provide replacement and enlargement of plant, and without these there can be no maintenance—not to say betterment—of the standard of living...

It ought not to be assumed that democratic economies are in all respects unplanned. No modern economy can be conducted without attention to certain broadly influential factors such as monetary and fiscal policy, conservation of natural resources, balance between the agricultural and non-agricultural sectors, volume of employment, and the international balance of trade payments...Public policy with respect to water supply, hydro-electric development, timber on the public lands and agricultural output is so greatly influential that private enterprise must adjust itself to government plans in these fields of activity...

But this inescapable planning...bears no resemblance to totalitarian planning. In the first place, while making room for social security,...it does not take welfare out of the hide of the farmer and industrial worker. Secondly, it is not centralized, is not the narrow prerogative of pundits drawing blueprints in an ivory tower. Thirdly, it does not come down by fiat, from

> *above...It leaves room for personal initiative, personal*
> *inventiveness, personal rewards. Above all it leaves room*
> *for the kind of imagination and readiness to take risks*
> *without which there is no economic advance...*
>
> *Totalitarian planners can copy, they can struggle to*
> *respond to market demand for products and amenities they*
> *had no part in creating...[but] the power of initiative*
> *is denied them as it is denied all bureaucrats, whose*
> *first rule must be Metternich's "surtout, pas de zèle," or*
> *in the American idiom, "Don't stick your neck out."*

Hoover-Puddington, box 199.

341. Butler Library, Galantière Collection, box 4.

342. Ibid.

343. Butler Library, Galantière Collection, box 1.

344. Ransom Center, Alfred A. Knopf, Inc. Records. Knopf_128_5_004.

345. Numbers 24 and 18 Quai de Béthune, respectively.

346. Butler Library, Galantière Collection, box 7-001.

347. Ibid.

348. In the early 1950s, Europe's intellectuals derived satisfaction and a sense of self-importance from criticizing American culture as materialistic, superficial, and vapid. That mindset was a tonic for the humiliation of their countries' wartime and postwar dependence on America's military and financial assistance. And it was an opinion that Soviet propaganda was ready to reinforce. *America and the Mind of Europe* was Lewis's response. He and nine fellow writers did not claim the superiority of America's culture; some of the opinions expressed were critical of the United States and of Europe. For example, Raymond Aron talked of the pigheadedness of European intellectuals, and the nontransportability of America's brand of democracy to Eu-

rope. Denis de Rougemont, noting the desire of people to believe in something greater than themselves, observed that

> the sterilizing oversimplification of mass media...
> operates against diversity and therefore paralyses true
> individuality.

And Arthur Koestler described, with extraordinary prescience, the devaluation of discourse:

> words are no longer taken seriously. The ideological
> chaos created a semantic inflation and a semantic black
> market where words are traded at a meaning value entirely
> different from their official quotation.

Melvin J. Lasky decried the arrogance with which many Americans viewed Europeans, and cautioned that

> it may still be the destiny of the American to become a
> European in a way that no European ever could become.

But the ten writers were united in condemning the USSR's closed press, its suppression of dissent, and its persecution of dissidents. And their essays, including those critical of modern Western civilization, were themselves testament to freedom of the press. The essays from the *Saturday Review* were compiled into a five-by-eight-inch red hardcover book that was published in England and that became a best seller in Europe under the same title, *America and the Mind of Europe.*

Seven of the ten contributors to *America and the Mind of Europe* were either subsidized by or on the payroll of organizations subsidized by the CIA. The best-funded and most influential of those organizations was the Congress for Cultural Freedom (CCF), which organized prestigious international conferences, art exhibitions, and musical performances and published several intellectual magazines. Although the CIA funded the CCF, it did not dictate the CCF's activities. Arthur Schlesinger, who was then knowledgeable about the arrangements, later assessed, "It seemed not unreasonable to help the people on our side. Of all the CIA's expenditures, the Congress for Cultural Freedom seemed its most worthwhile and successful." This in a 1996 interview of Schlesinger by Frances Stonor Saunders.

349. He consulted for the department's Office of Public Affairs.

350. Butler Library, Galantière Collection, box 7.

351. Hoover—Puddington, box 29 folder 7.

352. Ancestry.com.

353. Jackson's announcement of Lewis's new posting:

> Mr. Lewis Galantière, who for the past several months has been an invaluable part-time associate of Frank Altschul's in radio propaganda policy, has joined the organization full time, in charge of radio propaganda policy.

354. Hoover, RFE Corporate Records, box 444, folder 2, images 312–346.

355. Arch Puddington, *Broadcasting Freedom: The Cold War Triumph of Radio Free Europe and Radio Liberty.* (Lexington: University Press of Kentucky, 2000), page 43, quoting Ralph Walter, who was later appointed an RFE director.

356. Ibid., 43.

357. Ibid., 42.

358. Van Cassel, *A Cold War Magazine of Causes.*

359. Special Guidance no. 4, excerpted:

> We must not...exhort our listeners to hope for liberation without giving them good reasons to do so...We must avoid altogether the idea which is in their minds, that if liberation is to come, it can come only from the outside, without action by them, and only as the result

*of war between the West and the Russians. Hope must be
planted in their breasts indirectly, through the display
of convincing evidences of Western strength and through
reports of Western life which show that the free world is
worth fighting to rejoin...*

*Gen. Eisenhower and his chief advisor on international
affairs, Mr. John Foster Dulles, have spoken with great
firmness...We of RFE, who do not speak as Americans*
[but as the voices of the Eastern Bloc reporters]
*cannot comment upon these statements with unqualified
optimism, for to do so would be to deceive our listeners
by inspiring in them exaggerated hope of a Western
intervention of which there is as yet no sign.*

> a. *Not a single word in these statements can be
> construed as foreshadowing or even promis-
> ing military intervention. The U.S. Government
> could not take such a commitment alone, and its
> Western European allies in NATO are almost cer-
> tain to reject such a proposal at this time.*

> b. *Not one word in these statements can be used to
> encourage militant anti-communists to go over
> from passive to active resistance in the expec-
> tation that such resistance will be supported
> by Western elements...*

*The foregoing displays that it would be cruelly dangerous
to our listeners and speakers if RFE were to allow their
hearts to run away with their heads in their comments
about these American expressions of concern for the fate
of our peoples...*

We may quote Eisenhower's declaration of August 26:

> *The American conscience can never know peace until
> the peoples behind the Iron Curtain are once again
> masters of their own fate...We can never rest and we
> must so inform all the world including the Kremlin
> until the enslaved nations of the world have, in the
> fullness of freedom, the right to choose their own
> path...Then and only then is there a possible way of*

> living peacefully and permanently with communism in
> the world.
>
> ... But we cannot warn our listeners too strongly—and in
> particular their eager and patriotic young men and young
> women—that these words bespeak only the awakening of the
> American conscience: they do not foreshadow, they do not
> even promise, early American action.

Hoover, RFE Corporate Records, box 444, folder 1.

360. In a 1986 interview, Paul B. Henze, deputy political advisor at Radio Free Europe in Munich in 1953, described the dilemma RFE then faced:

> we had a hellish time with activist-minded Republicans in
> Congress who claimed that we were broadcasting socialism
> and capitulation. We were accused of having too many
> Social Democrats and not enough anti-Communists, despite
> the fact that many of the Social Democrats were more
> anti-Communist than anyone.

**Hoover, Paul B. Henze Papers, box 32, Accession no.
2005C42-272, at 527.**

361. Special Guidance no. 8.

362. Here, an excerpt from Lewis's Special Guidance no. 9 from April 18, 1953:

> What RFE has so long prayed for has now come to pass—a
> Government in Washington which boldly announces that
> peace without freedom is not enough; which boldly
> declares that the strength of the West is greater than
> that of the Kremlin, which speaks directly to our peoples
> and says to them: "The status quo is not good enough for
> us; we do not accept your captivity as a condition of
> peace with Moscow."
>
> ... liberation was an idea; thanks to Eisenhower it has
> become an article of policy.

Hoover, RFE/RL Inc. box 202, 14.

Special Guidance no. 9 was based upon Secretary of State John Foster Dulles's statement of April 18, 1953:

> One of the illusions we must be most on our guard
> against is the illusion of a settlement based upon the
> status quo. The present status involves the captivity
> of hundreds of millions of persons...It is of the utmost
> importance that we should make clear to the captive
> peoples that we do not accept their captivity as a
> permanent fact of history.

363. Griffith memo to Lewis, May 8, 1956:

> [For the satellite country rulers] slavish following of
> the Soviet Union in everything...[requires] appreciating
> psychology of fear of imminent Western military attack
> which Stalin had built among Soviet leaders, with
> resultant desire to "hang together in order to avoid
> hanging separately.

Hoover, RFE Telexes, May through July 1956.

364. Butler Library, Galantière Collection, box 1.

365. Among the others was FEC vice president Spencer Phenix.

366. Here, further excerpts from Nathan's Special Guidance no. 12-A:

> The events which have occurred in Czechoslovakia and in
> East Germany the beginning of June call for a change in
> RFE's approach to listeners. We are now in the position
> to proclaim the beginning of a new stage in the fight
> against Soviet imperialism and prepare the peoples of
> Czechoslovakia for spiritual mobilization and the first
> beginnings of preparation for effective resistance...
>
> It is essential that our listeners be made to realize the
> extent of the crisis in which the Czechoslovak regime
> finds itself...Once the peoples of Czechoslovakia disabuse
> themselves of the notion that they are hopelessly at the
> mercy of a powerful regime, they will begin to understand
> the truth—namely, that they are in the process of again
> becoming masters of their own destiny...

*In other words, the time has come to call Moscow's bluff
and to force the hands of the stooges who claim to be
the government of Czechoslovakia, by increasing passive
resistance and by taking all positive steps of which
fighters for freedom are capable without jeopardizing
the even more active role they may have to play in the
future...*

*On every front of the world struggle for freedom against
tyranny, the Kremlin is in retreat...Nothing less than
the freedom of the captive peoples is acceptable...*

*... If the time is not yet ripe for open action and
resistance, the time is right to make a beginning. Our
people must alert themselves, look about for the means
with which they can act.*

Hoover, RFE box 444, folder 1.

367. A. Ross Johnson, *Radio Free Europe and Radio Liberty: The CIA Years and Beyond* (Washington, DC: Woodrow Wilson Center Press, 2010), 52.

368. Lewis was "frontline" in the sense that, unlike Nathan and his ilk, he visited RFE's Munich station on June 6, 1953, and, from there, Belgrade, Athens, Istanbul, and Paris, and consulted extensively with Griffith, Nowak, and Henze.

369. Lewis would later (in a 1961 aide-mémoire) describe Nathan as "a maniac. The personal enemy of communism." He condensed Nathan's simplistic (and thereby fervent) Eastern Block philosophy into this:

*We must know how evil it is. We must show that Khrushchev
is a liar and a blunderer. We must show that the
Communists can't win because they are Communists, and
that the East European peoples can overthrow their
regimes because they are the people, and all strength
resides in the people.*

Butler Library, Galantière Collection, box 2, folder 2.

370. A. Ross Johnson observed, "Liberation" was American political rhetoric, not U.S. foreign policy. It was essentially an American election

campaign red herring, a by-product of the breakdown of foreign policy bipartisanship in the early 1950s. Johnson, *Radio Free Europe and Radio Liberty*, 48.

371. Special Guidance no. 19, May 25, 1954:

> Beginning at the end of this month RFE will face the anniversary of the show of weakness by the Soviet rulers and their agents in the "satellite" countries which marked a turn in the tide for the peoples we address.
>
> The death of Stalin [on March 5, 1953] precipitated the inauguration of a "new course" in the Soviet orbit which had been delayed only because nobody round the sick old tyrant had dared point out to him that it was long overdue...There is truth in Tocqueville's dictum:
>
> "A people who have long borne oppressive laws without complaint will throw them off violently as soon as the burden is lightened."
>
> ... [We shall show] how the regimes have grown progressively weaker and the peoples progressively stronger...
>
> ... We do not intend to rouse our listeners to...action... We are content with the resolute spirit which exists today among the peoples we address, and intend only that the spirits shall not subside.
>
> **Butler Library, Galantière Collection, box 2.**

372. Imre Nagy was Chairman of the Council of Ministers of the People's Republic of Hungary from 1953 to 1955, and then again in 1956.

373. Hoover, RFE/RL Inc., box 332.

374. Unique among the Iron Curtain countries, Tito's was not a puppet regime. He had led Yugoslavia to self-liberation from the Nazis and still possessed a military capability that could challenge a Soviet invasion. No other satellite country was similarly situated. In the mid-1950s,

Tito was exhibiting pro-Western sentiments at a time when Khrushchev needed his allegiance to the Soviet Bloc. Khrushchev flew to Belgrade, met with Tito, and hammered out the arrangement that came to be known at "Titoism."

375. At the twentieth (Communist Party) Congress, Mátyás Rákosi (whom Stalin had installed to rule Hungary and who, as of April 1956, still held power) pledged:

> Hungarian workers, working peasants and progressive
> intellectuals have received the directives of the
> U.S.S.R.'s Five Year Plan...with rejoicings and
> enthusiasm...We Hungarian communists have always regarded
> and will continue to regard the glorious CPSU, founded by
> Lenin, as our example.

By June, with the program of de-Stalinization underway, Rákosi lost his job and was recalled to Russia, where he spent the rest of his years.

376. In a July 10, 1956, critique of a CIA situation paper, Lewis noted that Russia needed to expropriate the satellite countries' resources and ship them to the Middle East, South Asia, and elsewhere "not for their benefit, but in furtherance of a program of 'economic competition' with the West which Soviet Russia is unable to carry on out of her own resources." CIA International Organizations Division memo W-7871, July 6, 1956, and National Committee for a Free Europe memo, July 10, 1956; both were furnished to the author by A. Ross Johnson.

377. Eisenhower's speech, August 24, 1955:

> Eagerness to avoid war—If we think no deeper than this
> single desire—can produce outright or implicit agreement
> that injustices and wrongs of the present shall be
> perpetuated in the future. We must not participate in any
> such false agreement. Thereby, we would outrage our own
> conscience. In the eyes of those who suffer injustice,
> we would become partners with their oppressors. In the

> *judgment of history, we would have sold out the freedom*
> *of men for the pottage of a false peace. Moreover, we*
> *would assure future conflict!*

**Address at the Annual Convention of the American Bar
Association, Philadelphia. August 24, 1955.**

Eisenhower speech, Christmas 1955

> *...the American people recognize the trials under which*
> *you are suffering; [and] join you in your concern for the*
> *restoration of individual freedoms and political liberty;*
> *and share your faith that right in the end will prevail*
> *to bring you once again among the free nations of the*
> *world.*

Hoover RFE/RL Inc., box 202–1746.3.

378. Hoover RFE/RL Inc., box 444, folder 2.

379. Excerpts from Lewis's Guidance no. 26, "The De-Canonization of Stalin":

> *After three years* [since Stalin's death], *the struggle*
> *for power in the Kremlin goes on unabated. The rivalry*
> *between the Khrushchev faction and a faction that now*
> *seems to be headed by Mikoyan was scarcely veiled at the*
> *Congress itself. When Mikoyan attacked Stalin personally,*
> *he went out of his way to name two Ukrainians executed by*
> *Stalin, unquestionably with Khrushchev's connivance.*
>
> *... The quick-thinking Khrushchev, seeing how well*
> *Mikoyan's personal attack on Stalin...had gone down with*
> *the delegates, snatched the ball away from Mikoyan and—in*
> *the uncompromising speech behind closed doors of which we*
> *have no text—ran with it himself...*
>
> *...* [As of now, the satellite] *states make a pretense of*
> *sovereignty; the parties...cannot pretend independence*
> *from the CPSU* [the Communist Party of the Soviet Union]. *
> In our opinion it is futile for Western opinion to look*
> *for national communism ("Titoism") as a stage on the*
> *way to ultimate democracy through free egression of the*
> *peoples...(This does not in the least mean that the*

> captive peoples cannot meanwhile press for liberalization
> of institutions...within the limits of decrees and
> promises announced by the regime leaders themselves.)
>
> ... At the XXth Congress, Khrushchev went so far as
> to express toleration for non-violent parliamentary
> "transition to socialism."
>
> There is no likelihood of military action by the West to
> liberate our peoples.
>
> ... there is no present likelihood that any degree of
> liberation, beyond some slight lifting of the Iron
> Curtain, can be achieved by diplomatic negotiation...
>
> To talk of "self-liberation" is self-deception.
>
> **Hoover, RFE Corp Records, box 444 folder 2.**

380. Ibid.

381. The following are excerpts of Dunning's April 2, 1956, memorandum
to RFE director Egan.

> These defects [in Lewis's Guidance no. 26] reinforce,
> and make unavoidable, a decision to withdraw which could
> well be based solely upon the improper and deliberately
> insubordinate manner in which this paper was issued by
> your Political Advisor...
>
> Moreover, the withdrawal should be made quickly. Any
> considerable delay can only be interpreted, by RFE
> personnel, as evidence of indecision and inability to see
> and judge clearly the shortcomings of the paper.
>
> I...recommend that you assign Messrs. Sears and Nathan to
> prepare a paper to serve as Guidance 26...
>
> ... these proposals demonstrate so dangerous a
> contempt for the intellects of our audiences, and
> such recklessness in gambling with RFE's credibility
> and standing...that their dissemination within the
> organization is destructive to exile morale...

> *... To allow this uncomprehending and defeatist concept of the opportunity [of de-Stalinization] to stand is to do great discredit to ourselves.*
>
> *... we want to be certain that relaxation of rigors shall not induce the captive peoples to drop their guard and diminish their fundamental opposition to the Soviet-dominated regimes.*

Ibid.

382. Hoover, RFE/RL Inc., NY to Munich messages, March 28, 1956.

383. May 18, 1956, memo from Griffith to Lewis:

> *even a partial emancipation of the human mind must lead in time to the undermining of the prescribed doctrine and, by the same token, of the system which is based on it. It therefore lies in the most vital interests of the people that the current liberalization should last as long as possible and should extend to its utmost possible limits.*
>
> *In planning our propaganda campaign during the "fallout" we must therefore seek answers to two questions:*
>
> > *A) How can we help the people to prolong and extend the "thaw," to perpetuate changes which are based on technical assumptions and therefore may be deemed by the regime to be transient?*
> >
> > *B) How can we make it more difficult for the regime to change the present course, to revert to the reign of terror and silence the people again? How can we make the liquidation of the "thaw" as costly and as unprofitable as possible for the Party?*

Hoover, RFE/RL Inc., telexes, May–July 1956.

384. Galantière to Egan, May 26, 1956, Hoover. RFE/RL Inc.

385. Galantière to Shepardson, June 26, 1956, Hoover, RFE/RL Inc., memo.

386. National Archives, Military Personnel Records Center, St. Louis, MO.

387. Richard Helms, another World War II OSS member, who would later become director of the CIA, wrote:

> One of the least remembered RFE [intelligence]
> achievements came in late summer 1956 when William
> Griffith, the Munich-based policy advisor, and his deputy,
> Paul Henze, spotted a changing mood in Eastern Europe,
> and gave warning of a likely confrontation between the
> indigenous populations and the Soviet Forces in East
> Germany, Poland and Hungary.
>
> Helms, Richard and Hood, William. *A Look over My Shoulder: A Life in the Central Intelligence Agency* (New York: Random House, 2003) p.363

388. In June 1955, the American embassy had criticized the Voice of Free Hungary staff as too propagandistic. The embassy's concern was that RFE was contributing to "wishful and speculative thinking" and "false hopes" of liberation. This was worrisome because the broadcasters' screeds had been the very reason that many of VFH's audience had tuned in. In September 1956, the State Department drew similar conclusions after listening to the VFH broadcasts. Puddington, Arch. *Broadcasting Freedom*, 96.

389. Hoover, RFE/RL Inc., box 1766/18133.

390. Ibid.

391. Katalin Kádár Lynn, *The Inauguration of Organized Political Warfare: Cold War Organizations* (St. Helena, CA: Helena History Press, 2013), citing Cissie Dore Hill, "Voices of Hope: The Story of Radio Free Europe and Radio Liberty," 7 *Hoover Digest* 7, no. 4 (October 30, 2001).

392. Lewis, Special Guidance:

> riots and revolts are not likely to improve matters in
> Poland, for the police may be given an opportunity for
> reprisals which only make things worse. No government

> *which bases itself exclusively upon the tanks and*
> *bayonets of the armed forces will endure. But the Polish*
> *people must husband their strength and hold on for the*
> *time of freedom.*

Puddington, Arch. *Broadcasting Freedom*, 93.

393. Egan to Shepardson, FEC memorandum, July 6, 1956.

394. July 18, 1956, cryptographic message from Griffith to Lewis:

> *we can no longer necessarily accept the previous*
> *political balance within the various immigrations. I*
> *think it is therefore, seriously open to question*
> *whether we can adhere to the same balance within our*
> *desks...we have experienced difficulties in the past, I*
> *think increasing ones, in respect to response of our*
> *exile staff to the...Developments of liberalization*
> *within their countries. We cannot shut our eyes to*
> *the possibility that some staff personnel changes*
> *may eventually be necessary. I am of course far from*
> *proposing that we should abandon the concept of*
> *partnership or the "illusion of freedom," but half*
> *measures will not do.*
>
> *In addition to this, I think we must contemplate*
> *the possible necessity of the judicious and tactful*
> *application of a somewhat greater degree of positive*
> *American control than has taken place in the past. Our*
> *functions, I feel, have all too often been limited to*
> *negative control, to preventing the wrong things from*
> *being said. It is often proved the easier course—and*
> *we have too often justified it by the principle of*
> *exile initiative—to be satisfied with somewhat less than*
> *complete positive implementation of guidance.*

Hoover, RFE/RL Inc., telexes, May–July 1956.

395. Hoover-Puddington, box 29, folder 7.

396. Paul B. Henze, Hoover, RFE/RL Inc., box 32, Accession no. 2005C42-272. Interview of Henze on June 5, 1986, by Martin Schwartz, in PhD dissertation, appendix G.

397. The source of this and all subsequent references to the Voice of Free Hungary broadcasts during the revolution is a report by William Griffith to Richard Condon, RFE European director, titled "Policy Review of Voice of Free Hungary Programing, 23 October–23 November 1956" as reported in Michael Nelson, *War of the Black Heavens: The Battles of Western Broadcasting in the Cold War* (London: Brassey, 1997), 214n27.

398. The creators and broadcasters of the "Armed Forces Special" programs were Julián Borsányi (speaking as "Colonel Bell") and Gyula Litterati-Lodz.

399. *New York Times*, September 28, 1996.

400. From a June 8, 1993, interview of Griffith by Michael Nelson, cited in Nelson, *War of the Black Heavens*, 215n54.

401. Hoover, RFE/RL Inc., box 1766 / 18133 11211.

402. Ibid.

403. Charles Gati, *Failed Illusions: Moscow, Washington, Budapest, and the 1956 Hungarian Revolt* (Washington, D.C.: Woodrow Wilson Center Press, 2006) 112.

404. Ibid., back cover.

405. Ibid., 164.

406. In a November 24, 1957, letter to Adolphe Berle (then a leading corporate lawyer and economics professor at Columbia; chairman of the Twentieth Century Fund, a progressive think tank; and a founder and still a member of the Free Europe Committee), Lewis expressed his exasperation with the decline of Radio Free Europe:

It is my opinion that except in Poland, where RFE still has a strong grip on its audience thanks to the skill of Griffith and Nowak, RFE has never been less influential in its target countries. The primary reason (in my opinion) is the transfer of its main attention from affairs in the Soviet Orbit (chiefly our target countries) to the world stage and specifically the Washington-UN stage...

...the top management of the Committee has little conception of the fact that our only weapons are ideas and words. Our mission is defined for us as "To say what freedom is and what freedom does." An excellent cliché; but even so defined, the mission cannot be carried out under a management which repeats that "the only people who count are the doers" and refers to others as "smart boys," with some grudging appreciation, but mostly with explicit assurance that the "smart boys" are not going to have anything to do with running the show...

This is for your own eye, of course. Understand that writing it is a painful matter for me.

Ever yours, Lewis

Butler Library, Galantière Collection, box 7.

407. Johnson, *Radio Free Europe and Radio Liberty*, 118.

408. When, in April 1958, Paul Henze told Lewis he was leaving Radio Free Europe, Lewis wrote him a one-page farewell letter, the majority of which was an indictment of Crittenberger:

April 9, 1958

Dear Paul,

Thank you for your letter, which I take as a special mark of friendship. The important thing is that, as you put it, the offer [of a new position] was "very choice." I am sure that nothing less could have persuaded you to quit your happy association with Bill [William Griffith], whose respect for you is as great as his affection...as it is of mine...

> I am not, socially and politically, an adherent of
> elitism. Nevertheless, I do believe that the good work
> of this world is done by men of good will; men who
> don't mind their pockets being picked because they have
> nothing in them which they would not willingly share
> with others. I believe, on the other hand, that there
> do exist men of ill will—ignorant, half-educated men,
> avid of power because they need to bolster up their
> psychic insecurity, difficult of direct attack because
> their motives as well as acts are equivocal—mixtures of
> confused good intent and ill intent—and evidence against
> them is almost impossible to disentangle and present in a
> small space. We have been going through a period in which
> such men have made life uncomfortable for some of us. I
> like to think that we shall see the end of that before
> too long (though I hasten to add that I have no evidence
> for this optimistic statement). But if ever these half-
> educated men, these terribles simplificateurs, as Bill
> likes to say, quoting Burckhardt, can be superseded, the
> organization you are leaving will take on new life, and
> Bill's side (or kind of man) will win in the end.

Hoover, Paul B. Henze Papers, box 3.

Lewis visited Munich between November 26 and December 5, 1958, and reported the shortcomings of the operation, including the loss of intelligence sources in the Eastern Bloc countries. Without targeting the Hungarian Revolution explicitly, Lewis concluded that RFE Munich had gone astray, that the organization had lost the respect it enjoyed at the State Department and the CIA, and that it was now viewed as a Voice of America equivalent (the "VOA" being a propagandistic rather than a news organ).

> December 11, 1958
>
> The [Munich-based Political Office] has [not]...been
> appreciated in New York...it is the only direct point
> of management contact with the Munich desks, which turn
> out 85 per cent of the RFE product. Guidance and control
> of the desks cannot be effective at a distance; they

cannot be bureaucratically imposed by paper definitions and prescriptions; they demand personal, day-to-day contact. They require an American management staff which will continue to demonstrate...that it understands... what is going on in the target countries; that it possesses superior political and propaganda instinct and skill; that it listens with an open mind to the desk people's own evaluation of events, particularly in their own countries. Only by these means can the American management be sure that what goes into the scripts— in tone as well as formal content—will be what the management wants.

The other principal function of the Political Office is the collection and analysis of political intelligence. Such analysis is of course the indispensable basis of RFE operational but the Munich product has turned out to be something more than that. The fact is almost unknown in New York—or if known is almost wholly disregarded— that the Griffith office has been the most highly prized source of "Iron Curtain" information and analysis which reaches interested quarters in Washington. The Griffith office has made mistakes; but I believe it is a fact that this is the RFE office which [the State Department] has, throughout, most admired and been satisfied with. Through that office, FEC has, at least once, made basic U.S. policy on East Europe, and has constantly influenced U.S. estimates of the East European situation.

Hoover-Puddington, box 29, folder 7.

Lewis incorporated these findings into a January 29, 1959, policy statement on the relationship of the FEC to "Washington," meaning (1) the State Department, (2) the United States Information Agency, and (3) the CIA. He noted that as late as December 1958, he and William Griffith had prepared policy papers to which the State Department had deferred. "In those years, FEC drafted policy and Washington reserved its right of veto. Today, the situation is reversed, except that FEC has no right of veto. FEC has not the reputation it

once enjoyed in Washington." Lewis noted that, since the Hungarian
"Rising," some officials at the State Department had questioned the
utility of RFE's broadcasts. The Standing Committee on Broadcasting
(comprising representatives of the three) had decided that it, and not
RFE, would thereafter define RFE broadcast policies through "unannounced policies." When no "unannounced policies" ensued, RFE de-
volved into a Voice of America variant. Lewis laid the blame squarely
on FEC president Crittenberger and his predecessors.

`Ibid.`

409. By Christmas 1959, it was clear to Lewis that "RFE has been thoroughly denatured and thoroughly emasculated" and he told Alexander that he wanted nothing further to do with it.

> *Dear Archie,*
>
> *I'm going to make myself a Christmas present. I'm going
> to take a load off my mind by tendering my resignation
> from the Committee, which I should like to become
> effective at the end of January 1960.*
>
> *To do so is no longer the emotional wrench it would have
> been when I first had this impulse, three years ago—before
> RFE was "Americanized" without committee presentation of
> counter-arguments, before the Committee was thoroughly
> bureaucratized, and before all but one of my old
> comrades-in-arms, who had my respect and affection, had
> been harried out of the Committee.*
>
> *Of course, it's an expensive present, but there are times
> when a high price has to be paid for self-respect. I have
> not been earning my pay; and not, I think, through my
> own fault. The things I can do best...relate to the only
> function of the FEC I consider of decisive importance
> in our field of action: the defeat of Soviet purposes in
> RFE's target countries. In 1956, management disagreed
> with the working staff about my competence in this field,
> and I was kept out of it by Gen. Crittenberger; I have
> not been brought back into it by you.*

*I do not think it was inevitable that FEC should cease
to be the principal arm of Western action and influence
in the target countries, and should cease to be the
authoritative source of Eastern European intelligence and
propaganda policy drafting in Washington.*

*I do not think it right that the primary function of
RFE should be to fight the US government's diplomatic
battles and concentrate on such purposes as (for example)
persuading East European peasants that Peiping China does
not deserve a seat at the UN (not that I want Red China
in the UN).*

*I do not think it was wise to scuttle the successful
practice of American-exile staff partnership in the
discussion and determination of propaganda lines (within
the framework of American-made policy) in favor of the
setup in which exile workers face American bosses and
there is no sympathy or real comprehension between them.*

*I do not think it was wise to substitute bureaucratic
(and ineffectual) control of script content for the kind
of control which consisted in the presence of an American
staff that was respected by Desk personnel for its
thorough knowledge of East Europe and of Soviet-settling
relations and its sound and imaginative grasp of the art
of propaganda.*

*RFE has been thoroughly denatured and thoroughly
emasculated. Up to three years ago it was a power in
East Europe, an object of respect and admiration in
Washington, and a prize exhibit of the [FEC] executive
committee. Today it arouses no particular interest in
East Europe (Poland may still be an exception), it is
viewed with distaste and disapproval in Washington, and
it is an object of worry to the executive committee. All
this is openly acknowledged. What is not faced squarely
is the reason for this degeneration: a bureaucratic
management which dislikes exiles who think for themselves
(deemed to be troublesome employees), dislikes political
action and finds it easier to carry on a simpleminded and
ineffective holy war against communism, conceives its
first function to be the defense of US diplomacy and the*

> *belittling of Soviet strength, and allows the Soviets to*
> *proceed unhampered with the rebuilding of their power in*
> *its target countries. This seems to me the wrong way to*
> *spend $12 million or $15 million a year.*

Butler Library, Galantière Collection, box 7.

In an October 15, 1960 letter to Alexander, Lewis again said he was resigning:

> *Archie:*
>
> *I very much regret that I must maintain my decision to*
> *resign from Free Europe Committee and ask you to release*
> *me at the end of this year.*
>
> *There are two reasons why I must resign. The first is*
> *that I have not been participating in the work of the*
> *Committee. At the level indicated by my position and my*
> *salary, this means that I have not been participating in*
> *the making of Committee decisions. A glaring example is*
> *this: for weeks you have been discussing the Oder-Neisse*
> *question* [the determination of the German-Polish border].
> *But not with me. I don't know what* [the State Department]
> *has told us about it; I'll bet anything it is what we*
> *will (and should) have told State at least two years ago,*
> *both as to Polish feeling and as to American policy.*
>
> *The only time I see you, the only time I am consulted, is*
> *in Planning Committee meetings; and the P.C. is not an*
> *executive. Data are not examined, views are not thrashed*
> *out by people who are given time to study subjects. Plans*
> *are not drafted and made to guide operations. Operations*
> *are not watched to see that they conform to plans or*
> *policy. Nothing happens in the Planning Committee beyond*
> *the vague airing of off-the-cuff views and occasional*
> *assignment of tasks for which those assigned are*
> *not, in fact, held accountable, except in connection*
> *with entirely superficial problems (what to do about*
> *Khrushchev's visit, etc.).* [Khrushchev visited the U.S.
> in September 1959.]
>
> *The other reason is that FEC is a bureaucracy, and*
> *not even a particularly efficient one. I know* [of] *no*

*department... which is seriously engaged in squeezing
the best out of its resources... A kind of easy-going
mediocrity is the rule, against which every attempt
at hard thinking and at creative imagination of close
planning... is bound to fail.*

*If I were allowed to leave you with one piece of specific
advice it would be to concentrate now on the radical
reform of RFE. The day of the exile mentality is long
since over. RFE should become a Western station, by which
I mean the station delivering the liveliest, solidest,
most enlightening and most intelligible information
that is available in its target countries. Information
conveyed as news, as "news analysis," and as personal
expression by European and American personalities. As
regards the third category, which would not be pegged
on the news, but would be very broadly cultural, social,
scientific, etc., I would suggest an "international
series" of daily talks in English, French, German and
Russian—all of course re-delivered in the language of the
audience at another hour...*

Butler Library, Galantière Collection box 2, folder 2.

410. December 8, 1960, memorandum from Lewis to Alexander:

*What I have in mind in proposing that Brzezinski, Griffith
and I work together in the quick production (once we get
started) of the following papers:*

>   1. *An estimate of the power position in RFE's
>   target countries ...*
>
>   2. *A set of recommendations to serve as a basis
>   for RFE operational guidance and programming.*
>
>   3. *A suggested topical outline for background pa-
>   pers on each of the target countries, the out-
>   lines to be filled in by RFE/Munich information
>   analysts...which will in turn serve...for the
>   drafting of RFE individual country guidances.*

Hoover-Puddington, box 29, folder 7.

411. Galantière to Hamilton Armstrong, Mudd Library, March 9, 1961, Hamilton Fish Armstrong Papers, box 30.

412. *Foreign Affairs*, July 1961.

413. Seven years later, William Griffith wrote of the devolution of Czecho-slovakia under the "peaceful engagement":

> Last month [January 1968] Czechoslovakia's long-lasting Stalinist; Antonin Novotny, was replaced—in a free vote in the Central Committee!—as party head by Alexander Dubcek, the young, nationalist, anti-Stalinist Slovak party leader. How did it happen?... First and most important...was Czechoslovakia's economic stagnation, caused by its economy being so centralized and administered by incompetent party officials rather than by efficient managers. The young pragmatic Communists realized that this stagnation could only be overcome by drastic decentralization and rationalization of the economy...Second was the collapse of the moral authority of the Communist leadership...[Finally]...was the revolt of the Czech (and Slovak) intelligentsia, notably the writers and students, against the sterile dogmatism, the lies and hypocrisy, the incompetence [of the government leadership].
>
> **Los Angeles Times, February 27, 1968, 5.**

414. Lewis addressed a draft of the same letter, dated February 22, 1961, to "John." The recipient was likely John Hughes, FEC's chairman. Butler Library, Galantière Collection, box 1.

415. Butler Library, Galantière Collection, box 2, folder 2.

416. Hoover-Puddington, box 29, folder 7.

417. January 10, 1964 memo from the Munich RFE station director

> January 10, 1964
>
> Lewis Galantière
>
> Counsellor to the President
>
> Free Europe Committee Inc., New York
>
> Dear Lewis:
>
> The last instalment of your series on the Negro Problem was broadcast on December 27, 1964. I had a chance to re-read all live scripts now and I wish to express to you our warmest appreciation for agreeing so graciously to help us and for this brilliant piece of programming.
>
> Your series fully met our expectations. It is lucid, beautifully balanced and presented to the audience with your incomparable skill. What is most important for us— it is not defensive in its approach, but is facing the problem squarely and frankly...
>
> I know that you have other important assignments and we are particularly grateful that you found time for us in your tight schedule.

This handwritten notation appeared at the top:.

> Dear Lewis,
>
> I agree and am very glad these were so well received. JR.

Ibid.

418. Johnson, *Radio Free Europe and Radio Liberty*, 134.

419. Firestone Library, PEN Series 1, box 5.

420. Butler Library, Galantière Collection, box 1, folder 2.

421. Firestone Library, PEN Series 1, box 5.

NOTES TO CHAPTER 12

422. Immigration and Nationality Act of 1952, a.k.a. the McCarran-Walter Act.

423. The Latin American experience differed from that of Eastern Europe insofar as U.S. actions had often been *the cause* of popular resentment: oppressive Latin American regimes had been supported by U.S. businesses and by successive U.S. administrations, both Democratic and Republican. The instrumentalities of exploitation had included the Alliance for Progress (a program of crony lending and the repatriation of interest charges and profits by the U.S. government and corporations, directly and through foreign cartels) and natural resources sweetheart deals involving United Fruit, IT&T, and copper and phosphate natural resources commodities brokers. Additionally, the U.S. military had intervened when U.S. geopolitical interests were at stake in Cuba and the Dominican Republic. The commercial profiteering and military adventures goaded Latin American intellectuals, including most of its authors, to look more kindly upon Castro and Communism than upon the United States.

424. Lewis described the founding and purpose of PEN in an article published by the *Saturday Review* in its coverage of the 1966 PEN congress:

> In 1921, when International P.E.N. was founded in London, the hope that the First World War had been "the war to end war" was fast receding. For the Russians and the Poles, the war was in fact not yet over. Germany was filled with civil strife. And in East-Central Europe one result of President Wilson's noble "self-determination of peoples" had been to rouse fresh tribal hatreds and create border problems that were to prove a primary cause of the Second World War. The half-score treaties

signed in the suburbs of Paris and at Geneva were written along nineteenth-century lines of power calculations and in response to popular emotions; they laid no viable foundations. At the newly established League of Nations the old-style diplomacy continued to bar the way to what our Founding Fathers in their day had called—see your dollar bill—a novus ordo seclorum [new order of the ages].

Yet there were everywhere, in government and out, men and women concerned to work for an end to war and for world understanding. One of these was an English novelist, Katharine Dawson Scott, whose death P.E.N, mourned last year. She brought to John Galsworthy the idea of a world association of writers to be called "The P.E.N. Club," P.E.N, standing for poets, playwrights, essayists, editors, and novelists. Galsworthy responded warmly and energetically. He recruited H. G. Wells, Bernard Shaw, and E. M. Forster, among others. Anatole France agreed to become the first president of the French P.E.N. Center. Gerhard Hauptmann in Germany, Maurice Maeterlinck in Belgium, Benedetto Croce in Italy were won over. An American Center was formed in 1922 by a committee of which the eminent publisher John Farrar is the surviving member. Its first president was Booth Tarkington; and one of his early successors was the first editor of The Saturday Review of Literature, Henry Seidel Canby. Today there are seventy-six Centers in fifty-six countries.

Saturday Review, June 1, 1966, 23.

425. The United States representatives to the Tokyo congress were John Hersey, John Dos Passos, John Steinbeck, and Lewis. Steinbeck wrote to his wife from the congress, reporting, tongue-in-cheek, that the American contingent, including himself, was "shockingly masculine," and that

Galantière would make passes at a lady streetcar. All in all, we have given P.E.N. a bad name.

But when Steinbeck became ill, his countrymen came through.

> *Hersey and Galantière have been wonderful to me.... Dos*
> *Passos has been an angel also. What a nice bunch of*
> *people.*
>
> **John Steinbeck, *Steinbeck: A Life in Letters* (New York**
> **City, Penguin Books, 1989 568-569.**

426. During the CIA's first two decades, it covertly funded pro-Western journals and cultural events, laundering the money through legitimate nonprofit foundations, corporations and associations. The Ford, Rockefeller, Farfield, and Carnegie Foundations were among the conduits.

The CIA's own sources of funds were congressional "black budget" allocations and money siphoned from the Marshall Plan. The Marshall Plan was a program for the industrial modernization of Western Europe in sums that eventually totaled $13 billion. In a neat piece of chicanery, the plan required that countries receiving U.S. aid circuitously deposit, to a CIA-controlled bank account, the equivalent of 5 percent of the proceeds of U.S. funding. That money was used for CIA projects, including America's anti-Soviet propaganda efforts.

One of the agency's major recipients was the European-based Congress for Cultural Freedom (CCF). The CCF had offices in thirty-five countries; published about two dozen "intellectual" magazines; financed conferences, art exhibitions, and musical performances; and paid for the travel and living expenses of the participating artists and performers. The CCF and similar organizations were not CIA creations and the agency did not direct their activities; it just furnished them with money it needed to pursue its own agendas, which coincided with those of the United States. CCF had an American sister organization, the American Committee for Cultural Freedom, which was based in New York.

John F. Kennedy joined PEN after he was elected president in 1960 and he, as well, would have known of PEN's Farfield contributions and CIA connection.

427. Galantière Memorandum to Congress File, U.S. State Department, February 3, 1966, PEN Archives, box 160, folder 6.

428. Deborah Cohn, *The Latin American Literary Boom and U.S. Nationalism during the Cold War* (Nashville: Vanderbilt University Press, 2012), 37.

429. The Soviet and East European Exchanges office, the Cuban Affairs desk, and the Bureau of Educational and Cultural Affairs.

430. Cleveland to Galantière, April 28, 1965, PEN Archives, box 160, folder 6.

431. Cohn, *The Latin American Literary Boom*, 28.

432. Firestone Library, PEN Series 1, box 5.

433. *Washington Post*, November 2, 1965, A15.

434. *Washington Post*, November 12, 1965, A16.

435. Lyndon B. Johnson, 1966, *Public Papers of the Presidents of the United States* (Washington, DC: U.S. Government Printing Office, 1957–).

436. Galantière to Frankel, March 2, 1966, Cohn, *The Latin American Literary Boom*, 73.

437. Mudd Library, PEN America Center Records, box 160, folder 6.

438. Department of State press release, Joint Statement by the Departments of State and Justice, May 3, 1966, PEN American Center Records (C0760), box 160, folder 6, RBSC, Princeton University Library.

439. Author's telephone interview with Sidney Offit, March 12, 2015.

440. *Mundo Nuevo*, October 1966, 41–51.

441. Ibid.

442. The following is an excerpt from Carlos Fuentes's "El PEN: Entierro de la guerra fría en la literatura" ("The PEN Congress: The Burial of the Cold War in Literature"), *Life en Español*, August 1, 1966.

> the New York meeting was what it was. An act of liberation...only a science fiction writer might have predicted that in the brave new world of 1966, a Chilean Communist poet would be hailed by thousands of people in New York...And...five hundred writers—conservatives, anarchists, communists, liberals, socialists—gathered together not to hurl accusations, nor underline differences, nor to announce dogmas but, rather, to discuss concrete problems, recognize a community of spirit, and accept a diversity of intentions.

> ... in the brave new world of 1966, a Chilean Communist poet...[Neruda was] acclaimed by thousands of people in New York...[A] group of leftist writers...abstained from attacking the United States.

443. Rodriguez Monegal, "The PEN Club against the Cold War," *El Mundo Nuevo*, November 1966, 85–90n5:

> The PEN [Congress] was the first institution to break the boundaries of the Cold War after the war between the capitalist world and the socialist world.

> ... [We said] a final goodbye to the late Senator McCarthy. One could go further and say that the XXXIV International Congress of PEN Club will be remembered as the funeral of the Cold War in literature. It was the defeat of cultural isolation, which served only to increase international tension, and is a useless relic.

> ... the mission of the intellectual is not to perpetuate the old mental habits but discuss them; not say amen to the world but to question; not to hide, with contempt, in an ivory tower or bureaucratic niche, but to go outside

and risk saying what you have to say. If others disagree, they will respond with reason and arguments or with insults, slander or malice. All of this is predictable. But worse is to remain silent, or speak only with co-religionists. In the XXXIV Congress PEN Club in New York, all spoke with everyone.

444. The following are extracts from Neruda's statement of July 15, 1966:

My contact with American writers, with students, with my readers and the people of the United States has been a poetic and political experience of primary importance...

... Carlos Fuentes of Mexico, Martinez Moreno and Onetti, of Uruguay; Nicanor Parra, Chile; Sabato, of Argentina; Mario Vargas Llosa, of Peru; and I discussed the problems we face as Latin American writers...

I had the pleasure of speaking to men like Arthur Miller and the poets and novelists of the German Democratic Republic, Bulgaria, Poland, Yugoslavia, Hungary, Czechoslovakia and other socialist nations...

I read my lyrical, anti-fascist and anti-imperialist poems to vast audiences of American, Mexican and Peruvian people poems...and expressed my views on major organs of the press, radio, television and film.

... And I reiterated my friendship to the huge number of US intellectuals who have a courageous opposition to the aggressive policy of his government...[The] terrorist action of the U.S. government in Vietnam is the criminal act of our time...[So too] those Latin American governments that keep obeying [anti-Cuba] orders from the State Department. Much of my work and my actions have been directed at denouncing those intolerable acts and expressing my support for the great Cuban Revolution.

Rodriguez Monegal, "The PEN Club against the Cold War,"
***El Mundo Nuevo*, n.5, November 1966**

445. *Cien Años de Soledad* was published in 1967 and translated into English in 1970.

446. Ibid. Monegal, *El Mundo Nuevo.*

447. Ransom Center, Alfred A. Knopf, Inc., Records, Knopf_530_5_005, p. 187.

448. Cohn, *The Latin American Literary Boom*, 9.

449. Ransom Center, Alfred A. Knopf, Inc., Records, Knopf_530_01_002.

450. Butler Library, Galantière Collection, box 3, folder 1.

451. "The 1966 PEN congress is mentioned as a turning point in almost every history of Spanish American literature that studies this period." Cohn, *The Latin American Literary Boom*, 66.

452. Excerpt from Lewis's address upon resigning as P.E.N. president:

> I don't think I need to say that as a result of
> the congress the stature of American PEN has risen
> considerably in International PEN circles... .The primary
> cause has been the two years of service given to PEN as
> international president by Arthur Miller. ...
>
> I hardly knew Arthur Miller when we went to the Bled
> Congress two years ago. I still don't know him very
> well. But I have seen him at work. He is not a man who
> takes the chair at a meeting and disappears when it is
> over. I have rarely known a man so unconcerned with
> leadership and so gifted for it. He is a man round whom
> people gather—because of himself, not because of his
> presidency...
>
> Miller is not an orator, but he compels attention. He has
> the gift of fusing thought and moral feeling and anecdote
> in a way that converts abstraction into reality—but not
> cold reality, warm reality. For us, his great virtue is
> that he cares about PEN, and in a way that makes others
> care, at least while he is around. It was from him that

> *I learnt to care about PEN, though I dare say I should
> have cared less if I had not been carrying certain
> responsibility.*

Firestone Library, PEN Series 1, box 5.

453. Butler Library, Galantière Collection, box 1, folder 2.

NOTES TO CHAPTER 13

454. Bancroft Library, Helen Haines letters.

455. Lewis and Nancy were legally separated in 1953 but never divorced. And they remained companions to each other when her state of mind permitted. Lewis to Nancy regarding the filing of a separate tax return for 1953, Butler Library, Galantière Collection, box 30.

456. Newberry Library, Sherwood Anderson Collection, Galantière 1941–1944, box 34, folder 1821.

457. Ibid.

458. Extracted from a memorandum quoting the review. Butler Library, Galantière Collection, box 30.

459. Ibid.

460.

> *Dear Rose*
>
> *About finding somebody to write the story of Rose Fried and her gallery. I told you I had spoken to Dave Taylor at Columbia, and that he had said he would pass on to Professor Meyer Shapiro the idea that a graduate student might profitably make you the subject of a doctor's dissertation.*
>
> *This morning, Dave read me over the phone part of a letter from Shapiro...who received the idea with much interest. He said that he had in mind "at least one student"... He would like to talk to you in the fall, when he comes back to New York...*
>
> *Summer being a dead season, I don't know that I can do anything more for the time being. Meanwhile, when you get rested...*

*I want you to know that the nicest thing for me about
your giving Nancy a show, after the show itself, has been
to get to know you...*

With great affection, Lewis

**Lewis Galantière to Rose Fried, July 1, 1964, Smithsonian
Institution, American Art Institute, Rose Fried Gallery
records, 1944-1971, microfilm reel 2203.**

461. Butler Library, Galantière Collection, boxes 6 and 30.

462. A further matter weighed on Nancy's spirits during that fall of 1964. She had been waging a legal fight to recoup her dream home: a 330-acre ranch on the southern tip of the Baja California peninsula, overlooking the Gulf of California. She named the ranch "Eureka." In the 1950s, Nancy had loaned a Mexican national—Antonio Ruffo—the money to purchase the acreage, which Ruffo leased back to her for fifty years. Nancy and Ruffo signed a partnership agreement under which she furnished the money and he the labor to improve the land and some buildings. Nancy bought a truck and a tractor, pumps, and barbed wire, and Ruffo repaired about a quarter mile of aqueduct. On June 20, 1952, the governor of Baja California, Augustin Olachea, seized Eureka, acting in the name of the agrarians, a populist movement that demanded the return of Mexican land to its indigenous people. Nancy's Mexican attorney sent word, by telegram, that Ruffo had sold Eureka to the agrarians, and that she would not be recouping either her money or the ranch:

> *Dear Nancy. Received wire yesterday there has been
> trouble about Eureka with Agrarians. Seems Ruffo sold
> land affected by them. I stopped all work until cleared.
> Very doubtful Ruffo willing to refund everything. Letter
> will fully explain situation and possibilities.*

Nancy, in a fury, went to Mexico, found the governor standing on her property and addressing his townspeople. She demanded that he return the ranch to her and Olachea replied so that his constituents could hear,

> You are working agrarian property. Ask Ruffo for a refund and go elsewhere. You cannot take the fencing.

Olachea then climbed to the top of the aqueduct and shouted:

> Boys. Here it is! All you have to do is install your pumps.

More than a decade of legal fees later, Nancy had regained neither her money nor her land. But she would not relent.

Butler Library, Galantière Collection, box 30

463. Lewis to Nancy's psychotherapist, Butler Library, Galantière Collection, box 6.

464. Ransom Center, Alfred A. Knopf, Inc., Records, Knopf_ 484_9_002.

465. Rosanna Warren is currently the Hanna Holborn Gray Distinguished Service Professor in the Committee on Social Thought at the University of Chicago. She is an award-winning poet.

466. April 8, 2014, email message from Professor Rosanna Warren to the author.

467. Butler Library, Galantière Collection, box 7.

468. Ibid.

469. Ibid., box 16.

470. Ibid.

471. Ibid., box 30.5

472. Ibid., box 16.

473. Letter to Nancy from Bellevue Hospital:

> *11 March, 1969*
>
> *To: Mrs. Nancy Galantière,*
>
> *This is to inform you that the Medical Health Information Service, First Judicial Department, is available to you. You, or anyone on your behalf, may communicate with the Service or its representative, and avail yourself of the facilities of the Service; if you wish to do so you or such other persons may either notify us or call or write to the office of the Service at Bellevue Hospital...*
>
> *William T. Lhamon, M.D., Psychiatrist-in-Chief*
>
> **Ibid., box 4**

474. Paul Henze and William E. Griffith had managed RFE's field operations during Lewis's tenure. Paul served as CIA station chief in Turkey and Ethiopia for two decades after leaving RFE; Lewis maintain a letter-writing relationship with him and his wife Martha ("Martie").

475. Hoover, Paul B. Henze Papers, box 3, folder 1.

476. Lee Allyn Davis, *Natural Disasters* (New York: Facts on File, 2008); *Weather* 63, no. 5 (May 2008).

477. All correspondence between Lewis, Nancy, and Brahim is from the Butler Library, Galantière Collection, box 30-001.

478. Ibid.

479. Reports of Deaths of American Citizens Abroad, 1835–1974, —Nancy Davis Galantière, ancestry.com.

480. *New York Times*, December 20, 1969.

481. Butler Library, Galantière Collection, box 30-001.

482. Ibid.

483. Ibid.

484. Ibid.

485. Ransom Center, Alfred A. Knopf, Inc., Records, Knopf_ 530-5-002, p.184.

486. David Alethea, *Lewis Galantière: The Last Amateur*. Dr. Alethea was a professor of philosophy and chairman of the Humanities Division at the University of Hawaii. His unpublished monograph, *The Last Amateur*, was furnished to the author by Geraldine Malter, Professor Alethea's sister. Professor Alethea and Ms. Malter were first cousins to Lewis.

487. Butler Library, Galantière Collection, box 2, folder 1.

NOTES TO CHAPTER 14

488. Butler Library, Galantière Collection, boxes 1, 4.

489. The area of the Dakota's central courtyard is about equal to two-thirds of the footprint of its residences.

490. Stephen Birmingham, *Life at the Dakota: New York's Most Unusual Address* (Syracuse, NY: Syracuse University Press, 1996), 207.

491. Butler Library, Galantière Collection, box 3.

492. Ibid., box 2, folder 1.The following are more extensive extracts

> Mr. President,
>
> I rise to put before this meeting a matter of new business.
>
> Members have very recently received an invitation to attend a musical evening in the Clubhouse...accompanied by a female guest, the performance to be followed by a buffet supper on the third floor, that is, in the members' dining rooms.
>
> Let me put my cards on the table...this arrangement is in violation of the Association's by-laws...[on] "Ladies in the Clubhouse"...
>
> I ask permission to discuss this matter.... There is here a flouting—I shall go so far as to say a vulgarization—of the very purposes for which a gentlemen's club is organized.
>
> A men's club is sui generis.... A men's club is a sanctuary, a haven from the confusion and turmoil of the world.... A men's club is supremely a place where a man can get away from women. Women in the plural.
>
> I lay it down as a law of life that the proudest moment of a woman's life is when she is seated in public, at table, with four or five men. And the most trying moment

> *in a man's life is when he finds himself at table with four or five women.*
>
> *The aura generated by women talking together is whatever it may be. My own conviction is that it is incomplete. The aura generated by men talking together is wholly different. Men, after dinner, rejoin the ladies with a certain reluctance. Ladies, after dinner, are impatient for their arrival from the host's library. A woman entering the library is a disruptive, a foreign element. A man entering the drawing room is a welcome relief.*
>
> *It is on these facts that the raison d'être of a men's club is founded.*
>
> *...In the Century, more than anywhere else, at the Round Table in the East Room, in the different sectors at the Long Table in the dining room, talk moves from subject to subject with a freedom, a smoothness, a variety that enchant all participants, cement friendships, warm the heart...A club without tranquility and without fraternity ceases to be a club.*

493. Ibid. boxes 1 and 4.

494. Hoover, Paul B. Henze Papers, box 3, folder 1.

495. Jonathan Carroll is an American author who, for the past three decades, has lived in Vienna, Austria. The description of his afternoon with Lewis is reprinted, with his permission, from his online posting: https://jonathancarroll.com/at-the-races-with-hemingway-c46fbad-f07e8. For more information about Jonathan Carroll and his novels, visit https://jonathancarroll.com.

496. Butler Library, Galantière Collection, box 7.

497. Hoover, Paul B. Henze Papers box 3, folder 1; Butler Library; Galantière Collection, box 7.

498. Hoover, Paul B. Henze Papers, box 3, folder 1.

499. Butler Library, Galantière Collection, box 1.

500. Butler Library, Galantière Collection, box 30.

501. Amherst College Archives and Special Collections, Henry Steele Commager Papers, box 23, folder 8.

502. Mina married Henry "Harry" Tomlinson Curtiss on June 1, 1926. He died the following year. Throughout her life, Mina never again loved anyone as she had Harry.

503. Butler Library, Galantière Collection, box 1, folder 3.

504. Ibid., box 1.

505. Ibid., box 3, folder 1.

506. Ibid., box 1, folder 1.

507. Elda was an accomplished painter.

508. Butler Library, Galantière Collection, box 2, folder 1.

509. Paul B Henze was a CIA and National Security Council specialist in psychological operations. He was a CIA station chief in Turkey and Ethiopia during the 1960s and '70s and a deputy to National Security Adviser Zbigniew Brzezinski.

510. Hoover, Paul B. Henze Papers, box 3, folder 1.

511. Butler Library, Galantière Collection, box 2, folder 1.

512. Ibid.

513. Ibid. Pierre Louis Duchartre was author of *The Italian Comedy*.

514. New York City probate papers for the estate of Lewis Galantière.

515. Butler Library, Galantière Collection, box 15, folder 5.

ACKNOWLEDGMENTS

The researching of this book was one of the most enjoyable experiences of my life; writing the book—fitting the evidentiary fragments of Lewis's life into a cohesive narrative—was one of the most challenging. A friend, Professor Diana Lieb Sands (recently retired chair of the Political Science Department at New Jersey City University) read the first draft and gave me her verdict: it was swollen with facts that impeded the narrative, mightily testing a reader's stamina. She told me that I had to choose between an academic treatise and a narrative biography. She obviously favored the latter because she frequently noted in pencil the ways in which she thought I might improve readability. This was unwelcome news because it disabused me of the notion that my writing job was nearly done. Four complete rewrites would follow.

I gave the second draft of the manuscript to another PhD friend, Elizabeth C. Wesman, for what I thought would be the final editing and proofing. Betsy meticulously expunged misspellings, and errors of grammar and punctuation, and her fresh perspective and insights were invaluable.

My thanks also go to Dr. A. Ross Johnson, a visiting fellow at the Hoover Institute and former director of Radio Free Europe. Dr. Johnson confirmed my understanding of the significance of documents I discovered about Lewis's role at RFE, especially during the days of the Hungarian Revolution, and about the rise, fall, and resurrection of RFE during the 1950s and 1960s.

I am grateful to Karol Lurie, my wife, who helped me plumb the thousands of pages of documents at the Butler Library as well as the turn-of-the-century court records for the City of Chicago, and for her willingness to reread the successive revisions of the same passages of the text so often that the letters are now embossed on her retinas.

Thanks go to my sister Patti who, in addition to telling me of the existence of our late cousin, also provided editing suggestions. To Laurence Dubrana, granddaughter of René Arnaud, who told me about René's family and spent many hours translating his correspondence. To the author Sydney Offit, who shared recollections his time with Lewis during both the 1966 PEN Congress and at lunch in the dining room at the Century Club. To Seymour Galantière, Lewis's cousin who, at 104 years old, still recalled events and conversations with clarity; and to his son, Steven, who told me about his great uncles Joseph, Jacob, and Charles, and their descendants. To Richard Curtis, president of Richard Curtis Associates, a friend, for the benefit of his advice. To Tsipi Keller, whose post-typesetting gleaning for errata turned up several. And to Attorney Norman Soloway of Hayes Soloway P.C., for his copyright expertise and for his firm's dedication.

Finally, I am indebted to the following people and institutions, whose assistance and resources were crucial to filling out the Galantière saga:

Libraries

William Baehr, Archives Specialist, Franklin D. Roosevelt Presidential Library, Hyde Park, NY

Julianne Ballou, Digital Archive Project Librarian at the Harry Ransom Center of the University of Texas in Austin

Margaret R. Dakin, Archives and Special Collections, Amherst College, Amherst, MA 01002

Jane Gillis, Reference Librarian, and Anne Marie Menta, Reproductions Coordinator at the Beinecke Rare Book & Manuscript Library, Yale University

Paul Haggett, Archives and Special Collections Technician, St. Lawrence University Libraries, Canton, NY

David Kessler, Dean J. Smith, and Lee Anne Titangos, Bancroft Reference Letters, Bancroft Library, University of California at Berkeley

Deej Maker, Digitization Services at the University of Virginia Library

Andrea (Annie) Murray, Curator of Rare Books and Manuscripts Libraries and Cultural Resources, University of Calgary

Tim Noakes, Public Service Manager, Department of Special Collections, Stanford University Libraries

Stephen Plotkin, Reference Archivist; Stacey Chandler, Textual Archivist; and James Hebert at the John F. Kennedy Presidential Library

Bailey Romaine, Library Assistant, Newberry Library, for the Sherwood Anderson–Galantière correspondence.

Nancy Shawcross, Curator of Manuscripts Rare Book & Manuscript Library at the University of Pennsylvania

Bill Sudduth, Head of Government Information and Maps, Thomas Cooper Library at the University of South Carolina

Gabriel Swift at Princeton University's Firestone Library

Emily Walhout, Houghton Reading Room, Harvard University

Individuals

Ronald Basich, Independent Researcher, Hoover Institution Archives, Stanford University

Jonathan Carroll, for his generously allowing me to reprint his experience of an afternoon with Lewis.

Claudie Finney, for her excellent French to English translations of Lewis's correspondence.

Arbitrator Florence Gladel, of Paris, France, who helped me to track down Lewis's godson, Michel Arnaud, in 2014. Michel and I had lunch in August of that year; he was then 82 years old.

Conrad Lochner, Project coordinator for the Digital Archives, PEN America Center

Geraldine Malter, for sharing her copy of "The Last Amateur," a monograph about Lewis written by her brother, the late David Alethea, a professor of philosophy and the Chairman of the Humanities Division at the University of Hawaii – West O'ahu.

Honor Moore, author of *The White Blackbird.*, the life of the painter Margarett Sargent.

Kim Murphy and Christina Geiger, Bonhams Fine Art Auctioneers & Valuers

Stacy Schiff, author of *Saint-Exupéry*.

Anatol Shmelev, Ph.D., Project Archivist, RFE/RL Collection, Hoover Institution, Stanford University

Sim Smiley, independent researcher, for her work at the Library of Congress, Washington, D.C.

Robert Varady and Judith Varady, who reminded me that I should "show, don't tell."

Professor Rosanna Warren, for her childhood memories of Lewis.

INDEX

C

D

E

F

T

U

V

W